Americans the Beautiful

An Italian American Memoir: The Caravella Family

Duty, Honor, Country. Those three hallowed words reverently dictate what you ought to be, what you can be, what you will be.

Douglas MacArthur.

INTRODUCTION

What is special about America? Is it the finest country that has ever existed? What makes America great? Does America work for all peoples? America is about the American Indian, about all immigrants, about all of us born and raised here. What is unique about America? Given your choice of any country to live in for your entire life where would it be?

America is great because it offers to all citizens opportunities to become the best that they can become. America does not pay your way. America is not offered to you on a silver platter. America is about a chance, an opportunity, a process, a beginning, a start, an opening, a window to the future, and to whatever you want it to be. It is not about hope. No one will hope themselves into a wonderful life. America is a gift to all that chose to win, that chose to improve, that chose to become. It is a gift to those who want what is best for themselves and their loved ones. It is a gift that keeps on giving. It does not take, it does not steal, it does not cheapen life, it does not defeat. America is the greatest country on Earth because it offers to all that come here or are born here a better life. America is a better, safer, and gifted life beyond what most citizens of other countries may ever hope for. Here we do not hope. Here we know we will win. We are Americans!

Other countries such as Denmark or Norway may in general statistically have a happier group of citizens but do they have the milieu, the variety of all nationalities, and the ability to ward off all enemies? Can the Scandinavian countries defeat

Russia, China, or other aggressors? Not without America at their defense. Denmark and Norway exist because America exists. That's the plain and simple fact of life. American is an oasis of love, comfort, peace, and a future for nearly all of its citizens. It is not perfect. Heaven is perfect. Look into a mirror and decide if you do not chose America to live in forever, where do you chose to live? I guess it would be Heaven.

America is you. America is me. America is all of us pulling together.

America is safe from all outside armies.

America is Heaven on Earth.

America is You.

Philip Caravella, MD, FAAFP, Lt. Col. US Army (Ret.)

Introduction for Debbie

My wife Debbie, is a very interesting woman on so many levels and though not genetically Italian, her amazing mystic-like photo appears on the cover of this memoir.

Some have questioned why, when this is an Italian family memoir?

The answer is somewhat convoluted yet valid on so many levels. Debbie's heritage is twenty-five percent Cherokee. Her father was born in Charleston, West Virginia and was fifty percent Cherokee. Debbie also has Irish and German blood.

Being part Cherokee is so American and after all isn't this book about Americans. The American Indian is the greatest of all Americans and the Fathers of this amazing country.

For immigrants to arrive in America from so many foreign destinations is such an admirable goal for those who chanced an unknown life in a faraway land. So together, the American Indian, the finest descendants of all Americans, along with America's world-wide diverse group of immigrants are the backbone and proud inhabitants of the worlds safest and most productive of all nations.

At the age of fifteen, Debbie dated a gentleman named Greg Cecchetti; her first Italian Stallion. She later on dated, Phillip, another Italian of beautiful genes. Debbie grew up on "Number 3 Hill," a part of New Kensington, Pennsylvania, and a suburb of Pittsburg. New Kensington was primarily Italian in makeup and thus Debbie was surrounded by Italians, their culture, and their mannerisms from day one. Other Italians she dated were from the Luccetti, Demao, and Fazio clans. Debbie being so beautiful and desirable by the men she met, had no trouble finding men that she would fall in love with; at least on a temporary basis. The first car she ever drove was the Torino (Torino, the capital of Turin; a metropolitan area of Northern Italy) of Italian heritage, and of Ford design and production; not a Ferrari but very much Italian as Ford saw it.

Debbie loves Italian foods, clothing styles by Italian designers (such as Vince Camuto, Dolce & Gabbana, Moschino),

perfumes, cars (Ferrari, Lamborghini), shoes, and everything Italian; long before she and I had even met. Some people kiddingly say, she is Italian by injection. I can vouch for that. Debbie is a fun loving character who everyone knows, everyone loves, and everyone desires to be like. She dresses to the hilt in fashion and knows how to wow people of every description. Debbie knew everyone and everyone knew her or knew of her atValley High School. To this day she has not changed.

Debbie is on the cover of this book because she is as much of an Italian as anyone and fits all the requisites -- well, except **for a few missing genes. Listen!**

Let's not get fussy!!!

This is my book and I will do what I want with it!!! **LOL!**

By Debbies loving husband, Phil Caravella!

In Her Own Words:

Debbie Tells It Like It Is!

"I have absolutely no Italian blood, although I grew up surrounded by Italians. Many of my family members married Italians because those were the folks we lived near and spent so much time with. A few of my neighbors were actually in the Mob which afforded a few benefits which I will not review.

Also, from the age of fifteen, I dated Italians. My first boyfriend was Italian and I dated several more as time went on. I often spent time during some Sundays and holidays with my boyfriends at their homes for their amazing feasts and holiday traditions. I learned to make many Italian dishes from their mothers who I came to know quite well. So at the holidays, I went to every Italian family's home, after I grew to know them over time. I was raised outside of Pittsburg in a little town called New Kensington. Being surrounded by Italians, their friends, their families, their customs, their traditions, their love, and their graciousness was a wonderful beginning for my younger life. The pizza, the bread, and the pasties weren't bad either. "

From Debbie with Love.

Philip's Wife and Soul Mate.

Let's talk a little about the author

Philip Caravella, MD.

My twin Phyllis and I were born in Walter Reed Hospital, in Washington, D. C. , a US. Army Medical center of very distinguished origins. From day one, I was in the US Army.

After completing my internship at the Cleveland Clinic as a physician, I joined the US Army serving as a captain in the medical corps during the Vietnam War. Within a few short years, I left the army to complete my training in the field of family medicine, while attending the University of Illinois.

Later in life, and at the ripe age of sixty-four, I decided I had not given back enough for America, considering what it had done for my family. In 2009, after serving as Section Chief of Family Medicine for about sixteen years at the Westlake, Ohio, branch of the Cleveland Clinic, I decided to contact my Ohio Senator, Senator George Voinovich, of Ohio fame. He was kind enough to put through Congress in Washington a waiver that would allow me to return to the US Army at the age of sixty-four. I believe, I may be the oldest soldier to return to serve in the US military. Eventually I retired from the army and thus will remain a soldier for ever; from day one until I take my final breath?

I am a patriot in every sense of the word and would have accomplished even more if the chance would ever again occur.

After serving America as an officer and a gentleman, my true devotion is and always will be to my wife Debbie; my soulmate forever. She and I have always clicked from the moment we first met. Everything I think, desire, and hope for, is a part of her even before I speak of it. She knows what I want and what I'm thinking about better than I know myself. She loves me with a passion far beyond the norm. With time we have become one.

by Philip Caravella, Husband & Soul Mate of Debbie

At the end of this book is attached a copy of my resume referred to for physicians as a curriculum vitae.

PROLOGUE

In 1886, the Statue of Liberty, a gift from France, was completed and overlooks Ellis Island, New York.

On the pedestal of the statue was engraved a verse by **Emma Lazarus:**

Give me your tired, your poor,

Your huddled masses, yearning

to breathe free,

The wretched

Refuse of your

teeming shore.

Send these,

The homeless,

Tempest-tossed

To me,

I lift my lamp beside

The golden door!

Emma Lazarus

I wish to thank France for the gift of the Statue of Liberty that all Americans treasure and love beyond description. Like us, you have been at our side as a free country for over three hundred years.

Dr. Philip Caravella

Ellis Island became a portal for massive immigration. In some sixty years thereafter, over twelve million immigrants entered the United States.

From 1848 to 1890 almost 400,000 arrived from Italy. Much of this occurred as a result of political upheaval and revolution that evolved when Italy struggled to become an independent and unified nation. Difficulties persisted with massive under employment fueling more immigration. Earlier immigrants to America, wrote back home to friends and relatives living in Italy commenting that jobs were plentiful in America and that our "roads are paved with gold". As such, between 1890 and 1914, some four million more Italians emigrated to the United States. Most were from southern Italy and settled in New York, Chicago, Cleveland, and along the East Coast. Later groups emigrated to towns in Colorado and California where they found jobs in the mines.

The parents of my maternal grandmother and grandfather were both from Villanova del Battista, a Province of Avellino located just east of Naples, Italy. They had apparently seen the words engraved on the Statue of Liberty and had heard the reports of earlier emigrants from their own villages in Italy claiming the same: "the streets of America are paved with gold."

Along with many other families from Villanova del Battista, my great great grandparents emigrated to the United States. Antonio Franzolino, the father of my maternal grandfather, Lucian, arrived in New York in 1893 on a ship from Naples, Italy. Like many Italian immigrants, he arrived without his family in order to first obtain a job and housing and later send for them when he was finally able to.

Nunzio Borrazzo, age 44 years, the father of my maternal grandmother, Generosa, arrived in New York on July 1, 1896, also without his family. Of note, he arrived one year after the birth of his youngest child Santa, and only one year before the death of his wife Marra who died of influenza. There were several other Borrazzos on the same ship arriving with Nunzio in New York.

Nunzio Borrazzo now a widower, was overwhelmed with the idea of coming to America with his five children to start a new life. He believed his boys, all of whom were old enough could find work in America. But then he wondered, what would he do with his two daughters, one a toddler and the other about ten years of age?

He contacted a local Italian convent and asked if they would be able to take his daughters in, until he was settled in America. They agreed to take in ten year old Generosa but could not take on a toddler. Reputedly, after about three years, Nunzio managed to raise enough money to pay for Generosa's passage to America. He sent the money he had saved to an acquaintance in Italy to be used for his daughters travel to

America. Both the acquaintance and the money disappeared. Thus Generossa was forced to wait once again.

Finally when Generossa was almost sixteen years of age and preparing to enter the convent as a novitiate, Nunzio sent for her and told her that he had arranged for her marriage to one of two Italian men in America. Generossa would eventually become my grandmother on the Franzolino side of the family.

A little more than a quarter century later, in 1920, my paternal Grandfather, Filippo Caravella left his home in Agira, a village in the province of Catania in Sicily. Along with several other relatives he came to seek work and establish a new home for his family in America.

He arrived beneath the up raised torch of Miss Liberty in the harbor of New York. A year and a half later, having saved enough money for the cost of passage for Rose Teranova, his wife(it was common for Italian women to keep their maiden names) and for their two children, my father, Luigi (Louis) and my aunt, Santa;he was able to send for them.

The Franzolinos and the Caravellas both knew other Italians from their former villages in Italy that were living in Cleveland, Ohio. As such, they decided to make Cleveland their new home and moved into adjacent Italian communities in east-side neighborhoods of Cleveland.

Our mother was born in Cleveland and my father was a young boy, fresh from Italy and brand new to Cleveland. Both parents attended school in Cleveland with my mother graduating from John Adams High School. By the time my father was in high school, hisfamily numbered three children after the birth of his brother Robert.

It then became necessary for my father to obtain work in order to help the family's finances. Dad found a job in an affluent suburb of Cleveland, Lakewood, Ohio as an apprentice barber. Soon he was making a good wage and elected to work full time rather than returning back to school. From that time on, Dad was a sort of self-educated man. He read a lot and even got in the habit of reading the dictionary. As a matter of fact, I was a sophomore in college before my vocabulary appeared to match his.

My Dad met my mother when they were both in their twenties and he fell "head over heels" for her (as the expression went in those days). He worked diligently to romance her, apparently a feat of itself in that she was betrothed to another when they first met.

My father clearly adored my mother as was evident throughout his life with her. They were in their twenties when they married. They were all about God and family and raised us as such. Our parents were both fluent in Italian having been raised with the language but they rarely used it at home.

Unfortunately, we were deprived of learning the Italian language from them, because they feared it would impede our ability to learn English correctly. Because learning English had not been a problem for them, I am not certain why they believed it would be a problem for us to learn Italian?I think that they wanted us to be as much American as possible. They were both proud Americans.

My mother did have a few Italian phrases that were memorable in that she used them frequently in speaking to us. "What God wills", said in Italian, was perhaps the most frequently used of these Italian expressions.

Our parents stressed the need for us all to go to college and as such this was such a significant expectation that none of us children would have thought otherwise.

I wish to credit Wikipedia as a source of some of the historical dates and information provided in the *Prologue* of this book.

This book is not broken down into chapters because life is not about chapters. Life and living is an ongoing continuum until it is over. My book is about an immigrant family, the Caravella's, originating from Italy, who are Americans in every sense of the word.

AMERICANS THE BEAUTIFUL

Are you going to live Caravella?"Get up deck-side and I mean now," Major Nixon firmly yelled.

Spending the first five days of his ocean cruise gratis Uncle Sam, Robert or Orazio as he was known in Italian, convulsed with vomiting in a lower bunk, while crossing a gut retching Atlantic on his way to Liverpool, England in a ship akin to a barracks rather than a cruise ship. When his paper bag cache had been expended, he resorted to regurgitating into his military issued steel pot, a frightful sight, when considering its primary function of protecting the head. This device could come in handy when collecting bodily waste from any number of orifices should the need arise, never mind just protecting ones noggin.

Miserable as he was, he had been praying for an enemy sub to torpedo the ship rather than continuing this miserable if not tormenting odyssey. No enemy sub closed in to provide the relief he so tried to seek, so his sickening gastronomic nightmare persisted as his prayers went unanswered.

After this brutal ordeal, his basic training at Camp Haan near Riverside, California seemed like a day at the beach. He had left aboard ship for Europe on July 1, 1943. Was this to be his first and last voyage?

As time would prove, nausea and vomiting was not unique to Robert but seems to be genetically ingrained when it comes to the Caravella stomach and its relationship with most bodies of water with the exception of a bathtub, unless of course it is a large jacuzzi and then the same rule applies.

Colonel Land, also aware of Robert's plight, inquired of the Major. "So where are we with this crew, the Colonel asked? "A few of them are having medical problems but the Doc's working with them. They should be okay," the major commented. "They have to be before we land," the Colonel barked! We have less than a week to get these men ready unless the Krauts sink us first. "

Robert Philip Caravels, twelve years younger than his brother Louis, would be born on New Year's Day, 1924, delivered with the help of a midwife in their family home. As a friend of the family, the midwife provided the service for free and was given a hot loaf of fresh Italian bread as a thank you.

Later on in life, Uncle Bob at the age of eighteen would ultimately join the US Army during the most dangerous days of Weirather completing three months of basic training at Camp Hana, California near Riverside, he shipped out of Boston taking seven to eight days to cross the Atlantic, landing in Liverpool, England.

Bob, affectionately known by only a few family members as Felix, as in the cartoon character, had been given a reprieve from guard duty and KP while aboard ship. Plenty of opportunities for those skills would surface once on terra friarbird with his mahogany-colored hair and dazzling blue eyes inherited from his father, would go on to serve in three theaters; Great Britain, the Rhineland, and the Ardennes while earning three Bronze Stars for heroism, a Victory Medal, and other decorations and citations. Corporal Caravella served initially in Britain with the US Army Headquarters Battery, 125th Anti-Aircraft Mobile Artillery Gun Battalion or "Triple A" battalion, shooting down the V-1 "buzz" bombs flying over the English Channel, gratis Adolph Hitler. The V-1 of the Hitler. The series, was developed by the Nazi Luftwaffe and was code named Kirsch kern or "Cherry Stone". The allies referred to them as "Buzz Bombs" or "doodlebugs". Hearing these coming did not give one a sense of comfort but rather doom since where it would land was any one's guess. These rockets had a primitive guidance system and were the first of their kind.

So, what did the allies have to counter the threat? Our methods were primitive in comparison; however, they got the job done.

Robert's battalion had four large guns in Charley Company and four guns in D Battery. The men of the battalion, when not firing their guns, lived in tents holding a cubby of two to four men each.

The 125th would go on to shoot down seven hundred and fifty-one buzz bombs during Battery. The guns were unable to hit the buzz bombs and once out of range, the battalion commanders would send up American Air Force fighter aircraft to buzz the buzz bombs and tip their wings with their own wings enough to force them to crash willy-nilly. This was efficient and saved armaments. One thing it was not was predictable, though caution and judgment was used when the doodlebugs were near allied troops. Plus, these sorties allowed pilots to hone their flying skills.

The V-1 flying bombs also had a characteristic low pitched whining sound emitted from their rocket engine located just above the fuselage. The characteristic sound of the rocket provided a unique yet reliable way of identifying their location just before causing the mayhem they were known for when indiscriminately impacting wherever they fell with one thousand pounds of TNT. The good news was that the V-1's guidance system was so primitive that chance played a far greater role than targeting when it came to hitting any site large or small.

These were arguably the first cruise missiles. They were more terrifying than destructive since anyone within hearing distance of them were the possible subject of the mayhem they were known to deliver. The British suffered the Buzz Bombs tyranny more than others but they were also as tough as they came and were well suited to battle any enemy. Robert would serve his country until February 5, 1949.

He was a soft-spoken quite gentleman in the true sense of the word who never cursed, never criticized, and never misspoke about anyone. If he did, I never witnessed it nor knew of it to occur. Felix was really a gem of a man like no one else I ever knew then or even now. A man of his word, he was a trusted and honest friend and uncle, that lived unfortunately in his own world that few would ever understand much less penetrate. His PTSD was at times overwhelming.

My cousin Salvatore Torrisi would over time become a confidant of Robert if anyone ever could be. From Sam, as I called Salvatore, I would learn little snippets of information about uncle as time went on. Uncle Bob was not an open book; though at the end-of-the-day, are any of us?

My father Louis was ten years older than Bob, yet Bob remained very close to him and always looked up to his brother. Uncle rarely spoke of Dad and when he did so it was always in a respectful tone with loving warmth that would forever lurk within the realm of their brotherly relationship.

Beginning in 1940, Robert's first job was working in the produce department of Heinen's, a local grocery market and chain where he worked until he was drafted in 1943 at the inexperienced yet physically prime age of eighteen. Prior to working he graduated from John Adams High School in Cleveland and was an average student though apparently very likable.

Before the great WW II, Louis worked at Ohio Best Tools. A few months later he was drafted on June 23 of 1943, at the relatively old age of 28. WW II was also only the beginning of a four-year journey that Louis had also begun but in a different venue than that of Robert. After his basic training in Detroit, Michigan, Louis would serve four long years at the

Pentagon as a guard and an aide under General George C. Marshall, Chief of Staff from 1939-1945. Marshall was responsible for supplying, directing, and deploying over eight million soldiers; the largest army ever assembled in history. Did Louis ask for the Pentagon assignment? What do you think?

Louis was inducted when living in Cleveland and was told to report downtown for a physical and to complete the usual paperwork many of us before and since have become very familiar with. During the enrolling process, if you could call it that there're suddenly erupted a great deal of commotion from somewhere in the facility. A terrified woman had appeared crying and screaming for help. The staff recognizing that she was of Italian extraction went room-to-room looking for an interpreter. Louis, hearing of the Italian woman's plight, said, "I speak Italian. I can help. "Upon seeing Louis, the woman with tears in her eyes, grabbed him about the head and neck and began hugging and kissing him lovingly for what seemed like an endless barrage that few in the room would ever likely forget. And guess what? It was his mother who had only just learned of his induction. She had run down to Cleveland's Armory processing center and resorted to the usual Italian hysteria in times of desperation, while overreacting to the less than dire circumstances. Eventually calm was restored though an ego may have been bruised in the process? Grandma Rose had mastered the art of hysterics as her husband Grandpa Filippo knew all too well.

Louie, as he was called by his friends, would spend four snail-paced long drawn-out endless and tedious years at the Pentagon as a Private First Class while guarding General Marshall, giving him weekly precision military style haircuts, and learning the stateside ways of the military. Louis had become a master barber many years before he had begun working at Ohio Best Tools. Marshall knowing a good thing when he saw it repeatedly refused to let go of his multitalented assistant.

His skill as a barber, first acquired at age twelve to help support his parents, was his blessing as well as his nemesis, trapping him in the corridors and offices of the Pentagon for the entire war though he earnestly tried on many occasions to leave for Italy as an army interpreter. On one apparent disappointing occasion he made it to a departure bus only to be plucked off in the nick of time, at least from General Marshall's perspective. The famous general, pulling rank after hearing at the last minute of his departing aide taking leave for Europe had him figuratively yanked off the bus. "My barber isn't going anywhere and that's that", Marshall exclaimed.

Dad would serve at the Pentagon for the entire duration of the war. Many would have been pleased with that wartime sentence though Louie was not.

He had a passion in his blood that would be realized in many future adventures. Italians are a romantically passionate and nationality driven group of people that sail beyond the limits of social mores finding solace and pleasure in the arts, in their Ferrari's, in their love of food, music, and opera.

But and I mean "but", at the end of the day nothing is more important to them than their love and concerns for their family. Family is everything too family. Family will always be there for you because the family bond for each other is without peer. Crossing "the family "or its members by outsiders is a perilous mistake met with unpleasantries and consequences that too many have experienced and many will yet continue to experience, because nothing changes for full blooded Italians. The family is "the family".

Some soldiers fought the war with rifles, while some supported the others stateside. An army travels on its' stomach and is supported by countless and less glamorous troops that serve a role that may seem thankless but remains indispensable for the benefit of the whole. Only fifteen percent of soldiers ever fire a weapon in combat.

For Louis, not making it to Europe was always a nemesis for a man that felt unfulfilled during the "great war". Would history repeat itself? What was in store for him and what would become his real genius?

The theaters of war varied worldwide though the goal was never in doubt. Victory was a certainty, since Americans could not grasp anything less. Among the countless nationalities blending and homogenized into Americans, these American-Italians, the older brother born in Sicily, and the younger in Cleveland were part of the backbone of a fighting team that would deliver Europe from its misdirected foes who unwittingly bit off more than they could chew. Nothing new here though! History is replete with misguided, under thought out adventures into other's territories resulting eventually in crushing defeats for many enemies not recognizing that freedom, a God given right, will ultimately prevail.

The Allies took a bit of time to get rolling, but once they did, the outcome was never in doubt. America's automobile factories were rapidly mobilized into building the machinery of war from heavy tanks, to world-class bombers, fighter aircraft, and support ships of every size and construction. American women flocked to the factories working tirelessly to support their men-in-arms. Times were threatening, though the outcome never would be in doubt. As the brilliant General George S. Patton once said, "Americans love a winner and will not tolerate a loser. Americans play to win all the time. I wouldn't give a hoot in hell for a man who lost and laughed. That's why Americans have never lost and will never lose a war, because the very thought of losing is hateful to Americans."

And General Douglas MacArthur also so poignantly put it, "It is fatal to enter any war without the will to win it."

My Uncle Albert Franzolino, my mother's brother, would serve in the Pacific with McArthur's navy. Another uncle and maternal brother, Anthony Franzolino, would also serve with the US Army, reaching the rank of Major. These men were part of the inevitable victory we all would so cherish and were Italian-American men of great honor, distinction, and purpose. With the exception of Louis, who was born in Agira, Sicily, the other men were all American born and served their country on many levels.

The Caravella family had its roots in Sicily, a magnificent island of mountains, farmland, laced with old crumbling temples, buildings of many descriptions and sizes, embellished by stone and rock formations rising above the blue-green ocean. It would become a melting pot for a dozen or more ethnic groups as time went on. The Sicani tribe of Mediterranean origin were interbred with the Elymi tribes who were later infiltrated by the Siculi descendants of the Central Alps.

One hundred years later in the city of Selinunte, temples would arise symbolizing wealth and influence only to be toppled and wasted by the Carthaginian invasion in 409 B. Ths. groups were molested by Greek and Etruscan pirates, and later the Senrites from Africas North Coast were to have their day.

Not to be outdone, these invaders were followed by the Romans, Goths, Byzantines, and the Muslims from Egypt, Syria, and Arabia. In 827 ADS, the Arabs brought with them lemon and orange trees that would become crops of major importance. The Normans of northern Europe took over about the year 1000, joining Sicily with Italy forming the Kingdom of the Two Sicily's. They introduced Western European culture to the island. If that was not enough, by the 1200's, German, French, and eventual Austrian rule would flourish for a brief century or so until the Italians regained their ground.

King Louis of Sicily on November 7, 1347, concluded a peace treaty with Catania and the Kingdom of Naples, which in that era claimed the Island of Sicily as its own. An earthquake in the 1700's would deliver another blow to the island, though more than likely, Sicily had reeled from similar jarring experiences in other distant centuries.

Finally, the Italian patriot, Guiseppe Garibaldi, invaded Sicily in 1860 turning over its control to the Kingdom of Italy as we know it today.

The beautiful landscape of Sicily includes mountain chains with the highest peak, Mount Etna exceeding ten thousand feet in height, and is one of the world's most active volcanos. In older cities like Arigento are seen delicate deserted ancient stone buildings not far from the ruins of Selinunte's temples laying in golden grace beneath the hot noon sun. In centuries gone by, Greeks planted the first olive trees on fertile areas of the island.

A magnificent island rising above the blue-green ocean, Sicily is composed of crumbling ruins of bygone centuries along with majestic mountains, sprawling irrigation fed farmlands, long rows of sweet grape-laden vineyards, flocks of densely wool covered sheep, and fields of wild flowers with rainbow-colored dresses approaching stone encrusted farm houses in all directions.

The lemon and orange trees brought over by the Arabs a thousand years earlier would forever influence Sicilian agriculture. Throughout the millenniums, as you now understand, every major Mediterranean and European power has invaded the boot's island oasis, leaving behind genetic material from Greece, North Africa, Spain, the mid-East, and everywhere in between.

The Germans, British, and Americans were no exception. During WWII, generals on all sides sooner or later had their eye on the Strait of Messina, a narrow body of water between the eastern tip of Sicily and the western tip of Calabria; a city near the southern border of Italy at the end of the "boot. "The Strait of Messina connected the Tyrrhenian Sea to the north with the Ionian Sea to the south and all-important bodies of water were located within the much larger and strategically located central Mediterranean Sea.

Some bodies of land just seem to be more important than others. A desirable location, sought after natural resources, splendid weather, or some other useful commodity has always garnered more interest than maybe any habitable site should ever endure.

Everyone knows a good thing when they see it and Sicily was no exception. This beautiful Italian island, in the central Mediterranean, with drawing cards of sun-bathed beaches and the richest of top-soils made it a desirable conquest, becoming a melting pot of dozens of ethnic groups. Its volcanic rain-washed soil provided abundant opportunities to grow olives, figs, grapes, almonds, and the staples Sicilians enjoyed. Amaretto, fine Sicilian wines, and tangy olives of all descriptions, would ultimately serve the economy over time but not without long periods of Sicilian poverty.

Saint Philip of Sicily, the Patron Saint of Sicily and more specifically the city of Agira, lying within the province of Enna, became known as the "Apostle of the Sicilians."

After thousands of years of turmoil and invasions, Sicily needed its own Champion. Saint Philip was the first Christian missionary to visit the island. Little else can be certainly stated about him, though notably he is a Patron Saint of the United States Army Special Forces. He was also known for his power to accomplish exorcisms. Saint Philip's feast day is the twelfth of May. He is also celebrated by the cities of Malta and the small town of Limina where he also had lived.

Sicily's roots are deep and long within the pages of history due to its strategic location at the toe of the boot of Italy nestled in the Mediterranean Sea midway between Italy and North Africa. All manner of men and conquerors from many European countries and those of the Middle East would seek to plant their roots in the milieu of Sicily's wonderful soil only to be uprooted by the invasion of the next Tribe, King, Ruler, Emperor, General, or Czar that believed the control of Sicily would give them a military edge over those passing through the straits surrounding the island. There was obvious truth to that strategic position and thus Sicily was likely the most sought-after prize of the Mediterranean Sea.

Plus, fantastic Sicilian wine graced by dishes of delicious olives and figs were not to be taken for granted. Beautiful Italian Sicilian woman were not an afterthought. Need I say more!

After over a thousand years of invasions from all varieties of European and Mediterranean beings, Sicily would become a melting pot of peoples, cultures, and mystery, controlled by the last victor, to be eventually assimilated, and ultimately replaced by a fun loving romantic and artistic people looking for happiness, family unity, and a quiet prosperous life. Few places on earth have been replete with such a variety of "want to be governors" lacking the power to hold a relatively small amount of turf. No place on Earth has ever garnered such attention and the need for men of all walks of life to conquer (for the moment) and control such a small piece of real estate.

Due to this extensive period of turmoil, rotating governments, and foreign rule, the Sicilians had developed an unrelenting distrust of all forms of governments. In turn, this resulted in unusually strong family bonds to the exclusion of outsiders. Thus, the evolution of the code of honor or "omerta" that forbid informing the police of crimes that were considered private affairs. One of the offshoots of this form of protectionism would later result in the evolution of the Mafia.

Paradoxically the Mafia triggered fear among the Sicilians while handcuffing the government's ability to control Mafia. Paradoxically would not and could not be coerced into revealing information about their camaraderie or paysans during government probes and thus the authorities were unable to make anything stick.

Of course, corruption at all levels further eroded any chance of government intervention, so the system never changed, and Sicilians were somewhat at the mercy of these local warlords often fighting amongst themselves for control and financial gain.

The Mafia was not unknown to the Taravella's or their future relatives, the Torrisi family. Both of these families would fall under the umbrella of Cleveland, Ohio, where as time went on, these families would flourish with a variety of interesting journeys of all descriptions.

By the early 1900's, most Sicilians were farmers, handcuffed by outdated farming methods, depleted land resources, no jobs, and an incompetent government; sort of the way the Sicilians apparently liked Taravella's a few Sicilian families saw their lives playing out differently. As this backdrop unfolded, Rosa Terranova the matriarch and Filippo Caravella her husband would find another way. Their destiny would not play out in Sicily.

Be that as it may, my grandparents, Filippo and Rosa would meet in Agira, Scicily, under not unusual but forbidden circumstances. Their blood and union would become a part of this intra-Mediterranean milieu. Rose Terranova, the product of well-to-do parents, plantation owners, and farmers were aghast over their beautiful, chestnut brown-haired daughter, running off with one of the plantation's surfs, Filippo Caravella. In Italy, surfs were not too far north of being slaves. Seeing past her lover's station in life and apparently knowing a good thing when she saw it, Rose would fall in love with her father's surf. Courtships and weddings were traditionally parentally controlled affairs, but not this time. Rose new what she wanted and at the age of fourteen her endorphins had probably altered her thinking for a bit. Get-out of my way, she thought. Her dreams would not be frustrated by a few overshadowing parental dictums. Sort of the attitude a good American would harbor when challenged. Rose and Filippo ran off, married, and had their first child Louis, when Rose was fifteen. Of course, in today's America that would be statutory rape saddled with many other unsavory connotations and consequences.

At first rejected, the wayward couple would soon be accepted by Rose's loving parents not embittered by their daughter's behavior. Returning to Agira to live, a coastal town in Southern Sicily where they had met, the couple began to establish their own roots, shallow ones though they may be, to start raising their family "temporarily" as Italians.

Married only briefly, they were experiencing the wonders of parenting while providing for two precious children, Louis born in 1912 and Santina, born six years later. Santina was a small happy child with a sweet smile and beautiful curly dark mahogany colored hair. Everyone would fall in love with her. She was such a sweetheart.

With a less than provocative future to behold in Sicily and hearing of a new country where the streets were "paved with gold," the Caravella's decided to begin planning and saving for another adventure across a vast sea separating the Caravellas from America only by time and patience. For years, Filippo had heard of America and was determined to do whatever was necessary to move his family to begin anew: a new life saturated with hope, freedom, and opportunity.

Rose had a financial and organizational bent while Filippo would work at any and all endeavors to acquire money enough to make the Atlantic crossing of a lifetime. They both knew of others that had made the move and thus those preceding Italians would prove helpful to them when the time would finally arrive to dive head on into a milieu of mystery and faith.

Times being tough in Italy, forced many Italians with spirit and hope to look for a new and seemingly better life in America. Compounding the Caravella's concern, was the unexpected death of Filippo's sister, found apparently murdered in a farmer's field near Agira. Almost nothing was known of her terrible tragedy and modern methods of seeking out the offenders was not to be. Her death remained an unsolved yet painful reminder of another reason for leaving.

Many Europeans knew of sorrow and poverty driving them onward into a future forsaking desperation and awakening within them a spirit never to be extinguished.

Saving enough over the years, my grandfather was able to eventually purchase a third-class ticket on The Dante, a five hundred- and three-foot-long Italian flagship steamer. He must have had a "James Bond" flair about him, having a manifest line number of 0007. Being short at 5' 3" tall, buff, with cool blue eyes, longish brown hair, and a highly tweaked sense of humor. He almost but didn't quite measure up to Bond's size (missing it by about eight to ten inches - but who's perfect?) and was lacking in financial prowess or British polish. Without a word of English in his repertoire and the lack of any Bond-like appearances would once and for all eliminate any pretenses of being James Bond, unless one considers the possibility that grandpa Filippo was the "first Bond" and totally unafraid of new beginnings. Yes, he was 0007 and let's not forget it. 0007 was an American long before Bond came into existence. James was a movie. 0007 was the real "McCoy."

Grandpa's ship departed Naples, Italy and arrived at Ellis Island on March 10, 1921, with 100 -first class, 260- second class and 1,825 third-class passengers. "Steerage" or third-class passengers traveled under miserable if not dangerous conditions. Many would become ill or would contact contagious illnesses being closely confined within the unfriendly holds of ships, not resembling in any way cruise ships as we now know them today.

Other notable Italians, including Columbus, had done this before but instead sailed "first class" with a fleet of small, sturdy, reliable, three masted ships of the "*caravels*" class; the Nina and the Pinta. The Italian Captain and Admiral, Cristoforo Colombo would sail alongside the *caravellas* in his official command ship, the Santa Maria, though he enjoyed the maneuverability of the *caravellas* that had the unique ability to sail backwards as well as forward. He arrived in the America's in 1492 landing in the Bahamas. "Columbus" would sale close to land with the *caravellas* because they could sale back out to sea, being far more maneuverable than the Santa Maria, which he left out to sea.

Time would prevail and with time others began to follow in the footsteps of Columbus. Though he was one of the earlier explorers, his accomplishments and that of others opened the door for thousands of other brave Europeans searching for gold at the end of their rainbow.

The first wave of European immigrants was the Irish arriving primarily between 1820 and 1860 landing on the quarantine island of "Gross Isle" located on the Saint Lawrence River just outside of Quebec City. These folks became Canadians. Gross Island arguably became known as the original "Isle of Tears. " It was notably labeled, due to many who died of cholera and later of typhus fever, acquired aboard ship. This unfortunate turn of events, resulted in the death of about three thousand Irishmen and women being buried on the island from those horrible outbreaks, as the decades wore on.

The next largest wave of immigrants, soon to become Americans, were the Italians landing on Ellis Island between 1860 and 1922 resulting also in many dying from contagious illnesses acquired aboard ship. This became the second "Isle of Tears," for many Italians who had family members that did not survive the passage or were to eventually die soon thereafter. Other immigrants would be returned to Italy when found to have contagious illnesses that were not lethal but never-the-less feared.

First and second-class passengers along with earlier travelers such as Columbus were not required tube quarantined on Ellis Island. The Caravella's of little means had sailed in the third-class quarters of the Dante and the Europa and would meet a different fate.

One year, five months, and nineteen days after the arrival of her husband Filippo onto Ellis Island, his wife traveling for unknown reasons under her maiden name of Rosa Terranova, arrived with her two children, ten-year-old Luigi (Louis) and six-year-old Santa (Santina) Caravella at Ellis Island on August 29, 1922. They had set sail for New York on the SS Europa, another Italian flagship carrying only first class and third-class passengers. They were initially quarantined for several weeks, just as other immigrants were, so they could be evaluated for communicable diseases. Rosa, and Louis were found to be healthy.

Unfortunately, a contagious medical problem had befallen Rosa's daughter, little Santa. Discovered during one of the islands routines "six second physicals" administered by overwhelmed physicians, her destiny would be deterred. While traveling aboard ship, she was infected with head lice and this seemingly benign condition by current standards conveyed concern among the local Ellis Island medical staff and officials. She was sent back to Italy aboard ship and not to be permitted entrance to America. Only two percent of immigrants would be shunned for medical or legal reasons and returned to their homeland.

The loss of their daughter's companionship would haunt the Caravella's for years to come. Many seemingly cruel though not unusual problems would dash the hopes of many immigrants. On the surface, the screenings appeared to be cruel, but fear in America was equally poignant, knowing how the plague and similar diseases had infested Europeans. Ellis Island's authorities would not chance fate, returning all travelers to their homeland that were thought to harbor infectious diseases acquired from their home countries or while aboard ship. This historical happening smacks of the fear many of us have experienced from the Covid-19 experiences of 2020.

The Caravella's would once again save money for six years before being able to send for their daughter. During this difficult period, arrangements were made for Santina to move in with her sickly Aunt Terranova who had been stricken with some form of crippling arthritis. This little child would care for her aunt until the age of twelve, when once again enough funds were saved by her grief-stricken parents allowing them to send for her. A missing daughter was no small price to pay, with family being so important to most new immigrants lacking a net-work of friends, much less relatives.

Life had never been easy for most new arrivals, but as time went on, good fortune would come to many that toiled and found sanctuary in America.

Louis was soon to be a teen when he entered America through Ellis Island. As time proceeded, he would remember little of Sicily either through intention or due to lack of interest while becoming firmly entwined with his newfound homeland and its culture. As time went on, he related little about his birthplace to others and rarely would speak of his past without some degree of prompting by others. Though as a young child, I remember my father telling me of a watering well in Agira. The well, centrally located in his town was a watering hole frequented by the townsmen during hot and humid days.

Filippo explained to his son the art of drinking water from a public cup. "When drinking water from the cup at the well, you must place your lower lip inside the edge of the cup. "This technique avoided having his son's lips touch the outer side of the cup thereby reducing his chance of acquiring an illness, or so my grandfather believed. Learning this from my grandpa, my father always drank in this fashion from cups and glasses whether at home or elsewhere. It seemed a bit odd to me but it worked for him. Old habits and customs sometimes never die and why should they?

Louis wanted to lose his Italian accent. He studied English and grammar, mastering the language to a degree exceeding that of all but the best educated Americans. Soon his Italian accent had nearly been completely abolished. Being not one to linger with the past, he would not educate his future children in the Italian language. He knew all about being taunted; "ginny", "whop", "grease-ball", "dayglo", but God help those who pushed it too dayglo very tough and strong and sometimes harboring a violent temper, those who crossed him would regret their actions. Their folly would not be repeated.

For most Europeans, wine believed to be more sanitary than water was the beverage of choice during many meals. In the "old days" good wine was more available to most than was good water. Italians are masters at distilling wine from many varieties of grapes they grow and have perfected the art over the centuries. Sicilians were no exception, if not the leaders in wine making when it came to family traditions. They would bring their winemaking skills to America. Any Sicilian worth his salt, could batch together a good wine from grapes of many descriptions.

My grandfather had a grape press and related equipment, needed to make a couple of hundred gallons or so of fine dark red-purple wine each year. This delicious purple grape also made for good eating. We gorged ourselves with fresh grape before most of the crates were turned into wine. Wine was a common gift among Italians and not usually sold as some would think. Bootlegging was not something that most Italians or the Caravella's were interested in.

Oddly enough the water well in downtown Agira, was the only experience my father would ever speak of as it related to his birthplace. Born at home by a midwife and fully adjusting to his new American homeland, he would never speak of Sicily as time went on. Putting his birthplace behind him with ease was easy to do for a man that always looked forward.

Of course, his youth allowed him to be very adaptive. Most new Americans adjusted rapidly to their new surroundings having little choice anyway. It was either adapting or returning to their homeland and most toughened immigrants would not accept failure, working at back breaking or menial tasks "to make a go of it" while providing for their families. Immigrants and migrants would flock to cities such as Cleveland from the end of the nineteenth century and the beginning of the twentieth century.

The first stream was composed of native-born migrants primarily from the eastern states such as New York and New Jersey and blacks from the Southern states. In the early 1900's, the second stream moving to Cleveland, were primarily foreign born initially from Northern Europe, and later many came from Southern and Eastern Europe.

Between 1900 and 1910, forty percent of Cleveland's growth came from immigrants. In the mid 1920's due to the National Origins Act of 1924 foreign migration dramatically diminished. During 1920, the peak year of foreign migration, the "foreign element" (the foreign born plus the native-born white with foreign parents) composed seventy-five percent of Cleveland's population. With that in mind, I and my siblings are part of the "foreign element. "

As a child, Louis had left Sicily behind both spiritually and physically and would never look back nor would he ever return. For Louis there would be no regrets but only new adventures. He would follow in his father's footsteps but would prove to be a relentless worker and a wonderful provider, as time would prove.

His Italian blood and heritage would leave an indelible array of "beautiful" characteristics, including Italian charm, a loving nature, a generous soul, humorous charisma, an unrelenting drive, a love of beautiful woman, and a pride unmatched for providing the best environment in Cleveland that the city would have to offer to an immigrant family. One of his most endearing qualities was a sense of humor that often carried the day. He was witty, charismatic, while dressing, and grooming immaculately. When older, he sported a closely trimmed mustache that was narrow and divided with a shaven "v" matching the cleft above his upper lip and nearly identical to the mustache sported by Clarke Gable in the role of Rhett Butler of Gone "With the Wind" fame. His dark brown hair was always well trimmed with wonderful waves just short of loose curls cropped over the top and crown of his head.

In another vein, Louis was generous to a fault, often giving money to those in need and eventually providing his sister and brother-in-law with a down payment for their home.

A beautiful and captivating woman he would eventually marry would also with time polish Louis's best qualities even further.

Knowing of country men living in Cleveland, Grandpa after arriving from "the old country," was open to advice on where to live. Their new lives began when Filippo, with help from a first cousin, would move his family, for a few short years from New York into a small apartment on 22nd and Woodland in Cleveland, Ohio. Good jobs were hard to come by though political connections, as has always been the case, would serve the purposes of Filippo who knew someone, who knew someone else, and who even knew someone else.

Through connections, Filippo found a job working as a laborer for the Cuyahoga County engineers. Cuyahoga County was the home of Cleveland and many other fine communities.

Some might think, now you call those connections? With connections like that, who needs connections. All joking aside, the job was a good job that paid well for a young immigrant and he appreciated this gift that provided a means into the future for the Caravella's.

Grandpa was a short, stocky and powerful man that could wield a good pickax with the best of them. Street, sewer repair, and construction would become his vocation as he toiled for a quarter of a century both above and below a myriad of hometown projects. The work was difficult but reliable. During his free time, Filippo, sometimes being called by a few as Philip, would work construction doing odd jobs for Zingale and Company.

Many of the details of the Caravella's lives were lost, since these things were not discussed, and if so, we're lost in translation as we children were never privileged to learn the Italian language. My folks had grown weary of prejudice, even before bearing the full blunt of language. Me did not want us to share in the "right of passage" that many before and many after us would eventually suffer. Possibly the scourge of the passage in "the old days" makes Americans what they are and what they will become.

For it is in the journey and the tribulations that build character, confidence, and "street smarts" harbored by immigrants of all descriptions. Many tend to be tougher and smarter than most Americans born "with a silver spoon" in their mouth. Once past their indoctrination, American immigrants bear the indelible marks of passion and experience forever wedding them to a culture and freedom not known by other less challenged peoples.

The Caravella's lives were somewhat difficult as were most others during the depression years. Money was closely held and children were expected to help provide for the family in difficult times. Education took a back seat to the demands of daily life forcing most to focus on the day-to-day struggles of survival.

Italian traditions, family unity, and Catholic teachings would shape the Caravella destiny, as time moved on. Italian-Catholic feast days were honored as they should be with remarkable displays of food and fun but not before God was given his due at Catholic services.

Grandma Rose was a kitchen artist with such skills, that Emeril would be challenged to duplicate. Later on, Grandma's daughter Santina would overshadow her mother with kitchen creations that were so luscious and delicious as to be beyond compare and description.

Louis Philip Caravella would attend Brownell Junior High School located at East 14th and Erie Street, on Cleveland's near Eastside. He would later attend high school but would never finish. At the age of sixteen he felt he had to help the family and became interested in becoming a barber after talking with family friends who were also in the trade. He learned the skills of barbering from a close friend who saw in dad his eye for perfection and artistic abilities required to work the magic so sought after by businessmen of many descriptions.

At the end of each week, after receiving his pay from his hair cutting skills, Louis would return home and put his pay under his mother's pillow.

Though intelligent and clever, his business mind would eventually drive him in a different direction. Schooling was not a Caravella strong point due to pressing family financial needs. Santina likewise would not graduate from high school but like her brother she attended Brownell as well. Survival and financial relief would be more in keeping with Louis's immediate goals.

The Eastside Cleveland neighborhood included large numbers of Italians, Jewish, and Slovenians. Friends and families often congregated in the streets to play baseball or other activities that would materialize sometimes at a moment's notice. Automobiles were not common on side streets but were left primarily to the main thoroughfares surrounding Cleveland neighborhoods.

During the early years, the Caravella's when residing in Cleveland would require a larger home. They went on to rent a place at 2267 Hazen Avenue, near Saint Joseph's Catholic Church on Cleveland's East Side. This home which would serve the family well for about seven to eight years. In the backyard was a small garden from which vegetables were harvested beneath a trellis strewn with grape vine hanging from the wooden overhead crosshatched beams and sporting precious purple grapes when the season was right.

They even had a small grey-white coated goat that roamed about and provided milk for the family. The Caravella goat went by the name of Caesar and in sharing the backyard would be occasionally challenged by Princess the family pet poodle. Sometimes being caught off guard, Princess knew when to back off before the going got too rough. Princess delivered several litters of her own. The pups were given away. As Filippo would denote, when it came to pets, the fewer the mouths to feed the better, though a little companionship was always a good thing. Later on, Princess eventually died and was followed by a scruffy yet powerful mutt named Tarzan who also had the run of the property.

Eventually the Caravella's were able to save enough money to purchase a larger duplex with an upper apartment serving as a source of rental income. Their new three-bedroom home, acquired a few years after it was built, was located at 3640 East 147th street near Kinsman Road about a stone's throw from Shaker Heights.

The home had a small stunted back porch that was rarely used due to its diminutive size and would thus serve more as a bird landing than anything else. It had an average sized kitchen, with large white ornate carved wood along with beveled glass covering the cabinets. The white large cabinets were streaming around the entire periphery of the kitchen, surrounding a medium sized solid white oak Italian crafted table that was butch enough to support a small car. Of course, the kitchen table was the center of attraction for all Italians especially when only a few guests were about.

For the most part, the kitchen exceeded in importance the dining room, though Grandma Rose's dining room sported a dark brown massive Mediterranean-Italian style table and chairs, a large buffet cabinet, along with other furnishings. When the "the family" would gather for Sunday feasts or holiday parties the dining room due to its size would become the main gathering point.

The kitchen table served as a coffee-pastry hub for guests and visitors sometimes relinquishing its primary function as a mealtime gathering place. Countless stories of intrigue, adventure, hearsay, gossip, and make believe, were shared at that wonderful table only to be embellished as time went on.

A good story becomes a better story with time on its side, as long as it is told with enthusiasm, relish, and hysterics to add to the experience.

Strewn around the home were a variety of ornate trinkets from the "old country. "The most memorable were small toy like wooden, intricately painted two-wheel horse drawn carts with each animal sporting a circus-like red or yellow plum projecting from between their ears in an upright fashion. These represented festive examples of carts ridden and driven during Sicilian religious feasts and gatherings in decades if not centuries gone by. They were also more ornately painted than the more common and mundane carts used to bring fruits and wares to market.

Grandma was very religious as were the rest of us and had many Catholic statuettes and ornate religious items throughout the dining and living room areas with a crucifix hung on a central wall that I must have peered at a thousand times.

The basement had a second kitchen with a stove that grandma would use to prepare magnificent holiday feasts for loved ones when the main floor kitchen would not suffice. On weekends and feast days the basement stove was ladened with amazing sauces, roasts, mashed and baked potatoes of every description followed by mouth dripping desserts the likes of which would drop you to your knees in amazement, not the least of which were cannoli of several varieties. Cannoli being a uniquely Italian creation by a Roman statesman Cicero, in 70 BC, would harbor an amazing story to unfold much later in the lives of the Caravella's. Grandma Rose loved to cook and treated all of us to amazing feasts on many occasions not the least of which were all religious holidays, especially Easter and Christmas.

When growing up, all of our personal family holidays with mom and dad would begin in our Rocky River, Ohio home. "River" as we called it was a western suburb of Cleveland. Before the day was over, mom's small family feasts, would inevitably expand across town to our grandparents' homes on the other side of the city.

This was sort of fun but we children missed staying at home on Christmas to play with Santa Clause's generous presents. As my mother would say to us on so many occasions, "There's always another day". But of course, someday there would not be.

Grandma Caravella held a special place in her heart for first son Louis. He was her pride and joy because he had a good heart and a love for her that would always be.

Grandma's gifts of cooking and baking were passed on to her youngest, little Santina, who learned hundreds of recipes from the old country.

Aunt Santina or Aunt San as we called her, met and married James Torrissi when she was age sixteen to seventeen would go on to have four children, Rosemary, Nancy, Stella, and Salvatore. As time went on Santina became a fabulous and loving mother to her wonderful family. Her place was in the home where she continued to raise her children and made every effort to make Uncle Jim's life and the lives of her children as wonderful as possible. They had limited means but were still able to provide for their children.

With time, Santina would even improve upon her mother's cooking skills which were to begin with, a nearly impossible feat to beat. I guess you see a pattern here of persistent speaking of delicious foods and pastries conjured up by my grandmother and her children as well. Italians as a nationality are likely most recognized for their wonderful food, devotion to God, the Catholic faith, but especially to the needs of their families. Nothing is more important to Italians than their family, children, and love of each other.

My aunt San was very very very short, standing well under five feet tall and always displaying the warmest smile accompanied by a huge hug, upon entering a room, for everyone in sight of her. She was a saint in a similar fashion as was my mother's mother Generosa Franzolino.

Aunt San never spoke badly of anyone. She was generous to a fault in talking about others. Her baking was way over-the-top in quality, taste, and amazement. One cannot overly portray the scrumptious pastries she was capable of baking. Find the best pies you could ever imagine and hers seemed to be infinitely better. She really had the gift. I mean she had the gift. Her cakes of all descriptions were short on the decorative side but so long on taste, moisture, and texture that they could have been the Michael Angelo's of the baking world. Every time I would visit Aunt at her home, she would pop out on the kitchen table a cake, cookies, or pastries that would more than throw any other baker into hysterics if they could taste her delicious creations always deserving of the highest accolades.

Fine wine making was a standard old country tradition among Italian immigrants that became a rule in most households if they had a cool basement and the means to proceed with a masterstroke of Italian genius. Every year a large quantity of wine was made and given away by Grandpa

Caravella to his relatives and friends. He would purchase crates of fresh purple grapes pressed to a mash before adding sugar and other secret ingredients to arrive at a perfect blend somewhere south of a Merlot but just north of a Cabernet.

None was sold and his creative art was even more cherished during prohibition. Why let a few laws get in the way of long-term Italian traditions. Six-fifty-gallon wooden barrels lined the northwest basement wall. Each one rested on a concrete block pedestal to be brought into service when wine making began. Wine making was simple conceptually, though involved a lot of hard work to bring it to fruition considering the amount of grape required to make fifty-gallon batches of high-quality red wine. Twenty-five-pound crates of grape were passed down the home's coal shoot into grandpa's basement, through an opening at driveway level. A truck or wagon would deliver "the goods" to the driveway where grandpa stood helping the delivery man pass the crates down the shut while someone at the other end would grab and stack them nearby.

The grape was immediately fed into a grinder that ground the grape into a mash so it could be more easily pressed. No attempt was made to remove the vines, stems, seeds, or unfortunate insects that resided within. I remember often finding spiders and their webs in crates of grape on a regular basis. The alcohol killed any worrisome bacteria so the rest of the problem was purely academic. What you didn't see would never hurt or so I surmised. The entire grape blend was then placed in a large round wooden sided press. The press was layered with the chunky grape concoction from the grinder topped off by a layer of cheesecloth like material. Many layers filled up the press followed by a top wooden circular board that would crown the structure. Apparently, the layers of cheesecloth filtered the non-liquid matter away, such as spiders, grape vine, and all, leaving a rich wine like blend. Sugar was added appropriately to the grape mash and then the grape was pressed with the residual juices running down ward into a trough and from there into the fifty-gallon charred wooden barrels for fermenting. Grandpa made about two hundred gallons per year from fine blue and red California grape.

The grape juice would ferment for weeks or months and soon wine was the order of the day. The better the grape, the better the wine. Good grape growing weather accompanied by adequate moisture would insure a wonderful blended taste year after year. The wines flavor never really varied as per my palate. But what do I know.

Later in years when my father had his own home, grandpa's wine was delivered into a wine cellar that Dad had constructed in the basement of our home in Rocky River, Ohio. The wine was stored in a large wooden wine barrel similar to what Grandpa had residing in his basement. The wine was added through the top of his wine-barrel via five-gallon jugs until it was filled to the correct capacity. This would provide wine for an entire year for our family and guests. The dark red wine had a deep flavor with just the right taste, as my dad often professed.

At my young age of ten or twelve, I was certainly not a connoisseur and thus could not be a critic one way or the other. Give me a Coke and I was happy. Due to my families limited means, Cokes were much scarcer than wine.

Grandpa's wine was so consistent every year, that to my dad's palate it never varied. Dad was always pleased with the wine, enjoying two or three small juice size glasses every evening with dinner. He was very proud of his father's wine processing prowess and served it to guests at every turn.

Not far from grandpa's huge wine cellar was a small room fed with a coal shoot to provide for Cleveland's long cold winters. Cold weather could begin as early as the fall and be prolonged into senile spring. We were all very adept at wearing the warmest multi-layered clothing, heavy outer-ware, and gloves of endless descriptions from the flowery ornate that children loved, to the hard-core heavy coarse leather, cotton, or flannel lined varieties many used when working outside on the job or shoveling the white fluffy wonderful clumps and bottomless crystals of snow that often graced the evening skies, driveways, streets, and landscapes. Snowing, snowfall, shoveling is a way of life that all Northerners embrace and looked forward to especially in the early winter season when they had become fed up with raking leaves. Raking leaves is actually more of a hassle than snow shoveling especially in the era preceding the leaf blower. I never had a chance to use one.

The North Midwest is blessed with seasonally cold, wintery, snowy, Santa Clause laden days that have their own wonderful character not experienced by Southerners. Snow is the secret sauce that laces the season with a sense of Christmas coming down the road. Those who love sledding, skiing, snowball fights, and creating angels in the snow, would understand the fun of outward flinging legs and arms creating interesting wings and designs of several descriptions by excited children enjoying every second of play.

A deep crisp winter evening with fresh snow glistening in the moon and street lights has its own charm not equal to many other natural phenomena anywhere else experienced. Fine flakes of white snow would pass around and under the street lights in a beautify artistic way garnering wonderful photos taken by so many snow worshipers.

With time, as the winter dragged on, the beauty and artsy quality of the snow fall would lose its luster since on so many occasions it would have to be shoveled, plowed, or removed to the point that it became more of a pain in the neck ("ass") until we threw up our arms in disgust.

Another blessing of the first frost of the season is the deathblow to those pesky little flying creatures that too often light on your skin to suck your blood from its capillaries leaving behind a raised itchy red welt that takes days to resolve. Goodbye mosquitos.

My folk's had a gas furnace heated home that was always appropriately warmed with the flip of a switch or a press of a button. Of course, grandpa's furnace required regular stoking in the cold months to achieve the same magic of comfort we all enjoyed. Grandpa's home had a large coal driven furnace, fed by coal from a coal bin located in the basement and adjacent to the furnace. Stoking the furnace in the morning after a cold night was a routine that beefed up your men's biceps on a daily winter morn.

The large black shiny chunks of coal were fed through the same shoot used for fresh grape passage in warmer seasons (of course the coal shoot was cleaned compulsively in the spring before the grape was harvested) via an opening in the wall to the outside just a foot or so above ground level. The river of coal would pass downward through the shoot from the driveway into the basement whenever a delivery was necessary. Hard almost crystal cut coal had a rich shiny look to it and not the look that you would imagine it would have unless you have seen it in the "flesh".

Not being from the coal belt, I still have an appreciation for interesting shiny black geometric structures wherever they exist. Coal is a beautiful thing.

With that being said, I wish to acknowledge Debbie's father who toiled in the coal mines of Pennsylvania for decades, only to die of black lung disease, a horrible, if not the worst part of using coal to power America and heat the homes and businesses of so many people. I am sure many people who used coal, to their benefit, did not recognize the true and extreme health hazards it dealt to those who gave their lives for the rest of us so that we could enjoy the positive aspects of what coal could provide.

Debbie's father, William Walter Thompson who also went by the name of Dick, was born in Chattanooga, Tennessee, and was also part Dick, was to Pittsburg, Pennsylvania to be a coal miner and also worked as a farmer for much of his adult life. He farmed many acres of land on a huge farm belonging to an uncle of Debbie. Debbie would comment, "he grew everything imaginable," with the outcome of providing amazing vegetables for the family table. When time permitted, he was an avid hunter as well, providing even more food for the family to enjoy. He was a very hard worker and provided well for his very large family of twelve children.

Debbie's mother, Virginia Marie Thompson became the wife of William, her maiden name being Miller. She was a good woman who worked so hard at caring for her huge flock. Virginia was born in Pittsburg and lived her entire life there. Before marriage, she wanted to be an attorney or an English teacher but of course those plans morphed into so many other avenues of greater importance; primarily caring for so many children. Her motherly instincts did not lend itself well to following her dreams of teaching or practicing law.

Parents give up many personal desires to care for the needs of their children. It is what is expected and we can all relate to that as time goes on.

One thing they never gave up. Both Debbie and her parents were hard core Pittsburg Steelers fans. You know what that means, since the rest of us are hard core Cleveland Browns fans.

Debbie's mother, like my grandparents, was a master chef, providing wonderful and delicious dishes of all kinds to please her large family. She canned and made jams and pies along with fabulous home baked bread. And you know what that means. As my mother said on many occasions, "I could make a meal on bread and butter."

Virginia was so very proud of her beautiful and talented daughter, Debbie. She wanted Debbie to be a standout among her friends. She would often take her to Cleveland from Pittsburg for shopping trips, so that she could find clothing styles different from what her friends all wore. Debbie is a clothes hound and a fashion aficionado on all aficionado love of designer clothes, shoes, handbags, perfumes, and all other feminine "wants" or "needs" were likely partially related to her mother's hopes and dreams that would not play out in her life but would rather reach fruition in the life of her daughter. What she did not have, she wanted for Debbie.

Deb's mom was also very humble and very much into her faith and love of God. It is unfortunate that I never had a chance to meet her, since she was gone before Debbie and I had met. Both Debbie and her mother looked so very much alike. They could have been twins. Maybe that is why her mother treated her in very special ways. Debbie would enjoy many occupations that her mother could never realize for herself. The list of Debbie's past jobs included school bus driving, substitute teaching, dental assistant, sales offices, airport gate agent, barber, hair stylist, and most recently as an airline attendant for Delta.

That was a long aside though very deserving of it.

Getting back to my grandparents' wonderful home. In warmer months, the small back porch attached to their home was almost an after-thought. It graced the back of my grandparents' home to provide access to the back yard when someone had chores to do. Feeding the rabbits, peeps, and chickens confined to several pens behind the single car garage in the backyard was a daily event regardless of the season. These cute critters of many sizes and colors were raised for food or for eggs.

As a child I tried not to think about what their future had in store for them and only visited their cages once or twice during my entire childhood. The less I knew about what went on in the back yard and behind the garage, the better off I was. Ignorance is bliss under some circumstances. On the other hand, never having sat on the back porch due to its tiny capacity and lack of chairs, left me with little time to wonder about the happenings of the back yard eco-structure or environment.

The front of my grandparents, home had a more usable widened and elongated porch with two or three comfortable couch like lounge chairs to relax in. Though like the back porch, we rarely inhabited that part of my grandparent's home except on rare or brief occasions. And why was that? The action was never there. When visiting the grandparents, nearly all the fun and entertainment occurred inside their cozy, interesting, and very livable home.

Thinking about our home in "River," mom and dad always enjoyed the comfort of the Caravella living room where a small TV was nestled into the front left corner of the room adjacent to a large "picture window" overlooking Gasser Boulevard. The side windows of the large central window were covered most of the time by beautiful drapes. The central window pane with dimensions of about five feet tall and seven feet long was covered with a colorful floral drape that could be closed by pulling a draw string during the evening hours once darkness set in.

The TV was always tuned into the baseball or football game of the day that Dad enjoyed immensely. Mom had no interest in sports to speak of. In fact, mom had no interest in television either. She rarely sat down to watch a single minute. She always seemed to be busy in the kitchen preparing dishes to eat or cleaning up in any number of ways.

When watching TV, Dad sat in his own large chair that was very comfortable and located in the living room allowing for a good view of the screen. Though almost any place in the living room offered good seating when the time came to watch something special, usually selected by Dad. After an hour or so, Dad would inevitably fall asleep in his chair. Mom would eventually come into the living room around ten PM and would begin to coax Dad into going to bed with her in the master bedroom. Phyllis, I, and "little" Lou of course followed suit and were never up beyond ten PM even on weekends.

Of course, nearly every Cleveland native cherished the Browns and the Indians. In those days the Browns were a power to be reckoned with. The 1964 football championship was the last and ended on a good note when the Browns beat the competition 27-0. Cleveland has never played in a Super Bowl. The Cleveland Indians have not fare much better and would have average years but rarely great years. Some say God hates Cleveland. I don't think that's it at all. He's instead protecting us from all of the hysteria and mania that would invariably occur had we won something of importance. Now that's true love. Winning is too much of a hardship. Ask any Clevelander! When you win you have to maintain the same annual rituals; too much trouble! Way too much trouble! We are blessed. Pittsburg citizens where my wife Debbie heralds from can barely deal with all of their victories. I do have pity for them.

When in Rome; I meant at grandpa's home, Mom would visit with Rose. Dad of course hung out with the men, which usually included grandpa Filippo, uncle Bob, and sometimes uncle Jim of Torrisi fame. Occasionally a Torrisi would drop on by with their "kids" to be included in a fine dinner along with the rest of the Caravella clan. My cousin Sam Torrisi, would sometimes darken the Caravella door when dragged along with his parents, though he was three years older than I and had his own group of friends that he hung with. He and I would with time develop a much closer relationship not anticipated in my younger days.

Sam was a gem as was his cute little sister Stella and his older sister Rosemary. Stella was a little peanut standing well under five feet tall at her tallest. She sported medium brown hair, cute eyes and a smile that would draw anyone's attention. Rosemary in contrast was a real beauty with silky red hair somewhat garnered from her mother's genes. I loved them all; cousins and friends to the core. When I was with Sam, Phyllis would spend her moments of fun with Stella primarily and sometimes with Rosemary should she be around. Rosemary being a bit older often did not accompany her parents to our home and was rarely around when we would visit her home.

My grandparent's home had a reasonably large front yard with a couple of trees and respectable landscaping. I never saw Grandpa ever do a lick of work in the yard, be it in the back or in the front. Somehow things were maintained though I am not a party to the mystery of how that ever took place.

The back yard had a large grape trellis backed up in the near distance by a distant small white wooden pen located behind the garage yet butted up against landscaping. I pen was built off of the ground usually housing two or three fat white rabbits with pink little twitchy noses that were raised – God help us - for food. Yes, you read that right. They would become rabbit stew, rabbit legs, rabbit whatever – but I did not have the courage to ever tell my twin sister the bad news. These furry white critters, distantly related to the Easter Bunny would serve or be served at another time. Not unlike the chickens that were raised for eggs and food, the bunnies would also find their way onto the dining room table sooner or later.

When facing the Caravella home and located to the right side was a long narrow driveway sporting a narrow patch of grass growing down the central area separating one concrete tread lane from the other similar to a miniature boulevard but without the requisite trees growing within the grassy area. This arrangement reduced the cost of making the driveway and added to the natural beauty of the front yard. I have often wondered why this driveway's geometric concrete design had not become a staple option for most driveways. Maybe the upkeep of trimming these long rivers of grass would lead to their less than enthusiastic reception by the majority of new homeowners in the area.

Grandpa liked cars and always had one as a daily driver. Grandma Rose always referred to automobiles as "machines. "She would say, "Filippo, get the machine and take me to the grocers" or to some such place. Grandma never learned how to drive though I suspect Italian women did not. My cousin Sam's mother likewise never drove a car. This request to pull up the "machine" always made me laugh inside whenever I heard her say it. I was so used to her saying "machine" that I never questioned its origin or it's use but in today's era it would be thought of as quite odd if not humorous to the uninitiated.

Their home was a duplex rented out all of the years that I can remember. The upstairs tenants were said to be friendly but rarely socialized with the Caravella's and for that matter their business remained mysterious to me due to a total lack of information about them. It was as if they never existed. I never met them, never saw them, and never had a conversation with any of them over the thirty or so years I visited my grandparents. They will always remain a mystery to me on every level.

I eventually learned that there were two small families living in the upstairs apartment, if you could call it that. In the early years, Mr. and Mrs. Benheim lived there and later on were replaced by the Blankenship's. The upstairs unit, like the first floor of Rose's home, also had three bedrooms with the usual two baths, a living room, and a kitchen similar to Grandma's. Going on the premise that they were happy folks,

I suspect they were fine in their nest and that no news was good news.

The Caravella home was near Saint Joseph's Catholic Church, frequented weekly by the entire family. The family attended mass, an important Italian ritual. Grandma Rose had many religious articles scattered among her possessions and around many places in her home. As often as we visited my grandparents, we never however went to Mass with them because we would always visit them on a Sunday afternoon after they had already attended services. They were actively involved in The Church but on their own schedule.

After rearing her children to a reasonable age, my grandmother went to work to help support the family. She operated a power sewing machine making sweaters at a well-known clothing manufacturer in the area. She worked long days but enjoyed it and felt comfortable contributing to the family's needs.

My father Louis worked for years to help support the family as well. Many Italian immigrants were laborers, barbers, carpenters, or other tradesmen. His first job was as a barber becoming interested in the skill through a family acquaintance. He learned the trade from Alfonso, a skilled barber who taught Louis how to cut hair over a three-to-four-year period of time at the Detroit-Giel Barbershop in Lakewood, Ohio. Louis would take a one-hour trip on the streetcar across town from the Eastside of Cleveland where he lived with his mother, heading to the Westside winding up in

Lakewood, Ohio. Eventually he would buy a 1937 Hudson Terraplane; not exactly a Maybach but never the less a fine four-door sedan to scurry in back and forth across town. In that year the Terraplane had been selected as the number "1" car of the lower priced cars that were available.

The Detroit-Giel Barber Shop was located about five or so miles from what would become our future home in Rocky River, Ohio.

Being very gregarious, Dad enjoyed fun conversations and storytelling with his customers. Being a jokester from the get-go, he was always mixing it up with clients, friends, neighbors, and relatives. My dad was a character.

Louis loved America with a passion and never looked back after arriving on these shores. He cherished America and its ideals. He believed we could all live in relative harmony and that is where our power truly lies. We are adaptable, forgiving, innovative, clever, God fearing, capitalistic, industrious, protective, democratic, humorous, kind, grateful, progressive, and more, all in one panoramic society. Sure, this country has issues but Dad never thought any were insurmountable and though most were rarely trivial, they all could be dealt with whether racial or equal rights in character, or financial in nature.

My father hated to hear anyone besmirch his beloved country. He came here to seek the riches for his family that his father had spoken of. The streets are paved in gold for those who mine for gold by working hard at an honest day's work. Paying attention to reality was a God given attribute he had that worked for him throughout his life. He found gold and happiness.

My father and his brother Robert often spoke of the amazing qualities of Americans and the gifts America would bestow on his family. My father was a loyal American. My mother was his counterpart. We children were raised to love and respect America and were taught to behave, respect our neighbors, and their property.

Dad was a sharp dresser nearly on the level of an *Esquire* gentleman. He was always clean-shaven and I never ceased to be amazed by his skill in wielding a straight razor from side-to-side only rarely nicking his skin every other blue moon or less. At work, he always wore crisp white freshly laundered shirts from a dry cleaner near his own shop, requiring very brief yet frequent trips to maintain the look he always radiated. Later on in his career he switched from the standard white button-down dress shirt with tie to a more comfortable and "professional barber style" shirt with a white flap that folded down from his left shoulder angled in an open downward fashion towards the opposite side of his chest. It had more of a barber almost classic look about it without the pretentiousness of a white shirt and tie.

Dad's look remained extra sharp when he would wear a custom designed and crafted suit gratis Uncle John Kosalam mother's sister's husband, for decades was the head designer of Richman Brothers Men's Clothing Manufacturer located on East 55th Street in Cleveland's near east side. At one time it was the largest manufacturer of men's clothing stateside but eventually would become overtaken by foreign firms that were slowly suffocating many American businesses not only in the clothing industry but eventually including the manufacture of electronics, toys, and of course automobiles as time would prove. The Japanese and later the Chinese steamrolling methods of operation would eventually be outdone by their own success.

The Chinese caste system still remains, but in a toned-down version that could be considered progress as more of the disenfranchised become functionally better off. I suppose that really is progress. My father, like the Chinese understood the concept of competition, efficiency, progress, and innovation developing a host of new ideas in the operation of his two businesses that would later evolve with time. My dad was rarely critical of any business practices with the exception of always opposing the barber's union attempt to increase the price of haircuts every few years. He believed that every price increase amounted to a doomsday effect. Being such a skilled barber and a very likable man, his business never faltered no matter how much he pouted about it.

Getting back to the *Esquire* look, Uncle John was equally as sharply dressed as Dad and wore the most pristine clothing with the cleanest appearance I have ever seen. He could have modeled for *Esquire* or any similar men's journal.

Uncle set the tone and had the look. He was remarkable and soft spoken as anyone almost to the point of a whisper, yet firm in his demeanor while wielding the best smile as he managed his children and nephews whenever we visited in his home or ours. As my wife Debra would often say, related to her training as a Delta airline attendant, "You can say anything, to anyone and get away with it if you do so with a smile on your face".

Uncle John's "clean as a whistle" home in Euclid, Ohio, always had a manicured lawn and sculptured shrubs. His garage was cleaner than your finest room or office space. His home was several octaves above his garage in condition and cleanliness. A white glove test of his surroundings by a full Colonel would pass every time.

This man was immaculate to a fault. The only cleaner possessions he owned was his pristine black 1957 Chevy Belair. He always had a top-of-the-line model that was so squeaky clean, you could eat off of the engine or even the tailpipe for that matter. I mean you cannot get it, unless you saw these vehicles. They could easily pass for a "show queen" at any Amelia Island Concourse. On another note, my Aunt Edith never learned to drive. Uncle John was very domineering and maybe by limiting her ability to get around, it really became a control issue. Their marriage however appeared to any outsider to be pristine in every way.

In those days, little was thought about women of that era not driving. Many did not smoke. Many did not curse. A few did and I can attest to that. But women were always capable of being provocative; a God given gift for any woman beginning with Eve and her first bite of the forbidden fruit. I am sure, at the end of the day, my Aunt Edith achieved whatever she desired in a very quiet and secretive way since she never suffered from the lack of an attractive wardrobe or the finest food for her family. Aunt Edith was equally charming, clothed, and groomed but gentle and soft-spoken in every way. She was sweet and never rude or unlikeable. She was always dishing out hugs and "smooches" to us children. Her clothing was perfectly worn and majestically draped in fashionable ways that would put Queen Elizabeth on notice. Queen Elizabeth rarely smiles. My aunt Edith perfected the smile.

It is of interest to note that Uncle John was a full-blooded German by decent and Aunt Edith was an exceptional Italian with equal but different bloodlines. They were sort of the Axis World War II Powers tucked into one provocative Euclid, Ohio, household on the north and near east side of Cleveland bordering on Lake Erie.

America was easy to love by Dad, with a passion to a degree that he never looked back at his childhood life in Sicily once arriving on these shores. He cherished America and its ideals. He believed we could all live in relative harmony and that is where our power truly lies. We Americans are adaptable, forgiving, innovative, clever, God fearing, capitalistic, industrious, protective, democratic, humorous, kind, grateful, progressive, and more, all in one panoramic society. Sure, this country has issues but Dad never thought any were insurmountable and though most were rarely trivial they all could be dealt with whether racial or equal rights in character, or financial in nature.

My father hated to hear anyone besmirch his beloved country. He came here to seek the riches for his family that his father had spoken of. The streets are paved in gold for those who mine for gold through a hard and honest day's work. Paying attention to reality was a God given attribute he had that worked for him throughout his life. He found gold and happiness.

Uncle Bob, as we called Robert, and my father often spoke of the amazing qualities of Americans and the gifts America would bestow on his family. My father was a loyal American. My mother was his counterpart. We children were raised to love and respect America and were taught to behave, respect our neighbors, and their property.

In his own way Dad was very giving, kind, and generous. He treated my Uncle John to a fine haircut whenever uncle visited our home. It was one of Dad's things. Dad had this special elevated chair in our basement adjacent to mom's washer and drier where a bare light bulb hung from the ceiling directly above the chair. We all frequented that chair on a regular basis. He cut and sculptured our hair with magical designs hoping to please us in every way and to show off his skills among out neighbors and friends.

Dad was a good soul and everyone loved and respected him. His majesty was in his gift of thinking of the needs of others. He was not a saint in that he would occasionally have a fit of anger now and then but never towards family members. Other associates that crossed him would meet with their just desserts. He was not to be messed with. Keep it honest and fair and he was good to you.

The Caravella family originated from Sicily while my mother's side of the family, the Franzolinos were from the boot of Italy hailing from Naples.

During the early part of the 20th Century the Franzolinos were evolving as newfound immigrants patterned somewhat after Dad's family. My mother Adele's father, Luciano (Louis) Franzolino had immigrated to Cleveland to stay with his brother John Franzolino. Ironically Louis Caravella and his future father-in-law had the same first names.

Together Luciano and John would later on purchase a duplex on East 93rd street in Cleveland, Ohio. During this period, he was working as a stone and cement worker until being laid off. During the offseason John moved to Hoboken, New Jersey, so he could live with friends.

Luciano would eventually become a tailor, though with a specialty if you will of hand pressing expensive dresses and gowns for the social elite of Cleveland. He always went to work wearing a suit and tie, and many felt he dressed as a banker. Being fussy about his appearance, he was handsomely groomed at all times. Standing just over six feet tall, he was quite stately in appearance. Upon reaching work, he would change into lighter more appropriate clothing to avoid perspiration and soiling of his suit and shirts from exposure to uncomfortable heat during much of his workday. His cute smile and humorous mannerisms would endear him to all that he would meet.

Luciano had heard of a beautiful young maiden, Generosa Borrasso, who had arrived in New York from Naples, Luciano's own home town. Beginning at age five, Generosa was raised in an Italian orphanage by nuns after her mother's death from influenzas lived in the Padua Italian orphanage until age 20. Her younger sister Cecilia had moved years before to America with her father and four brothers. Her brother Carl arranged for his sister to immigrate to America, narrowly missing a marriage arrangement in Italy. She moved to Hoboken to live with her father where she was eventually introduced to Luciano who was at that time living there as well. Generosa was a cute little thing standing two to three tads south of being five feet tall. Being raised by the nuns who gave no quarter, she was very pious, soft spoken, a hard worker, and enjoyed an endless devotion to the Lord. Her main gift, the love of the Lord was reflected in everything she ever did throughout her life. She was a saint and could have been another Mother Theresa under similar circumstances.

The newly married Franzolinos' moved from Hoboken, New Jersey, into the upstairs flat of the duplex located on 93rd

St. in Cleveland that he and his brother John had purchased earlier. They would eventually have five children with Sylvia being born one year later after their nuptials. Sylvia was followed in birth by wonderful siblings named Ida, Alberto, Adeline, and eventually Anthony. Ida would have here name changed to Edith and Adeline had her name refined to Adele. Who does that? Apparently, women of strong character knowing what they want to fulfill their destiny. As was said earlier, Aunt Edith had more going on than met the eye. I guess the woman of the family were fairly tough minded or at least independent to a large degree yet respectful of others and loving in nature.

My mother with the given name of Adeline, was born October 18, 1915, and was named after an opera singer Adele, by her Godfather who insisted on adopting her for his own since he and his wife were not able to have children. My grandfather Luciano stunned by the thought, said the "idea was out of the question" and again, that was that. My mother's name gestated from that of the opera singer though I rarely heard my mother sing a note. She likely had a fine singing voice though her reserve nature was not one to release any operative sounds that I ever heard.

Luciano was loving but very strict, while Generosa was gentle and extremely religious, reading her prayer book at least one hour per day. At dinnertime all had assigned seats and no one was permitted to speak until after the meal. I suspect the cell phone lighting up at the dinner table (had it existed at the time) would have resulted in a flight into the trashcan never to be seen again. Grandpa would have been furious.

Birthdays were handled in a way never to show favoritism. As a birthday gift, each of the Franzolino children received a penny for each year of age. The coins were placed under their dinner plate. Generosa always baked a birthday cake for each of her children on their special day. For Christmas, Luciano would buy a five-pound box of chocolates for everyone to share. Gifts were limited to a few handmade articles. Times were tough.

The Franzolinos were very thrifty but strongly believed in home ownership and encouraged their children to do articles. Times off their home as quickly as possible was sacrosanct.

Adele would remember her mother to be the "sweetest person on earth. She never yelled at us or spanked us. I loved the way she talked to us. My mother, being so close to her own mother named her youngest daughter Jennifer, after her mother, Generosa.

The Franzolino home was on Crestwood Ave just off Woodland near Luna Park on Cleveland's near east side. My mother would walk several blocks to school attending Anthony Wayne Grade School. When growing up she assisted her mother in household chores and helped in making lunches for her siblings. Mom was always neat and clean with polished shoes. While in high school she at times assisted the school's nurse in the dispensary and was awarded a Florence Nightingale pin. She was an avid reader, often walking to a woman's home in the neighborhood to borrow books to read. Doing well in all subjects, she would later graduate from John Adams High School at the unusually young age of sixteen. Her youth acted against her in the job arena in that no one would hire her at first due to her young age.

She desperately wanted to become a nurse, but during the dark days of the depression she was unable to continue her education. A future grandchild however would later fulfill that dream that my mother could not. After graduating from high school, mom eventually worked at the height of the depression with her sister Sylvia, earning twelve dollars per week at the Gottfried Company making house dresses. She would give her father about eight dollars and would spend $1. 25 a week to ride the streetcar. She kept the rest for spending money. She was grateful to have work. Being seen as very bright, she was later hired as the manager of a Kroger bakery in a store next to The May Company on 4th and Prospect in downtown Cleveland. The May Company was very similar to the Dillards style of department store.

Mom was good with money and bookkeeping. At the end of the day, she would purchase bread at half price and from then on never felt her time was worth baking bread and so she never again would do bookkeeping. At would sometimes purchase three loves of golden iced raisin bread for a quarter.

Her other siblings worked at various jobs to help out during the tough times of the depression. Anthony, called by his friends Tony, worked at the corner chicken store where live chickens were sold to the neighborhood residents. A patron would walk into the store, select a chicken, and then it would be killed and plucked before being sold. After a long twelve-hour day, my Uncle Tony would be paid at the end with three chickens, cleaned and dressed which of course the family greatly appreciated.

Attending church each Sunday became a routine for all of the Franzolino clan and for that matter for most Italian Americans. Generosa, being such a devoted Catholic prayed daily and through her example encouraged her children to remain close to The Church as well.

Mom had a special Jewish friend, Estelle Golden and by association was often believed by many to be Jewish herself. In fact, her neighborhood had a high concentration of Italians, Jewish, and Slovenians. They got along well, socializing in many ways. The younger boys often played baseball together out in the center of their street when traffic was manageable.

In Greater Cleveland, social dancing became a craze from the 1920's and well into the 1950's. These establishments however were looked upon as "potential havens for moral laxness between the sexes" leading to Cleveland passing

Ordinance 690 with restrictions on liquor sales, gambling, and smoking restrictions limited to designated areas. The ordinance also established guidelines for behavior and appropriate dress.

Every Sunday Luciano would give each of his children a quarter. The girls would save up their money until they had $1.00. As older teens, mom with her sisters and friends would spend 25 cents for a streetcar pass and 75 cents for admission to a dance hall, The Crystal Slipper at 9810 Euclid Avenue. When it opened in 1927, it became "the largest and finest of the city ballrooms. "The Franzolino girls looked forward to this social engagement at the end of each month and even more than most other activities they had enjoyed. Dancing was the craze and they were crazy about language. My had come to notice boys. Spinsters they were not to be.

Another favorite past time was playing bridge with each other and their friends until they became so good at the game it began to lose its luster. I told you they were smart and clever. Bill Gates plays bridge to keep his mind sharp. Using one's noggin slows the onset of dementia. Chew on that for a while.

During this same period, Louie Caravella was popular and attended parties and get-togethers when he could. Mom being no slouch was also given to such past-times, but never without a sister in tow. She was attractive and popular, standing about 5'5" tall, very trim, with light brown hair, brown chestnut eyes, high cheek bones, perfect "peaches and cream" complexion, and a class act smile that could be provocative when called upon. Wrinkling skin for her would never be a problem even well into old age because she avoided the sun, spending most of her time indoors when working or helping with her family.

Adele was introduced by a special girlfriend, Fanny Longo, to Louie one evening while he was playing cards at a mutual friend's home. Upon meeting her, he was discreetly swept off his feet, which for him would take a special woman indeed, since he was no stranger to the ladies being financially stable, handsome, strong, and desirable. She was swooned by his good looks, cleanly sculptured mustache, and a cute if not handsome smile that would ignite most women's fantasies. They were a pair that became inseparable.

He would show up every Wednesday at Kroger's at 6 PM to take her home. They courted for less than a year and on Valentine's Day, 1940 Louie gave Adele a box of chocolates in a beautiful walnut heart-shaped box. When the box was opened, a clear flawless 52-point diamond engagement ring replaced the center chocolate. My mother would later say, "she married the barber my mother never married."

They were married on September 28th, 1940.

During his earlier single days and off times, Louie would spend many an evening singing opera with his father at one of several clubs or opera houses in Cleveland. He had a wonderful voice frequently heard at home, in very brief stanzas, whenever the mood struck him. His Italian heritage and knowledge of the language gave him and similar immigrants a leg up on the others lacking similar backgrounds. Italians invented opera, another art form of amazing distinction with aristocratic aspirations for the initiated.

One of Dad's favorite clubs was the Guiseppe Verdi Club on 28th and Woodland. Dad had a bit of talent as an actor that few knew about, but it would be later expressed in one of his grandchildren he would never meet. In one play, he acted the role of a policeman. As fate would have it, one of his sons would also play a very similar roll over twenty years later. He usually performed on Fridays and Saturdays and practiced singing at home while performing other household chores. It was fun hearing him try to imitate the masters. He was a tenor but with a very rich full sounding voice probably not too removed from some of the contemporary opera singers of his day. With a little bit of formal training, he may have made a real go of it.

Most of his time was spent hard at work cutting hair five to six days per week. His good nature and generosity showed early in his working career. He was always good to his brother Bob and would leave him ten cents every week for the movies. They were always very close and in later years Uncle Bob would say to me long after his brother Lou was gone. "I loved the guy."

For about five years my parents tried fruitlessly to get pregnant and finally gave up. They just assumed it wasn't going to be. Then one day Mom told Dad that she believed she was with child and of course their long-time dream had come true. Dad was serving with the U. S. Army in the Pentagon guarding the offices of General John Marshall at the time of the amazing announcement. Dad would be delighted forever.

I was born in Walter Reed Hospital on January 4th of 1944. The entire event was a bit of a mystery from start to finish. When my mother Adele went into labor, she was rushed to the US Army Hospital, Walter Reed, and was admitted to the obstetrical floor. My father worried patiently in the waiting room. In those days the mysteries of birth were confined to nurses and physicians, while fathers toiled in another venue.

The hours went by and finally the moment of truth had arrived. A nurse presented herself to my father and said with a big smile, "Congratulations dad; you have a lovely baby boy with coal black hair and brown eyes but only weighing about four pounds six ounces. Because he is a bit early, he will have to stay for a while until he puts on some weight".

She then turned about and began walking away while leaving the astoundingly happy new father to think about his newborn son. After walking only a few steps away from Louis, the nurse abruptly stopped, turned about, and approached the Private First Class once more and said, "Oh by the way I forgot to mention one lesser thing. You also have a beautiful baby daughter as well. "

My newly minted sister was lean as well, weighing in just over four pounds. Dad was in shock and even more thrilled beyond belief, having no idea that Mom was carrying twins. Being premature was of concern to both my parents and the medical staff at Walter Reed. The Caravella's were told the twins would be staying for quite a while. I was released in two or so weeks after reaching the magic five-pound limit while my very special little twin had to tough it out longer. Twins had not been born at Walter Reed for a long time, so caution was the word of the day especially since we had reached celebrity status during our hospital stay.

From the very start, we looked quite a bit alike, though of course we had to be fraternal being of the opposite exit always amazed me as we grew up, how often someone would ask of I, if my twin sister and I were identical? Strange but true.

After our release from the hospital, our quarters were over-run by relatives from Cleveland all visiting and offering to help out. We were a demanding couple of kids early on but help had arrived in spades. After getting off to a slow start, we began to flourish and developed normally with cute smiles and good dispositions.

During our stay in Washington, fellow service men often covered for Dad during times of illness or need. He reciprocated with free haircuts. Dad was also given good cuts of meat and other foods from friends that he knew at the commissary. They seemed to take special interest in our family since the twin thing was a bit of a novelty. During our time in Washington, numerous visitors and extended family members darkened our doorstep on a frequent basis to assist Mom with us kids. Things went well until the end of the war and soon the Caravella's would be heading back to Cleveland. Of course, their first challenge was to find a home to live in with their fledgling family.

After a bit of research, looking for something affordable, my parents became aware of temporary housing that was becoming available for WWII veterans and their family. Mom and Dad were granted low-cost housing provided for veterans settling in Cleveland. These barrack-like structures were far from luxurious but they were just what the doctor had ordered. In Lakewood, Ohio, a suburb of Cleveland, a miniature golf course had out lasted its usefulness and was replaced with housing for veterans of the war. It was located off Detroit Road between Lakewood and Thoreau Avenues and ran north to the railroad tracks.

Residents of Lakewood, Ohio would walk the tracks at times finding golf balls that had strayed off their given course. The Detroit golf complex, including a driving range was built in 1931 but was closed in 1942. After being vacant for years it was selected by Lakewood, Cuyahoga County, and the Federal Housing Authority as a place to build "50 metal-roofed Quonset homes. "These were stark inside by most standards, being akin to small barracks, devoid of beauty, but beautiful in the eyes of those who had no other place to live. They provided an opportunity for transition into a new life for military personnel after leaving the service.

Louie and Adele took full advantage of what "the projects" had to offer while planning their futures for themselves and "the twins. "They knew this could be a step in the right direction allowing them to get a foothold economically. "The projects" were very unique in that they were occupied by former military and were composed of small buildings placed close together with narrow driveways and streets separating the units. They were sparse by most definitions but functional and appreciated by the tenants. Each of the "huts" had a small living room, two small bedrooms and was similar to army barracks in construction. A small furnace in the living room provided heat. An icebox served as a place to store perishables.

My twin sister usually accompanied me around the projects since we were inseparable for most of our childhood lives. We discovered many things especially the railroad tracks. The northern border of the projects was limited by railroad tracks heavily used by the Baltimore and Ohio Railroad, the Chesapeake and Ohio systems as well as the Nickel Plate Line, all of which were well-known railway systems, in their time, within the Midwest and Eastern United States.

I would spend hours standing by and holding on to the tall corrugated metal fence watching the huge steam locomotives pulling one hundred car-long trains. Often the trains had car after car laden with full-grown beef cattle heading for market. Those cars had an interesting odor to them that for some would be offensive but to me was fascinating yet troubling, seeing those poor critters heading to the unmentionable slaughter house and later onto our dinner plates. What a sight to behold, were the locomotives sometimes two of them back-to-back pulling exceptionally long endless trains streaming far into the distance. Billowing steam and smoke flowing out of their stacks with roaring ear-piercing whistles blasting before each street crossing was always a thrill as they thundered by at what seemed to be tremendous speeds. Their whistles would bellow out in long crescendos what could be heard for what seemed like miles away. The racket could not be mistaken for anything else. If anyone were ever stuck in their vehicle while on the tracks, which rarely occurred, they had better get out while the "getting" was good. The amazing sounds and power elicited by these "monster" machines were a welcome melody to my ears, compelling me to run over to the fence to watch as I was always amazed by the mightiness of locomotives and the clanking sounds of the car's wheels striking the rails. On rare occasions, it was fascinating to watch the "gandy dancers" work on rail repairs while riding up and down the tracks with their four wheeled tampers. They vigorously pushed up and down on the large seesawing lever of the tamper to move the small rail repair car along the tracks. Arriving at the proper location, these powerful men would hop off and perform repairs as needed along the course of the tracks.

    Occasionally the conductor on a caboose of a long train would wave to me as he flew by. Less often, a locomotive engineer would notice me by the fence and give a wave or even a train whistle as he likewise flew by. Trains to me were very fascinating though I never had a need to be part of the culture beyond playing with a Lionel train set early in my childhood.

The only other memorable thoughts I had of the "projects" was when the ice man came bringing to our small abode, huge hunks of ice cast over his shoulder atop a thick leather shoulder patch. He would trudge into each hut carrying a heavy block of ice to be placed in our icebox. Our iceman seemed powerful enough and could handle the large blocks of ice with ease. In that era, many people already had refrigerators, but most of us in the projects could not afford them. The iceman was a character and more than life-like in his own way.

Phyllis and I got along great during these early years and rarely if ever fought over anything, sharing our lives together and having as much fun as any two kids could have. She was a little angel and never got into trouble. I cannot ever remember having a significant disagreement with "Honey. "As a young child I was not able to pronounce my twins name, Phyllis, and began to call her "Honey. "This label stuck with her throughout my high school career and has been only somewhat diminished after we had both moved on. Her nickname has never totally gone unused though I remain the only person who has ever referred to her as Honey.

The nickname fit her perfectly, being sweet, gentle, and unassuming. She was also quiet and reserved and a big helper around our home. Mom complained incessantly about one thing when it came to Phyllis. She would "eat like a bird. "This led to ongoing mêlées at every meal. "Eat a little meat," eat this, eat that. I thought for the thousandth time, "For the sake of God, give it a break. "It wasn't that she was picky, it was just that she ate small amounts because she was little with tiny bones. Well maybe teeny portions were her norm. Hell, sometimes she missed the whole thing. The incessant haggling drove me just as crazy as it bothered my poor twin. How we survived the endless nitpicking about her dietary habits, I'll never know.

Phyllis was also extremely neat and well groomed. Every hair was well adjusted. Her clothes were perfectly pressed and her shoes cleaned and polished. Mom was a stickler for cleanliness and the lessons were not lost on Phyllis. She had silky dark brown hair, cut hanging straight over her ears, straight as an arrow across her brow, and then layered and cut perfectly around the back of her neck, just above her shoulders. Dad masterfully cut her hair at least once or twice a month. It was a clean shapely cut similar to what an Egyptian Princess would have worn. And she was a Princess for sure. Dad loved her to pieces. Phyllis enjoyed dresses and always liked to look pretty. Being reserved and never a behavior problem, she was always well liked by everyone including teachers that would come to know how sweet she was.

One time in second or third grade, a very unusual incident occurred while we attended gold wood Elementary

School on Center Ridge Road in Rocky River. We were in gym class together and some kid was acting up. The gym teacher, known for his fiery temper and red hair, became enraged, drew a bead on this luck blessed kid, and fired a volley ball across the room, missing the trouble-maker but taking out my sister. Fortunately, she was not seriously hurt and he was very apologetic over the incident. Oddly enough, his future would fall into my hands later on in life in a less than expected way.

    Overall, discipline would prove to be a strong point in "River" schools, not too far south of what was dished out in the Catholic equivalent. Phyllis rarely if ever was truly out of line. I on the other hand got into occasional trouble more often than simply what would have occurred on the far side of chance.

    Phyllis and I just hung out together. On our walks to and from the school we would daily pass a small corner store Zak's, on the corner of Center Ridge Road and Wooster Road. To get to Zak's and to our school, we would first walk to the end of our back yard, then across the small street adjacent to our driveway while traversing a concrete sidewalk that made its way back to a field and woods behind the area in which we lived. A new street directly behind our house was under development at that time. We would reach another short street as we headed east passing by the home of one of Phyllis's favorite girlfriends whom lived very close to our grade school. From there we walked to an intersection near our favorite little store. Zak's corner store was a fun place to visit and was managed and operated by a very very very old husband and wife couple. In reality they were probably about fifty years old but to us they seemed ancient. Mrs. Zak new what we were there for just like what all of the other children would want when they would frequent her store. Behind a counter towards the back of the store was a glass shelf were groups of boxes holding "penny" candies of every shape and description were kept. The children of the area would take pennies into the store and would select whatever appealed to them on at least a weekly basis. We got used to handling money even when very young and got a taste of wonderful treats that would provide memories forever. I loved so many things but especially the little wax like bottle treats that had a wonderful cherry lime, or similar flavor within. They were about the size and shape of a tiny tiny bottle of coke and no taller than an inch and one half. To get to the sweet and tasty liquid treat inside those tiny wax bottles involved simply biting off the top of the wax "bottle" while slurping the contents out of the wax bottle until it was dry. What a treat these slick little waxy bottles were.

    We would usually stop at Zaks after school let out but never before classes. Our grade school was directly across the street from Zaks at a busy intersection controlled by crossing guards during the school day. The automobiles in the area watched the sixth-grade crossing guards that were protecting the complicated intersection where there were three areas that students could cross. Only the best students were selected for guard duty. The wore a white leatherette waist band around their waist with another band crossing from the bottom left of the waist band passing up across their chest, over their right shoulder, and finally down their backside attaching to the white band around their waist. In the center of the white crossing band and over their chest was exhibited a chrome police badge. My sister and I were never selected to serve. Though frankly, I do not remember that either of us even applied for a position sticking with our long-term insecurities.

Another interesting food we would look forward to enjoying, while attending grade school, was drinking a small bottle of milk distributed to each student halfway through the morning hours of class. Though we all had to bring in our "milk money" once a week to enjoy the treat, it was something everyone participated in. We all imbibed in the wonderful cool milk while remaining within the classroom over a short break. Our choices included white milk or we could choose white milk and that was that. We looked forward to the daily treat without fail.

One more comment about milk in that era. Mom had a dairy company named Dairyman's deliver milk to our home about two to three times per week. Home delivery was commonplace in those days. One form of milk that was such a treat was a slightly pink colored strawberry flavored version that was very special in taste. She would buy that for us on occasion as an extra special treat.

When walking to school or later on when riding the bus together, we were known as "the twins." We loved the special attention and felt empowered because of it. At least I did. Phyllis was more reserved and understated. Boldness was not natural in any way for her. Shyness around strangers was the rule, though around friends she was able to show off her developing personality.

In the immediate neighborhood where we lived. As we got older, my friends and I often stopped into Roger's Delicatessen near the southern end of Gasser Boulevard. The "old man" had an amazing selection of candy bars, ice cream, cheap gifts, more cheap gifts, and a lot of really cheap gifts. But the highlight of the store, for us young men, were his girlie magazines that we could not afford but would take a quick glimpse at a current center fold whenever the owner wasn't looking. Playboy had the finest center folds and the most amazing photos of the best-looking women I have ever set an eye on. In those days they usually were shown with skimpy bathing suits; very skimpy but not naked. You all know what I'm talking about; only in my dreams, guys and gals. Only in my dreams. I'm telling you these women were amazing but of course at the age of ten or twelve I really had no concept of what women were all about. In fact, at my current age, I still have no idea what they're all about.

Having very few options, my main interest in "the old days" leaned in the direction of Roger's ice cream cones, though at ten cents apiece, they were expensive even for that era. You could buy two loaves of bread for that. A pack of cigarettes was about a quarter. A gallon of gas was also about a quarter, if that. In any case I only bought a few of those cones a year. Money was hard to come by. Ice cream remains a passion and it should be for most of us. As time went on however, the ladies became more of a passion but still limited to my dreams.

On the other hand, my father's favorite treat remained a glass of homemade ride red wine, to go along with viewing many of the photos he had taken of the children he so cherished. Almost every photo taken included Phyllis and I in some interesting scene or activity. He had taken thousands of photos over time, an expensive undertaking in those days when it was costly to have them all developed. The initial ones were black and white and later on color photos became affordable.

Eventually we could buy inexpensive throw-a-way cameras that would take about ten to twelve photos. When finished taking the full number of photos in the camera, you would turn in the entire camera to the store to have the photos developed. The cost of the throw away camera was actually about the same cost as a good roll of film. They were great for vacations especially whenever you forgot your camera at home. Their quality was not the same as a fine camera though fairly acceptable when considering the inexpensive cost involved to have them available at any time.

Dad loved spending time with us children. On occasion he would take Phyllis and I down to the Central Market near downtown Cleveland. The market had a huge variety of vendors that sold items and foods of all descriptions. We would visit the fruit stands first and Dad would always buy a crate of twenty-four yellow figs when they were in season. Italians love fresh figs because they were commonly grown in Italy and Sicily. I loved the ripe yellow juicy ones though Phyllis had a different more refined and selective taste shying away from many of my choices.

We would bring back a watermelon whenever they looked good. Dad would select a melon from a vendor through some mysterious percussion method, listening for a certain sound or echo indicating a state of ripeness. The interpretation of this method escaped me though the stand owner appreciated the method and concurred with it. After Dad selected the watermelon of his choice, the vendor would plug the melon with a sharp pocketknife, cutting deeply through the thick green outer skin to reach the red fleshy interior. He would cut three times deep into the flesh of the melon in a triangular fashion. Out would pop a small triangular wedge of melon for Dad to taste. If it was to his liking, he paid for it and off we went. Can you see that happening today?

Chestnuts were often found at the market during the "Holidays" and several pounds would be purchased to be oven roasted when the time came. The chestnut search would begin for Thanksgiving because chestnut turkey dressing would be the order of the day. Mom would cut a cross like incision into each nut, place them in water to soak for thirty minutes, remove them from the water, and place them on a cookie sheet in a three hundred- and seventy-five-degree oven for about twenty to thirty minutes. When the cut edges started to curl upwards and away from the meat of the nut, they were usually ready to eat. Over cooking is less of a problem then under cooking which lessoned the flavor and the nutty taste. If undercooked, the chestnut would taste flat rather than rich and creamy. Chestnuts rapidly become moldy if uncooked, while sitting on a shelf for more than a few days. It was best to bake them almost as soon as you walked in the door from the market. Leftover chestnuts would be easily frozen and used later in dressing for turkeys or chickens. Chestnuts are so delicious when properly roasted while having no equal when compared to anything else. They're kind of in their own stratosphere, so-to-speak. Here is an opportunity for some new recipes to be explored in the realm of cooking other forms of meats besides poultry. Let's get started!

Dad and mom were also very much about family including the extended family. Every weekend, Dad and Mom would pack us all into his dark navy blue 1949 Chrysler Windsor with a fluid-drive transmission, and sporting velvet navy blue seats with a wonderful softness that would cuddle your back and bottom with delicious enjoyment. The dash was chrome laden from end-to-end sporting a decent radio and a small yet attractive clock. Digital fonts had not yet arrived so we were blessed with wonderful ticking time pieces the likes of which have been long forgotten.

Sometimes one of us would be given the opportunity to sit in the center front seat between Mom and Dad though we usually resided in the comfy back seats. The back seats with very limited visibility for short little kids was not as much fun. Seatbelts had not been invented so a little rough housing and horseplay was often the order of the day, until Dad had had enough of it and would let loose a screaming yell that would rectify the problem immediately. Of course, my sister Phyllis was "always" the problem. I was so well behaved. Except when I wasn't.

Spending Sunday afternoon became a tradition that to some extant grated on my mother's nerves. She was a bit miffed by the fact that her mother's family, the Franzolino home was not given the same respect as the Caravella home. We rarely visited her mother's place due to the outrageous food displays that Rose would bestow upon her son and his family. Dad could not pass up these gluttonous displays of extravagant foods stretching from one end to the other end of a dining room table. These smorgasbord affairs were not to be equaled by most mortal women also made even more outlandish by Grandma Rose's love for Louis.

She was always trying to impress. This scenario was also provoked by the fact that Grandma Generosa was not as gifted in the culinary arts and thus frequenting Grandma Rose's table more often than not became the rule. Of course, everyone knows that their mothers cooking is always the best and we felt the same about ours.

Rose's ability to season and prepare foods and sauces to say nothing of special desserts was nothing short of miraculous. She had the touch. Plus, because Louie was her favorite, she hoped to see him weekly and provide wonderful meals to entertain him whenever possible. Along with the camaraderie afforded to him with his father, brother, and brother-in-law Jim, the visits were enjoyable to all; well almost to all. Phyllis and I had little to do at these visits and we tolerated them but would have preferred to be at home with friends or involved in other more interesting endeavors that suited us better.

Having said that, I lived to eat where on the other hand, Phyllis ate to live. These "boring" visits had to be much more annoying to her than they were for me.

On rare occasions a few of our Eastside cousins would drop in and that then would provide entertainment for all of us. Our cousins were older and had established other social circles for their enjoyment other than what we could provide for them. My first cousin Sam was very well liked and always seemed to have something going on in his neck-of-the-woods and thus rarely showed his face at these food and card playing festivals. When he was there, he attended for an hour or two at most and that was that and off he went. The rest of us were often there for the entire afternoon and were not leaving before nightfall.

Dad having to work the next day at his shop would finally leave for home packing us all in his Chrysler once nightfall began in earnest. Driving home was fun looking out of the car windows at the oncoming headlights on the other side of Lakeshore Boulevard. Lakeshore flows past Cleveland's share of wonderful, dark, and mysterious Lake Erie. Boat docks were visible from the Terminal Tower's lights shining in the distance and staring right at us from Cleveland's downtown Public Square.

During that era, the Terminal Tower was the second tallest building in America after the Empire State Building. The Terminal Tower was the home of railroad passenger trains that would pass through the center of town and under the Tower's primary structure to load and unload passengers heading to all points east, west, and south. Why not north? Well, north would take you straight into Lake Erie.

I remember taking a train from Cleveland's downtown to other Ohio cities but only on very rare occasions would I have that opportunity. Car travel was the method of choice once the interstate highway system began to open up. I-70 was a major route heading from Cleveland to all points south.

Uncle Bob, my father's, brother, younger by about five years, would never leave home until the passing of his father first and later his mother well into her early 80's. Uncle could not stand change and though he allegedly dated a few women on and off and at least one already married, he could never break away from his beloved mother.

His married "girlfriend" was supposedly a breath-taking woman with brilliant red hair who apparently shared her attributes with my uncle quite willingly. No one in the family, with only one exception would ever meet her. At one time the possibility of marriage was entertained by the couple but for reasons known only to them this arrangement would never reach fruition. Uncle seemed to be insecure in most relationships, outside of the family or his work place, but he was a gem of a man in every other respect and loved us children to the "nth" degree.

Uncle Bob was also short in height but of equal stature to his brother Louie, both being about five foot seven inches tall. The two of them were very close as brothers and uncle would visit our home quite often and at least once every full moon.

His weakness was for sports, especially the Cleveland Indians but his true passion was really the horses. As years went on, he invested large sums of money into owning and racing thoroughbreds but would never achieve success in this venue. Thistle Down, a race track in Cleveland, was frequented on a regular basis by Uncle Bob. It was not a track that would part with its greenbacks very easily. No surprise here. Betting on the horses is akin to betting on a women's choice of handbags when she leaves home, if she has more than six or seven to choose from.

Uncle Bob remained a very private man and few relatives or friends knew of his "addiction" at least during his lifetime. He was not addicted to drugs, alcohol, and never smoked.

Being good hearted and generous Uncle Bob often took his nephews and nieces including Phyllis and I to see the Cleveland Indians play at the old stadium. The days of Bob Feller, Bob Lemon, and the likes of them were oh so familiar to us when growing up. In fact, I have baseballs signed by them. I

In time I would meet and get to know both Bob Feller and Bob Lemon. They were pleasant men but also men of very few words. Money and popularity are often a curse to most who have experienced both of them. They are not what you think they are and few if any can escape the hall of fame or the in the case of less noble men, cross of infamy once obtained.

When not following sports, uncle Bob worked for years at Cleveland's Murray Ohio Manufacturing Company founded in Cleveland in 1919. The company concentrated on automobile parts and then in the 1930's began manufacturing Murray bicycles. The Murray bicycles were premium at first but too expensive to manufacture and thus later on became more affordable when less exotic models became available. They were competitive with Schwinn and AMF bikes and of the same quality.

Uncle Bob often provided various models of these wonderful bicycles for us children at Christmas time. He was a "good old guy".

Uncle like his brother Lou also had an interest in exciting cars. He owned his share of Pontiacs, Chryslers, and Oldsmobile's. He was soft spoken, loving, and never on a single occasion ever cursed or swore for any reason. He never showed anger and had a smile and hug for everyone. He almost had a piousness about him to those who knew him. I often wondered what he was thinking about that would never escape his thoughts. He had no apparent dark side that any of us were aware of.

Being so private about personal matters, other family members would never glean any negative connotations about his life. Only his nephew Salvatore or Sam would ever have access to his private life because the two were close and confidants in many ways. With further thought, about uncle Bob's inability to form relationships outside of the family, it is likely that he was struggling with what we now call post-traumatic stress syndrome that was not recognized in the World War II era. After all, he was awarded three bronze stars for heroism during the European campaign to free Europe of the Nazi's. Only he knows what he saw, experienced, and faced under fire. I believe the psychological trauma of those events were always with him in a way, they suppressed his ability to form deep bonds to others outside of the family. He likely feared that by befriending others, he would lose them under terrible circumstances and maybe he could not face those horrible possibilities again. That is one of the stigmas of PTSD. His life and personality were forever altered by the war. Thank you for your service uncle, Bob. We all love you.

As mentioned, Uncle Bob was always an Indian's fan to the very end of his time. On June 15, 2006, at 2:30 AM uncle Bob hit his last home run. While residing at the VA home in Vermillion, Ohio, and suffering from long standing dementia, he rounded third, and headed home. We lost an incredible gift that was not here long enough for any of us. He was so well loved by all. I think of him often and usually in the context of his great love of Cleveland's sports teams. He is now with other family members that have preceded him.

Dementia was heartless for him as it is for others. It is worse in so many ways than other diseases but not because it steals the mind and later the body but because it often takes its good old time while doing so. It is a selfish, miserable, pathetic condition that takes on a life of its own and does not represent a man or a woman on any level. It is cruel and irresponsible. But in the end dementia is always defeated. It is defeated because it cannot steal your Soul. Your Soul always prevails and lives on for eternity unfettered by mortality.

We will all be together in the future and we will reign appropriately in a new place not yet known to us but on the other hand it is known to most of us on a level that explores the beauty of humanity in the eyes of God. We will all prevail. Dementia has no future, no place on any level, and is soundly defeated with the last heartbeat. It is a thief that will always be reckoned with. Dementia never has the last word. God dooms dementia and thus we will always win with our final breath. See how easy that is. Life can never end. We are only one breath away from eternity. Life simply just changes its appearance as it moves onto a new playing field. I will see you soon Uncle Bob.

As time goes on, I would become like uncle Bob in Sam's life, growing closer to him than anyone else I would ever know, other than my future wife, Debra. Having said that my siblings would also remain close to me as time went on but in different ways of course.

Another gem of a person in the Caravella family was Grandma Rose. She was very good to us children in pleasing us with her fresh baked cookies, cakes, desserts, and treats of all kinds whenever we saw her. She would always give us a huge hug as soon as she saw us walking into her kitchen. For Easter each year, she would make an unusual cookie like treat that reminded us of the crucifixion. She would take a hard-boiled egg and wrap uncooked cookie dough in a ring around the base of the egg that was left in its shell.

She then placed a piece of dough in across-cross pattern over the top of the egg and matted the ends down to the ring of dough around the base of the egg. The cross of cooked dough represented Christ's crucifixion, a beautiful Easter gift. The egg represented a new life rising from the dead. This large cookie was baked in the oven on a cookie sheet with a thin layer of shortening and "presto" out would come, you guessed it, a hard-boiled egg with cookie baked around it. This sounded strange, but it was an annual treat we looked forward to each Easter. The cookie had a sweet taste with a crunchy bite to it. We all enjoyed it and it was a way to get us to eat a hard-boiled egg. She was quite clever at times. After eating one of these however it was enough for a year.

Her other more interesting cookies were what we really enjoyed and could not be had from anyone else. She had a massive repertoire of cookies more varied than the names of Uncle Bob's racehorses. One odd but flavorful soft moist cookie was called, Castelli. It had an almond cinnamon flavor, and a moist rubbery uncooked dough like consistency that sounds quite unpalatable but turned out to be in reality a delicious pastry as good as it was so odd in appearance. An outsider may find it strange and less appealing but everything I was raised on seemed special and delicious to me as a child and later as an adult. Both of our grandmother's had a gift and they gave it away with zest. Frankly, I don't like the taste of zest.

Grandma Rose's forte however was her ability to throw together the most amazing feasts anyone could ever imagine. She had both the basement kitchen and the main kitchen going full blast when it came to her big weekend or holiday blowouts. Her daughter Santina often played a major role by helping with all aspects of meal preparation and thus she learned how to be an equally astonishing cook. Children were always served first and given preferential treatment in Italian families. They were commingled at the tables with the adults and not left to their own. This provided the little ones an opportunity to learn how to eat to excess as the adults had already mastered and to enjoy the same foods with even a bit of red wine thrown in now and then for the adventurous. Nothing was forced on anyone though it was easy to offend Grandma if you didn't "try something" or if "seconds" were not requested.

    The meals were served in a long dining room, with a table that could easily sit fourteen people, allowing for two on either table end, and the rest would sit along the table's sides. The table was made of dark wood having an Italian look but with Mediterranean massiveness. The dark brown ornately carved dining room chairs were well padded with black leather seating surfaces allowing for comfortable sitting for hours at a time. There was a long matching dark wood chest that must have been about eight feet long resting against the north wall of the dining room. The buffet went well with the table though it did not appear to be it an exact match, being more Italian and less Mediterranean in design while still providing ample room for placement of Grandma's exquisitely prepared dishes. Crystal wall lamps decorated each end of the credenza, hanging from the beak of a golden bronze like ornamental parrot. A large elongated gold toned crystal chandelier hung over the mid portion of the dining room table. The walls were adorned with family photos and interesting pieces of Italian art along with small sculptures that would be very ethnic and considered dated by today's decorators though were authentically Italian in their time. Many of these pieces came from Italy. Some art pieces were sent over from "the old country," while others were brought by visiting guests hailing from Sicily. All were uniquely Italian and thus not American at first glance but becoming more so as I thought even more about the assimilation of immigrants to America and bringing with them from the "old country" treasures of endless descriptions.

Soon Sunday or holiday meals would begin after the women had spent many hours working in grandma's two kitchens. Many of the foods were prepared days in advance. The ladies would scurry back and forth bringing the hot dishes to their children and men folk. The meals would take at least two to three hours to eat and were laced with "good" conversation spoken mostly in Italian. Not understanding most of the discussion, the meals would become a bit tedious as time went on for most of us younger ones not in tune with the conversations. Thus, with opportunity comes attempted and usually successful escapes as we would gradually slink away from the table whenever possible. Slinking became an art form in its own right.

The main meal would begin with Italian wedding soup composed of a light chicken broth, small chicken pieces, simple homemade noodles, and small if not bordering on tiny meatballs about the size of a marble but with the flavor and seasonings equal to the best meat confections any Italian chef could muster. Everything was made from scratch, using the finest Italian ingredients purchased from local Italian shops around the neighborhood. Grandma's noodles and ravioli were always homemade, having a special firmness or a-dente when prepared. Along with the soup, a large tossed salad made its appearance having small chunks of provolone, mozzarella, tomatoes, and homemade Italian salad dressing consisting of fine Italian olive oil and rich tangy vinegar that could bring your tongue to a curl. Occasionally small pieces of fresh salami were added to the salad for extra flavor. The salad could take on a life of its own. We Italians know how to eat.

My suggestion to you young ladies, should you be reading this book, is to find a handsome, funny, intelligent available Italian young man to be with - but only if you can love and appreciate, his relatives that will become part of your life.

Fresh homemade Italian oven baked, hard crusted, – I mean stone hard crusted-golden brown-beige tinted bread with soft steaming hot centers, hand-sliced, and ladened with the richest, smoothest, yellowest, thick, lightly salted butter, that could never be nor would ever be forgotten by us Italian Americans. My mother would always say, "give me the bread and you can keep the rest". She was passionate about her bread like others that crave their most scrumptious ethnic delicacies. She could polish off a half of a loaf in a few moments. Keep out of her way.

Spaghetti smothered with thick red richly meat seasoned sauce was then served with meat balls, pork, and pork neck bones smothered in even more of the finest and richest and thickest of red sauces imaginable.

The fine recipes responsible for fabulous Italian dishes were passed on from mother to daughter and were not usually written down. They were mastered through practice, tasting, and smelling while tweaked by adding a pinch of this or a dash of that. No detail was overlooked. Too much prestige rested on the outcome of their home cooked dishes.

Martha Stewart would appreciate, as would any reputable chef the techniques and methods employed by any experienced Italian master. A woman's pasta sauce not only gave her a sense of pride but would also become her personal trademark, rarely varying in taste or texture from meal to meal and would always be one of a kind. For Italians no other single dish has more significance than traditional pasta. A first-generation Italian woman would do better not to prepare anything than to overlook presenting a first-rate pasta dish in one of many variations. Each cook prepares their own dish, somewhat differently, using various seasonings, meats, secret ingredients, and cooking times that give each sauce a distinct taste not equaled by any other. Every Italian woman and most Italian men have within them their own magic blend of spices, meats, tomatoes, and secret ingredients that lock within their dishes a unique taste unequaled by others no matter how many you have the good fortune to sample. You go to a thousand Italian homes and you will experience a thousand different flavors. Mangier; pronounced "Mangier means eat.

The best sauces are blended from, as most ethnic Italians will agree, with some form of a fatty like pork such as pig neck bones, pig's feet, and or pork-hocks. Italian homemade sausage, and lesser portions of beef for flavoring were required additionally by the truly inspired. Let's face it. Good tasting entrees require various forms of fat or butter. Substitutes may of course be healthier but never tastier. Good pasta sauce can never have character or flavor without the real "goods". There are no exceptions to the rule that flavor requires fat in many forms. Get over it. The vegans are out of luck though they may live longer; if you call that living.

Likewise good desserts give new meaning to the use of fats in all variations of the word and ingredient. Sugar as well has no substitute. Desserts should have a sweetness often lathered with heaps of whipped cream, vanilla custards, or decadent chocolate dressings. Calorie counting never had and never will have any standing in an Italian household. Taste was king. And the ladies were nearly all a little or more than a little over endowed with some of the wrong stuff. The fat in the foods often found a new home in other places easily noticed by all but the least casual observer. The men often suffer from the same problem.

Cooking beef in sauce or in "gravy" as some call it, by itself will not bring out the true character of Italian cooking though admittedly what is really good to each of us is what is perceived by the buds of the taster. Some would turn up their noses when they hear about pig's feet simmering in rich red-hot sauces. Until one tastes the results, all conclusions should be withheld by the uninitiated. Without the correct blend of meats and seasonings the best taste and consistencies cannot be truly obtained. As with fine wines, there is no substitute for the real thing but only pretenders that pale in taste and texture. Many American pasta sauces prepared by no Italians cannot be appreciated on any level by ethnic Italians who have a different idea of what true Italian food is all about.

The master's meats would simmer for four to five hours in water mixed with rich tomato paste, garlic, sweet basil, onions, sugar, salt, pepper, and a few other carefully chosen ingredients. The meats chosen by various Italians, included in their meatballs varied based on what they were raised on. Good meatballs begin with fine meats, whole milk-soaked bread - not skim or 1% -spare us the humiliation- parsley, seasonings, and other ingredients including eggs in just the right quantities. Uniquely chosen ingredients were not precisely measured by these seasoned cooks but were added to their creations in an artistic and self-fulfilling way. However, approximations were most often closer to perfection than the space shuttle's foam insulation formulas. Techniques and methods were passed down from mother to daughter and the exquisite dishes were left to dazzle their fortunate recipients. Dazzling is the hope and goal of all Italian masters. They live and sleep based on wonderful dishes, beautiful women, and lovely charm, dished out in quantities and style not known by many other ethnic peoples. Don't forget Italian masters like DaVinci and Michael Angelo along with famous current designers such as Versace, Vince Camuto, and famous Italian wineries exhibit the mastery of the Italian culture. This of course spills over into the traditions, lives, and abilities of such a creative group of people which they shower upon their friends and relatives.

Traditional Italian appetizers such as salami, prosciutto, pancetta, capocollo, alone with brilliant cheeses, specialty olives, and exquisite breads with shovels of butter were intended to pique the interest of the connoisseur but never intended to fully satisfy the palate when a holiday or special occasion meal was anticipated. After magical pasta and its supporting cast had been partaken, either a stuffed turkey or dressed chickens with all the trimmings would make an appearance. Never to be omitted were tender, specially seasoned thinly cut veal cutlets soaked in milk and whipped eggs, and then smothered with seasoned Italian style breadcrumbs slowly cooked to perfection. Not far behind could there be a handsomely prepared, garlic impregnated pork roast, sizzling on the serving dish with an undeniably dazzling aroma.

Standing rib roasts, pork ribs, or steaks were not the usual fare of these extravaganzas and rarely graced the holiday table of real Italians. Those dishes are left to those who do not know how to, or do not wish to cook the Italian extravaganzas I have written of, or are simply interested in a quicker fix rather than serious eating that holiday Italians are used to.

Having said that, good cuts of meat and steaks have serious merit in their own way and in their own time when not competing with unusually tasty ethnic Italian dishes of countless descriptions. Put a great steak next to a great Italian pasta dish and the steak will less often be taken until the pasta has met its fate.

Occasionally home raised and roasted rabbit was part of the menu though I never acquired a taste for that dish. A variety of vegetables, mashed potatoes, and various gravies would make an appearance. Gravies in their own way were as exquisitely prepared as French sauces but in much heavier forms. Light sauces are for wimps or fish to bathe in but not for real Italians who savor their thick, rich, heavy gravies when drowning their sacred treasures just before the serious eating begins. The French of course have a different take on all of this. Of course, this is an Italian memoir and the French can write their own. I love the French. But Italian cooking, as good as the French is, has its own magnificence.

And let's not forget those unforgettable Italian homemade wines that grace the tables of Italians and are a mainstay at any respectable meal. These were almost always rich red or burgundy varieties much like Chianti but again with each having its own bouquet, flavor, and character.

Problems of being overweight, as we know it began more than likely with large Italian feasts. The reality of this extra girth could only be overcome with good fitness practices or hard physical labor now often foreign for many of us Americans regardless of our ethnicity.

Everyone was so stuffed after these glutinous affairs that desserts were relegated to an honorable mention. Desserts regardless of their magnificence other than a variety of special Italian examples played a much smaller role in Italian-American feasts when compared to the pasta/meat entrees. Cannoli were the exception. There are no two cannoli's alike and every woman has her own secret receipt just as her own special Italian sauce. Everyone saved space for at least one cannolo. They, along with a few other delectable cakes and cookies were left to round out the meals. Fruits though available were less relished, though some of us shelled a few nuts such as pecans, walnuts, and Brazil nuts. There was always a nutcracker laying around for regular use. I also enjoyed the fact that some sort of snacks was usually available in Italian homes simply for the taking and without the asking. Italians believe food is a gift to be shared with all. It is the hallmark of friendship and bonding between people. Food is a unifying necessity bonding all mankind together and if anything is a gateway to all hearts and souls. Italians understand that as much as any other culture. Italians are a gracious and loving people that love to give and do not expect anything in return, other than honor and respect. Food is the melting pot for all to love and enjoy culminating in a richness and fellowship that nothing else can compare with.

Yes, Grandma and Santina could cook. They were amazing. Unfortunately, most of these remarkable cooking skills have been lost on younger generations lacking the patience, interest, or time to learn or to explore the intricacies of Italian cooking and baking.

After the impressive Sunday or holiday feasts, the women got stuck with the clean up as well as most of the preparations. The men with full bellies would waddle or crawl into the living room and talk or watch the Sunday afternoon football or baseball game if they could stay awake after the gorging had ended. In those days double headers were common and we could all expect about five to six hours of sports action; unless we were sleeping.

The women migrated to the kitchen and participated in talking about children, grandchildren, and husbands; mostly husbands. Everyone was generally in a happy and gregarious mood on nearly every occasion. There was little if any friction in the family since everyone got along fine. There were no problems involving hard feelings on any level and all spouses were generally getting along with each other. The key here was that nobody owed anyone any money, "the root of all evil." Thus, that common source of irritation for many families was nonexistent within the Caravella/Franzolino pride.

After the women cleared the dining room table, for an alternative form of entertainment, out would come the playing cards along with fists full of coins and low denomination U. S. currency. Card playing was a Sunday afternoon and holiday staple if no important sports teams were playing. I enjoyed watching the card playing with small coins being thrown in and scooped out depending on the status of the poker hands. It was fascinating to watch the players with their interesting comments, cool gestures, and mannerisms. Grandpa was pretty clever but they all seemed to be fairly astute and appeared to win about equal amounts over time.

Dad and uncle Bob enjoyed the card playing rituals but rarely took any of it seriously and were unflustered by the results. Rarely did anyone get much of an "upper hand", which was good for peace. Good wine was a part of the game though drunken behavior was never encountered. Fighting absolutely never occurred. Laughter and occasional good-natured yelling were the standard during these exhibitions. No feelings were ever hurt. There was too much love to go around and thus everyone in the family remained close and reachable.

Having often little to do much, of the time, while visiting my grandparents, I would often go into the living room and sit down, lie down, and often fall asleep on a soft overly padded chair. If any of us laid down on the couch for a rest, that was the end of them for the afternoon. Grandma Rose's home was comfortable, safe, cozy, warm, and pleasant though boredom frequented many of the visits at least from my point-of-view and the view of several of the other children. All of us loved the food and camaraderie but the other pleasantries seemed to escape us most of the time pleasing the adults more than us children who were less entertained.

Early on in life, with interest and wonder, I saw sitting next to my grandfather's chair a unique looking metal container. I didn't know what it was, but once I looked inside and saw some sort of gross looking stuff lacing its bottom. Later on, I learned it was a spittoon not uncommon apparently in those days for those from the old country. Now in thinking back my father had the nasty habit of opening the car window at times and spitting out as he drove down the road. He never threw cigarette butts out the window if that's any consolation. In retrospect, he, his father, and I all had the same problem: allergies. In those days there was little to do about the problem from a medical approach so the spittoon came in handy. It was also less expensive than going through reams of "Kleenex" as we would do today.

Things have changed a lot in modern times and that's a good thing. Now we use steroid nasal sprays or antihistamines to handle nasty symptoms and post nasal drip. Then they used the less attractive methods but that is why times and customs take on a life of their own. The daily use of fluticasone nasal spray can go a long way in solving most nasal allergy symptoms as I have found out over the years.

Aunt San, as we called Santina, was my father's sister and a beautiful Caravella. She unfortunately suffered from severe asthma nearly impossible to treat in those years when only substandard medications were available. It reminds me of Saint Bernadette who suffered from the same asthmatic condition and died at the age of 32. Saint Bernadette, a French woman fell under the umbrella of Mary, The Mother of God, and as a result her body, though never embalmed has never decomposed over the centuries. Her body has been exhumed on two occasions over the centuries and remains the same in color and mobility as it was in real life. Science cannot explain this; but a miracle by Mary does explain it.

It was remarkable on how Santina was able to survive from one day to the next with her terrible asthma. Every day for her was a measured existence that could end up in disaster at any time. Her inhaler was always within hands reach and she seemed to use it more in frequency than how it could have ever been prescribed. Her breathing was always a struggle for her and it worried me endlessly though I had no concept of what was going on with her during my childhood years. It was actually frightening to see how often she struggled at times to stay alive with long shallow difficult wheezing breaths with each one bordering on her last one. Even with poor health she managed to remain pleasant and loving though always audibly wheezing even without any evidence of emotional or physical stress. For that matter she seemed to wheeze under any and all circumstances. Asthma and many allergies were not then well understood since corticosteroids had not made their presence known at least for the treatment of asthma during the 1940's. If on the other hand they were in use for the treatment of asthma, her physician certainly was not aware of it. There was also a cat or two around most of the time that likely played a major role in her struggles though the connection at that time may have never been associated with her misery. It is likely her physician was not aware of the fact that the Torrisi family had cats.

Aunt San loved children and always catered to us as much as she could. Stella Jean, her youngest child, and Rosemary another, reminded me most of her mother. Both of them had the same smile as their mother and a very caring way about themselves. Neither complained and both would do well in time, raising fun loving children. They were terrific cousins and I loved them dearly.

Sam, Aunt San's only son, was a special case and remarkable in so many ways as time would bear out. He was always happy, fun to be around, a little on the chunky side, likely related to his mother's amazing cooking, and seemed to be well versed in worldly things for a youngster. Sam, being older than I, was also a role model in many ways. When we were only a few years old, we would often play outside together whenever our family visited his small and modest home located on the East side of Cleveland. Sam had many friends and they would occasionally drop by. When that happened, I felt like a third wheel though cousin Sam always included me in whatever he did. He was always very clever and had a whit about him that was unending and enjoyable.

In that regard and as time went on, I developed the same characteristic as I grew more comfortable within my own being and not so insecure. Sam and I always joked around in a good-natured way, but would never play a practical joke on each other. Sam always had a great deal of respect for his parents and as time went on did whatever he could do to help out his family. He treated all others in the same way and always wanted friends and relatives to be comfortable whenever they visited. His father, uncle Jim, was a fascinating man as well and had a huge repertoire of home repair skills, auto mechanic abilities, sheet metal shaping, and cutting. He had a general knowledge on how to repair and build from scratch nearly everything he worked with either at home or at his new gasoline service station that would soon bear fruit.

Uncle Jim's real name was Vincent but he was never called that. On St. Patrick's Day, 1951, Uncle Jim purchased what became named as Jimmy's Service Center; a Gulf Gas Station that within a few years would become known for quality mechanical, body work, and paint jobs. He worked the station from 1951 through much of 1956 and then decided on a new adventure.

Uncle Jim sold his service station and decided to form a new company to manufacture cabinets for large retail stores that would prove to be more lucrative than the gas station business. Sam worked alongside his father who called his new business, Vincent Metal Products. His manufacturing concern designed and built heavy metal display counters for Ben Franklin retail stores, Neisser Brothers, Kresge's, and many other 5 & 10 cent stores of the 1950's era. These businesses existed throughout Mexico and the U. S.

Sam's job was to spray paint the finished display counters. In time he would learn all of the skills required in making the cabinets including welding, cutting metal, assembly, packaging and shipping. In my late teen years and out of curiosity I would occasionally visit Uncle Jim and Sam at his various businesses. They treated me like royalty and would show me around to observe what they were involved in at whatever business they were operating at any given time.

When Sam became of age, he joined the US Army entering the service on July 17, 1960 at the age of 19. I suspect this was a blow to his father who likely depended on Sam for his help, but everyone has to do what they have to do. At the same time, while Sam was studying and learning about the military life, I was a sophomore studying girls, I mean math and science at Rocky River High School.

Sam was busy becoming one of America's BEST. He entered boot camp at Fort Knox, Kentucky: Jump School at Fort Campbell, KY, Signal School, at Fort Gordon, Georgia, Advanced, Signal School, at Fort Jackson, South Carolina (where I also would serve someday), and was a member of the Electronic Warfare Department, Fort Huachuca, Arizona (requiring a secret clearance).

After serving as a paratrooper with well over fifty jumps completed while training and serving at Fort Campbell, Kentucky with the 101st Air-born Division he would move onto another part of the world where the Cold War was becoming hot. During his military training at Fort Campbell, he would pack his own parachutes while I was packing my own bubble gum. In 1961 he was stationed in West Germany as a Special Investigator with the 7th Army Signal Deport and the 504 Signal Battalion located in Mannheim, Germany.

He had a flashy uniform with a couple of brilliantly colored cords (red, yellow, and/or maybe blue) dangling from his shoulders, black spit shined boots with his military pants tucked into the boot top, and then bloused over the top of each boot. Yes, he looked pure military and one hundred percent army. He was "The Man". His military prowess fascinated me in many ways and I looked up to him while he served America here and overseas. As time went on, I suspect his service in the military would also be of influence to me to join the Army as well someday.

Sam was honorably discharged with the rank of Specialist 5 (E-5). Hewes a true patriot like his uncles who had served before him in the Great World War II. Upon leaving the US Army he returned at the age of 22 to Vincent Metal Products.

He designed and built a state-of-the-art spray booth for his dad's company. In 1965 his father opened another company, Regal Aluminum that made awnings. Sam again worked for his father at making awnings, selling them, and installing them as well. Sam would eventually own his own home improvement company known as Owners Installation, Inc. with annual sales revenue of three to four million dollars.

More than his work ethic, Sam was an honest, hardworking, respected husband, father, and devoted American. He married three times having two sons with his second marriage, Vincent Patrick and Christopher Scott. He finally found his true love later on in life when he married his long-term bride, Laura that I and Debra would treasure as time went on.

He always wore a smile on his face, and had a pleasant greeting every time we met, "What'd yak say?" was his unique greeting to me every single time he approached me on thousands of occasions. We would hug, discuss a few pleasantries, and move on with the days fun or plans and objectives. He never had a bad word to say about me or anyone else. NEVER! He held everyone he met in high esteem.

Sam and I were unique in that we had a very similar sense of humor. We could not say two sentences together without a funny crack, joke, or comment that had us both laughing. Anyone in earshot would also laugh. We were two characters cut from the say cloth. We were two comedians who never had a cross word to say to each other. NEVER. He and I were closer than brothers. Sam never had a brother so I guess he picked me. Over the years, beginning with childhood, and eventually until his last day when he moved on to a better life with God, he and I had the best relationship any two men could ever have. He and I were soulmates if that were possible for men to be. I would say that is a feeling or experience that would rarely be felt between any two men. When I think of him, nearly on a daily basis, it usually brings tears to my eyes.

During the 1950's medical care was fairly primitive for immigrants, not having medical insurance, and little if any "disposable income" available to them. Such luxuries as seeing a physician was usually afforded to a different class of people and many of us did not fall into that category. Italian immigrants rarely if ever frequented a physician. I remember on one occasion, when Grandma was ill, a friend brought over to her home when we were visiting her two or three "special" leaches that were placed on her upper arm where they attached themselves. The leaches did their thing and I found it interesting but had no idea what was going on. Though bizarre for me to witness, I do not recall any revulsion of the treatment nor do I remember the discussions of this event since they were conducted in Italian. Grandma recovered either due to or despite the treatment though she could not have been too ill since she had been sitting up in a chair in the kitchen during this entire "healing" procedure. Leaches to this day are used in some instances by plastic surgeons to reduce skin graft rejection.

While her children were becoming adults, Rose would eventually be found operating a sewing machine for a sweater manufacturer in the Cleveland area by the name of Bamberger. Robert would graduate from high school and would then work for various manufacturing companies.

A few years after the war, in the 1950's, Uncle Bob worked for the Murray Manufacturing Company that produced bicycles among other useful products. This proved to be a true family bonus because my father would purchase bikes at a discount through Uncle Bob's work place. Christmas often proved to be exciting with one of us occasionally finding a new bicycle under "the tree." This American tradition has gone overboard here in the States when compared to the gifting process in other parts of the world, though who is complaining?

Are you Italian or are you Sicilian? This opens up a whole new can of worms. Let's get this straight. There are Italians and there are Sicilians. Many of the Northern Italians had less than the best of thoughts about their Sicilian relatives. Sicilians lacking a pure blood line were considered a bit on the lower end of the Italian genetic milieu so to speak. Sicilians are a conglomerate of every nationality that ever-conquered Sicily. Italians may be essentially pure without any other nationalities in their blood, may be mixed with other Europeans, or even a mix of Italian and Sicilians as well. The real Sicilians were born in Sicily of course and the rest of us genetically endowed Sicilians are merely pretenders. Those who call themselves Sicilians feel that they inherited the better end of the stick. Be that as it may be, all Italians seem to be proud of their heritage regardless of which twists and turns their genetic material was derived from. American born Sicilian/Italians seem to enjoy the history and merits of being Sicilian and often want to be perceived as such. At least we hope we can kid everyone into thinking we're full-blooded Sicilians or close enough that most won't notice or know the difference. Of course, there are those of Italian heritage who don't care one way or the other but most seem to have an opinion of the entire spectrum of which Italians are best. When all is said and done nearly all Italians are close knit and feel like a poison or countryman regardless of where they reside or of what blood line they possess. They love to kiss each other on the cheek and often on both cheeks; sexual identity be damned, and they never seem to be on the outs with each other. They have disagreements aplenty, but not full-scale war as a rule and thus remain on speaking terms regardless of their differences.

Italians are masters at hand gestures, social touching, and romantic ideals. Squeezing cheeks or butts is not uncommon in the Italian culture. Italians have powerful opinions, but rarely to the exclusion of a loved one regardless of their errant ways. Ostracizing someone is not culturally likely, if not nearly forbidden in an Italian family. Problems are always resolved, apparently related to the permanent bonding of blood relatives in early life. Children being held in high esteem are treated like royalty, thus perpetuating an unshakable bond among Italians that lasts a lifetime. Italian-Americans are equally devoted to their country, having a love affair with people and their homeland unsurpassed by most cultures. How do I know? Italian's passion for life, love, and the lives of others is strengthened in America's culture of freedom and diversity. The Italian-American culture has a richness, a beauty, and a clarity that especially empowers their women, be they wife or mother. They are endowed with a passion to provide for, support, and love all family members and especially their children for all time.

Most Italians are warm, generous individuals as well as hard-workers. Dad being like many Italians, knew he could be successful through practicing a solid profession and barbering was his love and passion. He could make a living, have fun, socialize with a lot of people, and work eventually on his own terms if he was able to have his own shop. His secret was his gregarious nature and love of all from family, to friends, to customers.

A few hundred feet away from Lakewood's Saint Edwards Catholic High School for boys, was a barbershop at 13616 Detroit Road, where my dad began working. His average day was about ten to eleven hours per day when he was only in his mid-teen years. Child labor laws of that era were a bit lax. Detroit Road, Route 254, stretches west seventeen- and one-half miles from the City of Lakewood, through Rocky River, Westlake, Avon, and ending at route 57 near Lorain, Ohio. Some people erroneously believe it goes all the way to Detroit but it does not.

Dad had actually begun working at the shop before the war when another barber who owned it would take him under his arm to teach him the "tricks-of-the-trade". He would travel daily across town by trolley from East 147th Street, Cleveland all the way to Lakewood, a hefty haul to say the least. His first job at this shop had been arranged through a family connection. The shop was on the North side of Detroit Road between a beauty saloon and a butcher shop. In very bold and gold black script writing was spelled out, Detroit-Giel Barber Shop located above the main entrance door to the shop.

The shop was a keeper and well known to the locals. Men's haircuts were the norm, though children were also well received. My father had the envious position of giving many little boys of the area their very first haircut. Dad always loved children and often someone would take his photo with their nearby child sitting on an elevated platform atop the handles of the barber chair that dad had made for that specific purpose. Dad greeted everyone with a cheerful smile and he knew how to please his customers. He never rushed through haircuts turning every one of them into a Caravella masterpiece. He was a master barber in every sense of the word. He was a master human in the rest of the senses.

Above the shops were apartments rented to a handful of tenants that competed for on the street parking with local shops, though parking spaces were available in the back lots just north of Detroit Road. On more than one occasion this detail resulted in problems between my father and the upstairs tenants. They would often park in the spaces directly in front of his shop, which was their right to do so, though it interfered with his commerce. Louie had a nice talk with them reminding them of this point and as a favor to him, he would ask them during business hours to park in the back behind the shop and the apartments where their intended parking spaces were. Somehow they could not understand English or what my Dad was driving at, until one day, through some quirk-of-fate, the tires on their cars were slashed. Their cars astonishing enough were never parked there again.

Dad being a generous soul, often gave free haircuts to many friends and acquaintances on a very regular basis, sometimes at the shop but more likely at our home. He also got to know the local butcher very well who spent most of his time nestled in a shop next to Dad's place. Having a good relationship with the butcher, we never went without the best cuts of fresh meat or the finest food. The parent's funds were limited for restaurants, vacations, and traveling but not when it came to eating well and feeding us the best money could buy. Dad loved a good steak once a week and usually on a Saturday evening. His favorite was a thick T-bone cooked to his perfection with a pink but not rare center. When he cut into it, it would ooze pinkish delicious juice he would mop up with a piece of amazing Italian bread. Italian bread was a staple at all dinners. Dad always managed to give a bite to me whenever he ate his steak because I would hoover nearby when he ate and with a big smile, he placed an amazing, juicy, good-sized piece, in my wide-open mouth. After that choice delectable bite, I would leave knowing enough was enough. My sister, "Honey" did not care for meat and was not to be seen during these meat forays that I became accustomed to. She was not a food hound. That was great; really great because then I would get her bite! Honey was a gem.

My parents rarely went out to eat, because they believed and rightfully so that their money would be better spent for other more important needs. Plus, mom was such a great cook that little would be accomplished by eating out. At home, we always ate like "kings" throughout my childhood, never wanting for food or drink. My mother cooked amazing Italian dishes. Dad never cooked a meal and like I never had a desire to do so. His thing was cutting hair or the lawn and that was about it. His lawn cutting escapades ended once I was old enough to handle the lawn mower. Dad traded in the lawn mower for a set of golf clubs.

Though golf was his third love after his family and of course his barber shop. The shop had four barber chairs. The seats were firmly padded with a green vinyl like covering and white porcelain bases which could swivel in all directions and recline as well for the occasional hot lather shave that would be regularly granted to a guest of the house. My father was an artist in his abilities to cut, shape, and create hairstyles for children, men and women of all ages.

Louie was so well liked, with an enviable sense of humor, and a love for his clients. Thus, soon his business was flourishing and he was able to purchase the shop. It was called The Detroit-Geil Barbershop due to its location with the appropriate streets nearby.

The shop became frequented as time went on by happy repeat customers from all parts of the area. His shop served well-dressed businessmen, blue-collar workers, teenagers, and even countless children of all ages presenting with a happy but somewhat worried parent for their very first haircut. Louie was a master barber and had a special gift for working with children. After their first haircut to each and every one of them a lollipop or small toy was given to them upon completion of their adventure.

The buzzing shears and clinking scissors with hair flying in all directions accompanied by happy customers, was a site for my eyes to behold whenever I visited there. Dad would take me with him on some Saturdays for a few hours to watch the activity. I would often sit there for an hour or more while reading magazines and watching Dad work his magic with skillful hands while giggling and laughing with the customers he knew so well.

After each cut, he would sweep the floor around the base of his chair and gather the hair and dispose of it in a nearby container. When completing someone's haircut, dad would place his shears that were just freshly used into disinfectants living in containers on a shelf in front of a large mirror extending the entire length of the area behind the barber chairs. Cleanliness was important to him and his customers appreciated his attention to detail in all regards of the haircut and styling process.

Behind each chair was located the requisite sink, various barber tools, and warming basins holding hot towels. The hot towels were to be used in a turban like fashion placed around the customer's face for warming and moistening a patron's beard before shaving and descending upon the client's face with a flashing lightening sharp straight razor. Trust is the operative word in this relationship and not too different from a surgeon's task though anesthetics are not privy to barbers even though a slight slip can have less than ideal results. My father reminded me that in centuries gone by, barbers were in some circles the early surgeons.

The outside of the shop sported two large windows with the name of his shop in bold gold and black lettering. A barber pole with a red and white striped rotating cylinder stood to the left of the shop, next to the front door. Above the cylinder was a white-lit porcelain globe used to attract further attention from passers-by. A red, white, and blue striped aluminum awning ran the entire length of the shop on its outside to keep the sun's rays at bay. Every national holiday Dad would fly an American flag from the front of his shop.

Detroit Road stretching East and West in front of his shop was the street paved in gold that his father had spoken of when they were living in Sicily. With hard work and devotion, Dad was able to provide a good life for his wife and family. He would also later on purchase a fine gold ring that he truly enjoyed and it spoke to others of his success.

Inside the shop always stood an American flag in one corner of the shop located near the front bay window area. At the front of the shop were two large windows bordering the public sidewalk. There were huge shelf-like areas below the front windows to hold newspapers and various displays for clients to look at often recognizing local high school sports teams including the nearby Saint Edwards Eagles. These shelves also held all kinds of interesting items and advertising paraphernalia, often drawing attention to events from local churches and other non-profit institutions. Each shelf was about eight feet wide, four feet deep, and ended at the base of one or the other windows. The windows themselves stretched upwards towards the ceiling reaching every bit of ten feet from the window deck to the ceiling above. The shop had large slowly moving ceiling fans dropping from a white painted geometrically designed sheet metal patchwork covered ceiling. Air conditioning was not part of the equation. Opposite the barber chairs was a row of about fifteen chairs interspersed with small tables holding magazines and newspapers of numerous descriptions from *Newsweek* to the *Readers Digest*.

In the back of the shop and behind a wall with a single door, was an odd single dark poorly lit and sometimes dusty room with back hallways. The back room held supplies, floor cleaning equipment, and a few boxes of unknown contents, at least to us children. Phyllis and I were always afraid to go alone into the mysterious back room because it was so dark and of course scary to us during our early childhood years. We spoke of ghosts or dark creatures lurking in the dark confines of the back shop. They were there. They were really there. Venturing into the back was not an option. There was a connecting dark hallway in the very back of the shop, located behind closed doors separating the back from the bright and cheery shop front. These halls connected the barbershop with the beauty shop on the eastern side of the building. My father became good friends with "Burnie" (Bernard) McKay and his employees that operated the adjacent beauty shop. Now

"Burnie" had some fine looking attractive female hair stylists working for him. They were boss. On several occasions I along with Dad visited the other side as well but usually after business hours when Dad would talk with "Burnie". The shop seemed to be teaming with stylish and attractive women clients coming and going as would be expected to be the case in this sort of work environment. At this young age, I had not really discovered the significance, the importance, nor the relationship of the opposite sex. That would come with time, though having said that do any of us men ever discover or figure out anything about the opposite sex?

After leaving Mr. McCay's heady saloon, it was back over to Dad's place. His four barber chairs were generally manned by three long-term steady barbers one of which was Dad while the fourth member varied from month to month on whether or not he would show up. One of Dad's great barbers hailed from Kentucky, though over time he proved not to be very reliable, showing up now and then whenever the fancy hit him. Dad liked him and he cut a great head of hair and thus Dad put up with the man's inconsistencies. Plus, I believe it was hard to find good barbers.

The boss was usually able to keep good barbers for long periods of time because he paid them well and respected their abilities. His shop had a reputation for having good barbers and thus it would bring back a steady clientele year in and year out. It was not easy to maintain this degree of reliability because many barbers came and went for any number of reasons. My dad after many years of this had developed good rapport with the Barber's Union to help him find the right men when needed. This era preceded the now common scenario where many if not most barbers and hair stylists are women.

Though my dad had been in business for about 37 years he rarely was able to find a steady and reliable fourth barber. It was sort of musical chairs year-in and year-out with all sorts of barbers coming and going when it came to "manning" that last chair. It was traditional for a barbershop owner to man chair number one, with the chairs being numbered from the front of the shop to the rear. My dad never followed that tradition. He awarded the first chair to the barber who brought in the most business as a form of a reward. Leonard who had been there the longest and having the largest customer base, other than Dad, usually manned the first chair unless he was sick or on vacation. Dad always worked the second chair though he was the busiest of all and of course the owner.

The shop was busiest in the early morning and towards the end of the workday, starting at 3:00 PM., when clients would stop in after work. In midday, if things were slow, Dad and the others would drink coffee and read the Cleveland Plain Dealer, the number one newspaper in Cleveland of that time. Anyone in the shop by 6 P. M. would be taken care of regardless of how long Dad would have to stay. The hours of operation were firmly set by the union in those days, as was the price of a haircut. Louie was a strong union advocate, and never wavered from the rules though he fought each and every price increase thinking it would hurt business. He also feared that the price increases would cut into tips that were important especially around the holidays. Every night when he came home, he had a thick roll of bills as big as your fist. I was always amazed at seeing so much cash at one time. Sometimes he would let us count it. There were always many fives, tens, twenties, and an occasional one-hundred-dollar bill. Wow! Dad had the magic. A hundred-dollar bill in the 1950's was more like a thousand dollars in today's money.

Even more interesting than the shop itself was the variety of barbers Dad had working for him over the years. He always selected those with amazing hair cutting skills or they wouldn't make the "cut. " The most interesting barber that I had ever met was a fellow named Al. He was of West Virginia extraction and had a thick accent to go with it. He was younger than Louie though untamed in his mannerisms and style when it came to working with the public. These characteristics were overlooked and considered minor in that he could cut hair accurately and beautifully with speed and precision. On a Saturday in the barber business, you had better know how to cut hair because that was the bread-and-butter day of the week. If you couldn't cut it then you were sent packing.

One day in the middle of winter during a heavy snow storm and for reasons I can't recall, both my sister and I were somehow left stranded at the shop after closing hours with Al. I believe Dad had to run off and cut some dignitaries hair and he didn't make it back before closing. Al asked us kids if we wanted a ride home since it didn't look like Dad would be arriving anytime soon. Al wanted to leave, but as he wisely assessed, he wasn't going to leave his bosses kids there alone at the tender age of six or seven. We hopped into his "54" Chevy with a three-speed column stick. He proceeded to hall ass out of his parking space, fish tailing all over the place on the snow-covered roads while traveling at crazy speeds when considering the white out conditions. He was a maniac behind the wheel and the ride became one of terror. When coming up to a red traffic light, he would down shift into reverse to slow the cars nerve-wracking pace and all but avoid rear-ending or side swiping surrounding cars. His transmission must have been bullet proof to take this sort of abuse. For him this was his standard MOA; nothing unusual here. When we arrived at home and lucky to be alive, my mother knowing his reputation for wild driving was beside herself. When Dad had heard about what had transpired, he threatened Al's life and warned us never to get into a car of his again under any circumstances. In Dad's opinion, standing out in the middle of Detroit Road during rush hour would have been safer. Al continued to work for Dad but he was eventually lost to follow up.

When Phyllis and I were nine years old, besides the frequent winter snow storms, the Cleveland area on June 8th, 1953, was hammered by a killer tornado arriving at the Cleveland Hopkins Airport located on Clevelands far westside and very close to Rocky River. The storm tore through west side neighborhoods over a period of twenty-seven long minutes leaving nine dead and hundreds injured while destroying almost two thousand homes. One couple, Cy and Ethyl Field of Mortimer Avenue had a typical comment to reporters: "It lasted only one horrifying minute. We came out of the basement and our house was gone. " On nearby Worthington Avenue, at the height of the storm, a bathtub crashed through a bedroom window of the Anton Thomas residence.

The saddest death of all was of three- and one-half month-old Daniel Balint whose father rushed to his aid to save him as his home disintegrated around him. "I rushed to Danny's crib, I had my hands on it and was touching it. The wind tore the baby right out of my hands. Next thing I knew I was under timbers in my back yard." Later neighbors would find the remains of Daniel five doors away. The Ohio National Guard was activated to patrol and protect private property and keep onlookers out. The houses were replaced, but memories will linger forever in the lives and minds of those so damaged by this horrible event.

Horrible tragedies and bad weather aside, while thinking about my father's other barbers there was a good man named Bernard. Bernard was older than the others including Dad. He was extremely reliable and the perfect employee in many ways. He cut a great head of hair, was soft spoken, trim, well groomed, and stood about 5' 8". He like my father loved cars as well and one day showed up at the shop with a new "59" Plymouth Sport Fury harnessing a Golden Commando

361 cubic inch V-8 engine, a "torque flight" tranny, a large four-barrel Carter AFB carburetor, dual breaker points, and dual exhausts. This "mother" roared. It was a two-door coupe, two tone, orange over brown, with white wall tires, and a tan interior sporting swivel bucket seats with the sweetest belt buckle trim streaming down the seat backs. It had a huge "Sport Fury" emblem on each tail fin, and also sprouted one long aerial angled at 45 degrees rearward from each tail fin. Talk about sexy! This was the "machine." This thing would burn rubber all the way through first gear and then some, just before shifting hard into second. The torque was phenomenal only exceeded by the hood lifting up under full throttle with bellowing sounds blowing out of the dual exhausts. Fords and Chevy's had to take notice. It didn't handle worth a shit, but in those days straight-line acceleration was the ticket. Chrysler was putting out serious torque monsters then, though Chevy's and Fords were more popular. Why? I will never know!

Too bad for them! These less frequently seen Plymouths would eat them alive during stop light drag racing. Drag racing was a major event in the "50's." Many guys would soup-up Oldsmobile's, Buicks, or anything else they could get their hands on including Nash Ramblers. Pontiacs were also highway "queens" and streetlight heavies. Engines were easy to work on if you had any mechanical aptitude at all. Bodywork was tougher so the pros often did the paint and "nosed and decked" the cars. This was the practice of removing a cars insignia from the hood and the trunk to give a classy smooth look to the exterior body panels. The cars rear-end was lowered giving it a racy look of the times. Now car aficionados tend to lower the front end for the look and aerodynamics. In the last century few knew about nor did they care much about aerodynamics. The look was the thing.

My dream was someday to have Bernard's car but that was indeed a foolish thought. Bernard couldn't part with it.

Over the years I continued to go with Dad to his shop but much less often as time went on. He enjoyed my company. Phyllis not taking the same interest as I, generally stayed at home. Let's face it, it was a "man's" thing.

After many visits with Dad to his shop, I developed an aptitude even at a young age for discovering what was going on in the main part of Dad's barber shop. Centrally located in the middle of the long line of chairs and resting against the western wall of the shop was a shoeblack's chair perched directly across from Dad's barber chair. Dad hired a porter named Ernie who was a kind, trim, and black gentleman. He often kept me laughing when he would shine my shoes on very rare occasions.

His main responsibility was to keep the shop clean and he was paid appropriately by my father to do so. Being a fantastic shoeblack earned for him a fair amount of extra money polishing shoes to a luster beyond most mortal's abilities to perform the same.

While waiting for a haircut, a customer would climb into the shoeshine chair which was fastened onto a wooden platform perching the customer well above the rest of the clientele. Ernie would place each foot-laden shoe into a footrest and he would begin by soaping down each shoe to remove superficial grime with a softly bristled brush. He then dried off the shoe with a cotton cloth waiting an additional few moment for the shoes to completely dry while he prepared for the next step. Ernie added copious amounts of appropriately colored polish with a round short bristled brush. A little water taken from a small basin would be sprinkled onto the polished shoe to give the desirable "spit polished" look followed by a vigorous buffing with a horse-haired curved wooden shoe brush that flew from side to side and hand to hand with amazing dexterity and speed to bring out a highest possible luster. The brush motions would disappear in a rage of fury to provide "the look" as good as any master could master. This process was repeated until the luster met Ernie's standards. In practice, I was never able to even remotely approach the quality of Ernie's work though it was not from a lack of trying. Ernie rightfully believed that too often a man's shoes were mistakenly over looked but were in fact are one of the more noticeable aspects of being properly and attractively dressed. There are two things' ladies notice in a man, his watch and his shoes. Keep that in mind, gentlemen.

People's shoes are nearly always noticed first. If there is one accessory that needs to be right, it is your shoes. Next is your hair style. It is always noticed and it had better be right depending on who you're trying to impress. Hair styles come and go, though a class act look remains important under most circumstances and life experiences. If it is right, you will hit a home run. Dressing well and looking great is not intuitive and is a gift owned by a handful of people; beautiful women and handsome dudes. A great wrist watch also gives an impression of decent financial standing.

The rest of us are mired in yesterday's look, never realizing that we are a bit dated, underwhelming, and overlooked. Of course, going unnoticed is not necessarily all bad. Public figures would often love to turn back the clock to a quiet and more unnoticed existence, like before they became public.

Though my mother was an exception, women to advance their needs and desires figured out from the get-go how to be noticed. Italian shoe designers and artists have mastered the art of creating beautiful shoes, handbags, and dresses (function be damned), seducing women into complete and total states of submission with the exception of my mother who was not drawn into that morass. Part of the reason was that mom had all sorts of foot and arthritic problems that contributed to an endless amount of foot pain unless the proper orthopedic (read ugly) shoes were worn. Eventually mom required custom made shoes due to her severe osteoarthritis, a hallmark of Franzolino women. Her shoes, in all fairness, were atrocious in the style department. Gorgeous shoe designs would never be her thing. Comfort was the rule. Women of her ilk, if they had existed in any significant numbers, would have put the Italian Stallion designers out of business from the get-go. Fortunately for most shoe designers, women with her degree of arthritic deformities remain in the minority.

Many men are not as cognizant of the need to wear clean and stylish shoes. Apparently, they believe their shoes will go unnoticed since they are worn so low to the ground. In real life the opposite is true. A woman will notice a man's shoes more often than the rest of his clothing.

In the same vein they will sometimes give special attention to a man's car or truck if it is clean. A clean and polished older vehicle trumps a dirty unkempt newer model. Cleanliness is next to Godliness in the eyes of nearly all members of the opposite sex especially when it comes to the men they are with. Having said that a "sporty woman loves a sporty car". What is a sporty woman you may ask?

Along with sporty women, cars have always been an interest of most Italian men. Given a clear choice, most men, Italian or not, would pick a sporty woman over a sporty car.

As fate would have it, Dad's shop on Detroit Road was about two blocks east of a former Lakewood Chrysler Plymouth dealership; a place that would take on a special significance of its own, as time went on. Louie and Uncle Bob had a love of fast and attractive women, I mean cars. Dad genetically passed this gift on to me. Remember fast and attractive cars are a staple in the thinking of Italians, as over the decades they have created amazing cars including Ferrari, Maserati, Lamborghini, and several others.

Not in the same financial position as some Italians Dad still exhibited the same spirit and drive, and thus purchased several amazing American/Detroit cars over the years from his local dealer. The first one I recall was a "49" Royal Blue Chrysler Windsor. Dad bought the navy blue 1949 Chrysler Windsor with fluid drive from his pals. This car was stately to a degree with a massive chrome front bumper, chrome grill, and chrome dashboard. Did I mention the chrome handles, window trim, trunk garnishes, and everything else that could be chromed. This "machine" was the ticket. The seats were boss with a sued like medium dark blue cover. The back seat had a fold down arm rest separating the back seat into two areas. It had a 116 horsepower six cylinder, with a semi-automatic tranny requiring a clutch for reverse.

Uncle Bob would later purchase his first Chrysler through Dad's connection at the same dealer. It was a 1951 Chrysler Windsor, purchased interestingly enough in the color green on Saint Patrick's Day of the same year. Cars would always remain an interest and a desirable commodity of all male members of the Caravella family.

As earlier mentioned, Uncle Bob began working for the Murray Ohio Manufacturing Company. For about eleven years he was involved in some process of bicycle construction and assembly line mechanics. Then all of a sudden, the plant was closed and was moved to Tennessee where I suspect labor costs were less and unions were not around to contend with. He would not follow the plant but instead took a job at Pepsi for about one year and was unfortunately laid off and on the job hunt once again. Bob joined Cadillac Industries, which later merged with Bud Industries where he stayed for thirty years until he retired. He never lost a job because of not fulfilling his responsibilities. He had a work ethic as much as anyone and rarely if ever missed work for any reason. Uncle Bob continued to live with his parents as time went on.

In the late 1940's my father and mom in contrast to his brother were living in Lakewood, Ohio's housing "projects". Dad and Ad were planning their next move. The long term "projects" living didn't look promising and soon the government would be giving the tenants the boot anyway. The Lakewood projects were after all only a temporary stopgap method of providing housing for needy post-war veterans and within a few years they would be going the way of other short-term government housing projects.

The folks were a couple of smart ones and decided they didn't want their kids "to work as hard as they had to" over the years. Though neither one of them had an advanced education they both believed the wave of the future was for children to go to college. Among the Caravella's no one had ever attended college. The folks decided to change that. Not being able to afford private or Catholic schools they believed their best bet was to find out which Cleveland communities had a public school system in which a high percentage of high school graduates would be heading off to college. Their belief was in finding the right place to live would require a city with first-rate schools for their children to attend. They believed that better schools would provide for future educational opportunities that would lead to a college education. When exploring the Westside suburbs of Cleveland, they found that graduates of the Rocky River public school-system had an unusually high college attendance rate. So that was that. Rocky River it would be. "That's where we will live. " Or at least so they thought.

Sitting about ten miles west of Downtown Cleveland, "River" as we referred to our hometown, was a community of about twenty thousand residents living in pristine homes with well-cut lawns, first rate services, and the best schools on Cleveland's Westside. Many professionals and business owners lived there along with a few professional athletes. My parents felt the environment was perfect for raising a family though a few ethnic barriers would have to be overcome just as in the case of many peoples before us including the Irish, the Germans, the Puerto Ricans, and others of non-Northern European extraction. Hey you get through it and you move on.

In the 1950's and 60's advancing education would become the greatest paradigm shift for the Caravella Family. It was the substance of higher education that would hopefully transform our family into one of vigor and stature. My parents felt it would free us from the long years of hard work they had endured. The educational process of "Rivers" school system carried the day and became the most important reason for moving into that city leading to great opportunities for the Caravella's as time went on.

Rocky River, a bedroom community stretched about eight miles west of Cleveland and Lakewood, Ohio. It was named for the river that passes through the Rocky River Park Reservation adjacent to the city of Lakewood. The river had over millions of years, carved out a deep valley that passes through the park system similar to the Grand Canyon but of course on a much less grandeur scale; sort of like comparing a mole hill to a mountain. The river's size and depth varied widely, depending on rainy conditions or drought. During low water periods, it was possible to drive back and forth across low-lying concrete fiords to transverse the river. During high water you sat at the water's edge and looked across to the other side since the fiords were completely overrun by rushing waters.

The Rocky River valley walls rose about one thousand feet above the river basin. The reservation is part of a huge system of parks surrounding Cleveland called the Emerald Necklace. It is indeed a system of emerald like gems consisting of golf courses, archery ranges, parks, ball fields, camp grounds, horse stables, and beautiful woods, streams, and rivers where wild life especially rabbits and dear abound. In my time, I found plenty of snakes of several varieties as well as wild flowers of many descriptions. Fishing the river was another past-time and my friends and I did it on many occasions.

Many a fisherman has tested the river as did my father, sister, and I. Carp were easily taken though bass were less often caught. Carp were thrown back in to the river, being scavengers of all sorts of unappetizing river trappings. Yellow perch, when caught on special fishing trips aboard boats traversing the great Lake Erie were gems and tasted amazing. Dipping the prepared fish into egg and flour and frying those delectable gems was a Friday evening treat tasting even better than a good steak. Catholics on Fridays were supposed to give up meats as a penance of sorts but eating delicious perch from the lake was no penance; believe me.

Many a fisherman has tested the river as did my father, sister, and I. Carp were easily taken though bass were less often caught. Carp were thrown back in to the river, being scavengers of all sorts of unappetizing river trappings. Yellow perch, when caught on special fishing trips aboard boats traversing the great Lake Erie were gems and tasted amazing. Dipping the prepared fish into egg and flour and frying those delectable gems was a Friday evening treat tasting even better than a good steak. Catholics on Fridays were supposed to give up meats as a penance of sorts but eating delicious perch from the lake was no penance; believe me.

Dad would occasionally take us out to Lake Erie on a fishing charter to fish the waters for famous Lake Erie perch or fabulous bass. Catching a few was such a treat. The Caravella's stomach however would often show its ugly face with violent retching for all of us as we heaved and hoed over the side of the boat. Our enthusiasm for the lake waned as time went on. Fishing again; I don't think so.

As children, my sister and I would hope to visit the parks and ride our bikes down into the Rocky River Reservation (valley) to pursue all sorts of fun activities from skipping rocks across the river while also hunting for crayfish. Skipping rocks across the Rocky River was a fun and playful sport though not very challenging since the river was quite narrow in many spots. The secret to rock skipping is to find flat shoe heel sized rocks that would be flung onto the surface of the river landing as flat as possible at the moment of river impact. These flat smooth like pebbles were found aplenty on the shores of the river. They were easy to skip on the river for five to ten feet when thrown so that their flat side would land on the surface of the river. Thrown with enough force and dexterity, they could make up to ten or more skips sometimes even reaching the far side of the narrow river. With each successive skip becoming shorter and shorter, they would eventually lose their velocity and would sink to the river's bottom. The best of us could achieve five to ten skips of a stone occasionally making it fully across the river. This was doable when the river narrowed at various points along its course. We never grew tired of these shenanigans, though girls rarely took part in this adventure that tended to be more of a boy's sport.

The valley or metro parks also served as a destination point for many school projects. Once we found a praying mantis for a third-grade class. The insect was placed on a bush located near the front of our classroom and fed fresh grasshoppers by hand. He would eagerly grab the poor critter and then go to work. This was fascinating but at the same time it appeared to be cruel and somewhat revolting. The mantis would pull off the victim's legs and head and then enjoy the rest of the grasshopper while we all looked on with amazement and of course with disgust. Nature is not very classy when it comes to eating. After a week of this butchery, the critter was released into the wild looking plump and no worse for the wear.

Rocky River soon would become our new home if all went and according to plan. Mom, growing weary of cramped "Project" living wanted a new home that would be worthy location for raising her children. The folks looked around and found an empty lot they could afford to build on. The site would become 2785 Gasser Boulevard. I always found the name Gasser to be odd but no one seemed to have issues with it. I think Mr. Gasser was a man of importance in bye-gone days and was honored with his own street name.

After locating the new lot to build on, Dad with a few phone calls to the right friends and relatives soon learned of an Italian builder through family contacts by the name of James Thomas Restivo. Restivo was born in Accede Defuse, Sicily. Isn't that interesting?! James started his construction company after the war and soon he developed a good reputation as a fine craftsman able to build quality homes.

The folks met with him and felt comfortable knowing they could work well with him while building their new home. The plans for the Caravella home were drawn up for a two-story brick bungalow with a white peak. Dad submitted the plans to the Rocky River building department.

Rocky River was a city in the early 1950's composed notably of primarily white Anglo-Saxon protestants. No, do not misunderstand my drift. There of course is nothing wrong with this wonderful, English speaking Germanic group of citizens. However, it should be noted that Italians and other ethnic groups of that era were as common in "River" as ice flows were in the Mojave Desert.

Regardless of the reason or reasons, Dad and Mom struggled to receive approval from the building department over an increasing number of issues. After a few weeks, the City of Rocky River said the home was too low and didn't meet other building standards required of the lots location and they would not approve the plans. Adjustments were made. More adjustments were made. The house still failed to meet the city's standards. Even more adjustments were made. No luck. Rumor had it, that Dad was told to find a local builder who knew how to meet "River's" building regulations.

Over time, my folks feared a sense of some anti-Italian sentiment at work. This would be difficult to prove even if it were the case. Louis, at his wits end, notified the city in writing that he was contacting his U. S. congressman about possible discriminatory activity. That put a kibosh, once and for all to the city's delays, paper signing, further regulations, and grandstanding. The city's monkeyshines soon took a nosedive rivaling a Nazi aircraft being hit by one of Uncle Bob's on shore guns.

With the evaporation of city obstacles, the new home some stood magnificently at the corner of 2785 Gasser Boulevard and a small corner street that may have never been dedicated for it bore no name. The small street (not an extended driveway) separated our home from that of our future neighbor's home. At the end of this short street of about one hundred and twenty-five feet in length, began a small hill rising to a dirt path extending another one hundred to two hundred feet into the undeveloped land beyond.

Our home stood on the eastern side of Gasser Boulevard and was located nearly exactly at the midway point of the street between the north and south ends. It was a sight to behold for this relatively newly minted immigrant and his wife to ponder. Phyllis and I were so excited. It was a grand time; new home, new schools, new friends, new life. It is America.

We moved into our new home shortly after completion and were warmly greeted by the neighbors. In those days it was the rule rather than the exception to welcome new neighbors nearly immediately after the moving truck pulled out of the drive. Someone brought over a freshly baked cake for us to enjoy. Others brought over other tasty treats. It was a marvelous day especially for mom and dad; one that was hard for my folks to fathom. Their wishes and hopes had finally fully blossomed. They had finally made it. A Sicilian immigrant accomplished what he always knew he could do and as he said to me on many occasions, "Philip, the harder you work, the luckier you get. " America is a wonderful if not magical country.

Phyllis and I entered first grade at Wooster School off Wooster Road; another odd name to be sure. The older school, an original for the city was within walking distance from our new home. We would walk through the back yard path into the undeveloped land heading over to another street on the other side known as Morley Court. From there the school was only a stone's throw away on the other side of Wooster Road. It was an old school, earlier serving as a junior high school and before that even the first Rocky River High School. It had old wooden rickety floors, tall windows, and narrow staircases but enjoyed a special character all of its own. Don't forget. It was "River."

"River" was and remains one of the most prestigious suburbs on the Westside of Cleveland, though Bay Village residents would argue the point. Bay Village was also the site of an infamous murder of that era allegedly committed by Dr. Sam Shepard the husband of his wife, Marilyn Shepard. He was convicted on what seemed to be flimsy evidence and it was my belief as time went on and that of others, that he was innocent of the crime. Dr. Shepard after serving many years in prison was released and later met and married an attractive blond woman from Germany. He and she moved into Rocky

River after his release from prison and began living in a nearby apartment on Wooster Road not far from the school Phyllis and I attended. I actually would deliver newspapers to his address later on in years.

The rivalry between these two communities "Bay" and "River "was locally legendary. Fortunately, their energies were expended on the football field and the basketball court rather than in back allies. Well, everyone knew neither River nor Bay had any back allies. Back allies have never existed in these well-to-do, tree-lined and park laden communities.

Shortly before moving to "River" my brother Louis Philip Junior was born. Neither Phyllis nor I were given middle names because it was not as traditional then to do so. Lou as I called him was jovial, with a perpetual smile, and a very cute face. I teased him no end. He looked up to me, no end. We fought but never in a vicious manner.

Lou was well liked and fun to be around. He proved to be intelligent with a good sense of humor and an endless smile that at times had a mischievous character to it. He had large bones compared to Phyllis and I. We were tall and lanky and far from muscular. Lou had lighter hair but the same brown eyes as we had. Phyllis's hair was a very dark brown and was often referred to as black by those who do not know what black is.

In contrast to Lou, Phyllis was very soft spoken and a little lady. She was clean, neat, and always prim and prissy.

Her shyness may have gotten in the way of her social life, which seemed to bother her endlessly in that it seemed to be on hold a good portion of her youth. Phyllis was very pretty as a child and even more so as an adolescent. She knew how to dress and mom and dad took very good care of helping her with her hairstyles and clothing. She was neat, clean, and well spoken.

Phyllis had many friends but only a couple that were very close to her for most of her childhood. Patricia LaVoy, her best friend, was one of them and she lived within walking distance of our home. In fact, Pat lived much closer than we did to Wooster School at which we all attended for about a year or so until the new gold wood School had been completed. Gold wood Elementary School was further west of our home requiring a school bus ride to get there. Pat and Phyllis had a lot in common and spent many countless days together as the two of them grew up.

Our new home was special in many ways. It had two full baths, two bedrooms on the first floor, one on the second floor, a beautiful living room, a good-sized dining room, a large kitchen, a full basement, and an unfinished attic. The home was beautifully finished and sported a bold kitchen done up in yellow and bright red paint. It was bold yet exciting in the theme of the 1950's, a new era moving away from the darkness of the war and into the future of growth and prosperity.

The kitchen table had a yellow almost Formica like surface and six yellow vinyl like chairs with double chrome plated legs. Kitchen cabinets had wood toned doors set upon white painted surrounds. There was a large window facing East and a smaller one above the kitchen sink area looking south over the small street connecting our driveway with Gasser Boulevard. This window also over looked a path that led to the woods eastward from the side street we would share with a future neighbor. The woods along with nearby dilapidated green houses would later be built into a residential neighborhood and a small park. My mother would find herself peering endlessly out the small kitchen window above the sink while often involved in washing dishes, preparing meals, or observing the back and for movement of children and occasional adults visiting the nearby woods.

We soon became acquainted with several other kids on the street, spending endless hours with them, at homes, in classrooms, and on the playing fields. Most of our days were happily spent outside, in all types of weather, playing with our friends unless rain shortened our activities. It was commonplace for all of us to visit each other's homes to play. The mothers graciously provided treats of all sorts whenever we visited each other's homes. Mom always had homemade cookies for all. She made sure no one would outdo her and no one ever did. It was an Italian thing. Food is the drug of choice for enduring people together and is always appreciated.

A new home has its share of needs before one can really settle in. One of the biggest projects for any new homeowner is to establish a lawn and to landscape the perimeter. This is no easy chore and preceded the days of sod and even hiring firms to do it. Most new homeowners were into do-it-yourself projects. Asking relatives for help was by no means taboo and for Dad, being ignorant about how to carry out such projects would require all the help he could muster. Dad was clever in the business world though he had very few skills that could be honed for yard or garden work. He was not alone. I fell into "the same kettle of fish". I have never cared for yard work though a necessary evil that goes with the territory of owning a home.

Putting in a new lawn was a project Dad believed he could handle without a lot of fanfare but of course with a lot of help. He called his brother and father to help provide skill, muscle, and equipment. Grandpa Filippo brought a heavy home-made lawn roller to grade the land surface of our yard. It was made from a large left-over piece of orange ceramic like underground city water pipe. The orange two-inch-thick pre-casted sewer pipe was about twenty-four inches in diameter and thirty-six inches long. Through the center of this contraption passed a forty inch long piece of heavy duty plumbers pipe that would later be connected in sequence to additional pipes that would serve as a handle to pull the roller around the yard. During construction of this handmade roller, grandpa poured concrete into the orange sewer pipe that also housed another smaller central pipe of sorts. He had filled the twenty-four inch sewer pipe with concrete and then placed a smaller heavy-duty two inch steel pipe through the center of the roller before the entire wet concrete contraption hardened. Later he connected another set of pipes to pass through the center pipe and with right angles to each other formed a handle made up of all of these pipes to allow for pushing or dragging this homemade roller. It proved to be quite effective in evening out and smoothing out the surface of the ground that would later become the grassy lawn.

This entire project sounded like a lot of work. In fact, it was a lot of work. Putting in a large lawn with homemade equipment took on a life of its own. I became exhausted just thinking about this project before it even began.

Shovels, rakes, and bags of seeds were purchased or brought along and were in abundant supply. This endeavor turned into a sweaty, back breaking, elbow racking project for Dad and to a lesser degree for me, being younger and a bit more resilient. Planting this lawn in an oversized lot took days to complete. Just sitting out rocks and stones on the property where the lawn would be was a major project in its own right. Extensive raking and evening out the ground throughout the property was a job big time job for us folks. Hand thrown grass seed by Scotts to be later covered with straw over the entire lawn surface finally wrapped up the project; almost. Endless placement and moving of sprinkler heads for intense watering was required to help the seed germinate. Shrubs and trees were planted as well, and the property began to look special; lived in and lived on. Considering that landscaping was not this crew's forte, we had done a wonderful job.

Well with every well-planted lawn comes another related job. The grass-cutting and lawn edging chore was delegated to I, as were the car washing duties. Dad believed in hard work when at work, but felt that children should take on a few responsibilities as well. I never minded any of these tasks because I felt we should blend in with the rest of the neighborhood and it was important for all of us to pull in the same direction to gain the respect of our neighbors. In fact, car washing and waxing became one of my interests as did automobile repairs on a very basic scale at first. I made sure we had the best washed and waxed cars as well as the best maintained lawn and shrubs in the neighborhood. PERIOD. We were never to be thought of as second-class citizens. The best or nothing was how I felt about life.

As time went on one of my best friend Lowell Gaspar, said to me, that all of our cars were always amazing in their look and style. You could eat off the engine block and in addition they ran perfectly. As I saw to it, proper tuning and good carburation would be the answer to flawless performance. A minimum of once a year, I would purchase a new set of spark plugs for each vehicle, check the spark plug gap, remove the old plugs and replace it with the new ones. In addition, the points would be replaced. All of these adjustments led to a dramatic improvement in power and performance after the worn parts were replaced. Changing the engine oil and oil filter was also easy. Occasionally I would replace the shock absorbers as well to improve the ride and control of each car. Before winter would begin, I also switched the standard tires with winter treads knowing that without them driving would turn into a circus of slippery starts, wild skids, and dangerous performance. I loved working on cars but not enough to pursue it as a future.

Mom did most of the house hold chores though Honey got roped into dusting, sweeping, and washing floors, washing dishes, and worst of all, washing walls. Spic and Span worked well but I didn't. Whenever possible, I would pull a disappearing act but eventually Mom would catch up with me. These projects seemed to be endless but so was mom's work in raising four children.

My brother and I shared the second-floor bedroom using a single full-sized bed until we grew too big for one bed. On the Western wall were two unique wall paper cartoon-like wall hangings added to the room as a finishing touch. We would spend long periods of time looking at them before falling asleep, though I do not recall speaking of them in any meaningful way. Kicking and fidgeting early before falling asleep was the norm for both of us.

Lou being little and younger than I, probably got the worst of it, though I was never truly mean to him in any way. His memories may differ from mine. As we grew older my parents invested in twin beds that would then be used by us until we left home. They were unusual in that the headboards and foot boards appeared to be hand carved out of hard oak wood though they were not. They were very masculine looking while sporting hand wrought rusted looking steel pieces holding the bed posts to the head and to the foot boards. Very cool! Very boyish! They were indestructible and looked like the day they were bought after twenty or more years of use. I mean these beds were tough.

A rather humorous incident occurred involving Dad's 1949 Chrysler that I was a party to. The car sported a fluid drive transmission with a column shifter. This transmission was a cross between a stick shift and an automatic having some characteristics of each one. It was a throwback to the old days driven more like an automatic fluid drive tranny than a floor shift stick.

One day my two-year old brother and I were sitting in the Chrysler while it was parked in the garage. He began fiddling with the column shifter moving it up and down. Dad soon arrived. He started the car after little Lou had earlier inadvertently placed it into drive when he was playing with the shifter. The car being placed unknowingly into gear by my brother, while the car was not running, suddenly jerked forward when Dad started the car ramming the back end of the garage hard enough to push the back wall two to three inches off of its concrete foundation at the base. The incident was not enough to affect the integrity of the garage itself and it would remain the same forever. This maneuver gave new meaning to the phrase, ramming speed. In those days bumpers were real chrome bumpers held onto the cars frame with heavy duty braces and therefore no car or bumper damage occurred from the impact into the back wall. Dad never let on that he knew what had happened even if he actually did know. We remained speechless about fearing the full consequences of speaking up if Dad had found out what really happened. My dad never said much about it thinking apparently that it was his mistake. I never peeped a word about it. Little Lou was too young to figure anything out as well though he was the real culprit.

It was a forgotten incident and I have never mentioned it to anyone. Being as young as we were, it was scary and shocking when it happened. My father being a good-natured man would not have made a huge deal out of it even if he knew what had really happened. The garage remained intact over the years and never required a repair or an adjustment. The 1949 Chrysler was a moose. With today's cars there would have been major front end damage costing in the thousands to repair and repaint.

After every few years, Dad felt a car change was due and he decided to trade the "49" Chrysler in for a silver-blue and grey two-toned four-door Plymouth hardtop (meaning no B pillar) giving the car a sporty appearance. Cars without B pillars looked sleek and sporty. Due to rollover regulations with modern cars, the B pillar centrally located is a must to prevent roof collapse killing the occupants in a rollover accident. The new and stylish Belvedere had a V-8 with a three speed pushbutton torque-flight automatic tranny to go along with its large tail fins. He chose this number to save money over the cost of another Chrysler.

Let's face it. A Plymouth is not a Chrysler and thus he was never fully satisfied with the car as was proven two years later, by trading it in on a new 1959 Chrysler. His new Chrysler was a real looker. It was a huge white car with a two-tone white and red trimmed roof, accompanied by a long red chrome surrounded accent stripe on both sides. It had a 383 cubic inch Golden Lion engine that moved it along fairly well. The monstrous fins on the back were incredible to behold. The Chrysler sported a red interior with swivel seats that moved outward when lifting a chrome lever on the forward part of the lower seat cushion. It was the ticket. The Plymouth being a little too tame started off on the wrong foot. Anyway, it had to go. It was not Dad. Dad was Chrysler.

These were the years of excess automobile design supporting the newfound optimism Americans had for the future following the great World War II. Americans were bold and their cars showed the same theme. Americans were winners and their new cars and homes were built and sold with modern themes.

Americans hopes and dreams were also exhibited throughout their lives including with the fun they had when they were not working. Along with their love of new and amazing cars and homes, they enjoyed movie theaters, shopping centers, and malls that began to evolve in the 1950's. Even theme parks were big ticket items, including Ohio's

Cedar Point and Disney's Disney Land with amazing theme rides, fun houses, roller coasters, fireworks and all of the cotton candy one could ever hope for. The 1950's was a rebirth of a nation exploring all of the fun and interesting aspects of life after surviving World War II. It was not about excess. It was about experiencing all things possible in a new era that would precede the "space race."

The "Cold War" be damned. America's Americans were proving their mettle, their love of their country, and their amazing scientific and engineering capabilities exceeded by no other country. America was gifted. America is gifted. America is America and shall never be overcome from outside influences. Inside political foolery is another matter.

As time went on, Dad found that owning a home was a big responsibility and he became interested in home improvement ideas from time to time as time moved on. Beginning with several ideas, even though our new home was new, Dad had discussed with mom a few thoughts he had to improve the property. Lacking deep pockets he would explore any and all ideas that would increase the look and comfort of the new home that he believed he could tackle by himself. The unfinished basement was on ongoing target that would bug him until he finally decided what to do about it.

Eventually he would decide what to do. He decided we all needed a "recreation room" that could serve many purposes. It was silly to let the unfinished basement remain and so his imagination took over. After a few discussions with mom, Dad would begin the lengthy project of finishing the larger half of the unfinished basement that was essentially empty. It could become a functional and attractive recreation room for any number of activities including adding a new television to the basement level. The other half of the basement held the furnace, laundry, and wine cellar. The unfinished half of the basement sported a brick wood-burning fireplace located centrally against the eastern wall of the basement. This large and wonderful room would begin a new and interesting chapter for the Caravella's new home.

Dad began his long-term project by first installing 12" x 12" black and maroon rubber floor tiles with white and beige speckling along the entire length of the floor using a gooey black cement. Having limited time off, only on Wednesdays and Sundays, would limit his ability to complete new projects in a timely fashion. But what was the rush?!

Thus, it would take months for him to complete the floor installation by itself. After the floor, Dad began to installed knotty pine wood planks along the four walls of the primary basement area where the fireplace existed. He attached wood faring strips upon the entire circumference of the basement's four long walls. Now this was another job and a half that took many months to complete. The tricky part of the entire job was to encase the four outside basement windows with wood envelopes. Now that was tricky for someone who had never done any form of carpentry. But where there is a will there is a way. I took after Dad in that regard. Just because I had never done something and just because I had no specific training in a given area, never stopped me from jumping right into something that I felt good about completing.

When all of the wooden planks and window coverings had been completed it came time to wrap the project up. Dad finished-off the room with fluorescent light fixtures and standard incandescent light fixtures placed in strategic locations to light up the room when ever needed. The fireplace was outlined above with a wooden knotty pine valence.

While working on the wood valence, a nail that he was hammering into place flew backwards striking the glass of his spectacles. In those days corrective lenses were made of glass and not plastic as they are today. Some of the shattered glass flew into his right eye and around the orbit of his eye. Grasping his face in shear pain, he ran upstairs and my mother rushed him to St. Johns Hospital ER in Lakewood. This was a disaster of course and he was rushed to an eye specialist, Dr. Raft who suggested surgery. Dad decided on a second opinion and saw Dr. William McGannon, a highly respected eye surgeon who recommended leaving the glass splinter where it was, feeling it was too dangerous to go on a fishing expedition into the globe of the eye since his vision was relatively intact.

Dad eventually would recover but it was an incident that was never to be forgotten and would have a major impact on the life of my brother. My Dad, after this experience, avoided projects that he felt were dangerous. As time went on My father as a whole was not mechanically inclined and rarely attempted repairs of any sort, and often would hire the best workers he could find to do a job.

He also learned that there are no short cuts or freebees when it comes to good appliances and thus always purchased for mom the best appliances available to avoid replacements that over time were more costly than doing it correctly from the beginning. He believed you got what you paid for and for the most part he was right.

Well after the car shifting fiasco, my brother Louis continued to have a penchant for mischievous activity. One year during grade-school, Phyllis and I along with a few classmates painted a large mural about six feet tall and fifteen feet long. After it had outworn its usefulness in school, we were granted the opportunity to take it home and keep it. We attached the paper mural with tape to the southern wall of the knotty pined covered wooden wall in the finished basement.

My brother became interested in the mural for other than its artistic beauty. He was experimenting with matches and set the end of the mural on fire. Panicking, he ran upstairs and told mom who then called the Rocky River fire department. Racing downstairs, she ripped a fire extinguisher off a nearby wall fortuitously placed in the stairwell to the basement. Little Lou grabbed an empty milk bottle, filled it with water and at first tried to throw some water from the bottle but realized this was a useless idea as the flames grew larger even after smashing the bottle against the wall onto the burning mural.

Being nearby and thus within a few short minutes the fire department arrived in force and in full battle gear, while smoke was pouring out of the basement windows. The firemen danced around the shards of glass during the process of extinguishing the fire and later asked about the glass apparently thinking someone had thrown a Molotov cocktail.

The fire department performed a masterful job with minimal serious damage considering the various possible outcomes, ranging from bad to really bad. In retrospect the mural was becoming a bit of a bore anyway.

Aside from some of life's challenges, Dad did well when it came to dressing sharply and remained current with clothing styles for a man of his means. The family was blessed to have my Uncle John Koesel, mom's brother-in-law, as a frequent visitor to our home along with his gifted family. He was the head designer of men's suits and clothing for Cleveland's Richmond Brother's Company, the largest American men's clothier of its day.

Uncle Johnny as he was called by most of us, was a master designer and tailor. He would design, cut, and hand sew the finest custom suits of the day for Dad and myself to enjoy. He would provide at least one suit per year to each of us at no cost. Dad would return the favor by cutting Uncle John's hair whenever he visited.

Both Uncle John and Dad were meticulous about their looks, grooming and dressing as sharp as any executive of any corporation. This was not a lie. They're cleanly pressed white shirts and carefully selected ties were accompanied by a matching hanky for the left breast suit pocket, gold toned cufflinks, and a solid gold watch my dad wore religiously.

Dad was allergic to most common metals suffering the consequences of nasty rashes on his wrists or fingers when exposed to metals other than gold. Dad only tolerated gold jewelry and he looked great sporting the beautiful and solid gold Longines Wittnauer watch on his thick boned left wrist. Later in life, he began to wear a gold one-half carat (actually 52 points) diamond ring on his right ring finger. He never wore a wedding band nor did most other men of that era. The men's wedding band craze is surprisingly new, possibly due to the fact these folks lived through the depression and a ring for your lady was one thing but men often could not afford one for themselves. They had more basic needs to deal with. Their word was hopefully good enough. My father was an honorable man and conducted his life accordingly.

Mom was no slacker in the area on how to dress to the "T's". Neither spent much on clothes but when they did, their clothes were elegant and of fine quality. Mom's hair was perfectly groomed by Dad, a couple of times per week or whenever needed based on social activities. Her hairstyles and clothing were rich and gorgeous to match her peaches and cream complexion, her vibrant personality, and her handsome figure. She wore little makeup except for a touch of rouge and a bit of lipstick. Lacking sun exposure throughout her life, her skin was wrinkle and blemish free. Minimal eye shadow if any was required. She always looked beautiful and was pristine in how she handled herself around others.

An interesting development developed a short distance from our home on Gasser Boulevard in 1954 that would temp all of the ladies of the area for decades to come. What could this be? Westgate Center, the first shopping mall in the greater Cleveland area and the first suburban mall in Ohio opened up on Center Ridge Road less than a mile from where we lived. The mall covered fifty-five acres of land. The original anchors in this open-air plaza included a three level upscale department store, Halle Brothers Company, a two level Federal Department Store catering to the less financially endowed, and a Krogers Supermarket. A movie theater was also part of the fare.

This wonderful shopping center would have much greater meaning to mother other than for shopping purposes as time would go on. Mom was not a clothes hound nor into the latest styles though her practical instincts would kick in later on in years as it pertained to the plaza which would eventually become an enclosed mall late in the 1960's. Halles would eventually be replaced by Higbees of similar but of slightly less stature. Until then, mother's trips to the mall were fairly rare as finances and the costs of raising four children would always remain a challenge. This was even more true, when in later years a major disaster would strike to the core of our lives.

My parents rarely fought about anything and when they did it was usually about some money issue with Mom usually getting the upper hand. They were fairly frugal and thus had no significant debt after paying off their new home within the first ten years of ownership. Cash was their standard modus operandi while credit did not apply. If they could not pay cash for something, they did not buy it. Along with a trade in, Dad paid cash for his cars avoiding loans at all times. If you didn't have it, you didn't spend it. That was that. Mom and Dad were cut from the same cloth when it came to money issues.

Cleanliness and a crisp clean-shaven appearance were another one of Louie's trademarks. He would rise every morning at about 6:00 AM and head for the bathroom to shave with a straight razor and thick white lather taken from a mug. A shaving cream brush with a white handle and bristles of about three inches in length was his main tool. He would add a small amount of hot water to the white cup like dish holding the round one inch high and two-inch diameter shaving soap bar. The brush would be used to lather up the soup with the warm to hot water to reach just the right consistency. He would apply the thick warm suds to his face and neck with his shaving brush and then sculpture his look with a fine well sharpened razor, removing the twenty-three hour and fifty-five-minute old beard that had grown and run its course from the previous day. He never went unshaven. He spared the crisp appearing mustache on his upper lip that was as much of a trademark as it was a decorative reminder of his masculine Italian culture. Only once in his life was, he briefly and completely clean-shaven, only to be later admonished severely and to such an extent by us disbelieving children who did not recognize him as our father. Taking the criticism well, he grew the mustache back within weeks never to be removed again for the rest of his life. If there was one taboo that we children forbid, that was it. He was not Dad without it. PERIOD.

After finishing his bathroom activities, he would sit at the kitchen table where Mom would prepare a light breakfast of two slices of white buttered mahogany toasted toast accompanied by a slathering of deep colored grape jelly and several cups of black coffee; no sugar thanks you. An occasional soft-boiled egg resting on top of a shot glass with the top shell carefully removed was served two or three days per week. On weekends Dad sometimes began with a raw egg yolk, separated from its white and placed in the bottom of a tumbler filled with his rich red Italian wine to be swallowed in one large gulp.

The Cleveland Plain Dealer was always close at his side each morning but only to be scanned and later read between customers at the shop. His customers would also have access to the same paper. When finished eating, he folded the paper in half and placed it next to his packed lunch that Mom always prepared for him and for us children as well.

Upon finishing breakfast early each morning, he would then dress for work. Wearing a clean white crisp shirt pressed to perfection by Mom, was the usual uniform. Only in later years did he switch to a barber's shirt that was easier to clean and required little if any pressing. Dad's always immaculately clean white barber's shirt had four snap like fasteners over the left shoulder. When he felt warm during the hot days of summer, the shoulder flap would be unfastened, left partially opened, and draped downward over his upper chest.

After dressing, he would leave every morning at about 7:20 AM driving through eastern "River" and heading down Hilliard Road to Franklin Boulevard and into Lakewood. Arriving ten minutes before 8:00 AM and just before his clients would begin to arrive was his general routine. There were often however two or three customers already waiting, hoping to catch the first spot.

My sister and I would start the day just before Dad. We began drinking coffee with milk and sugar as early as I can remember, probably by age four. I would eat two slices of white bread toasted with margarine or peanut butter smeared thickly over one side. Occasionally I added some jam of one sort or another. My favorite jams varied from cherry and apricot and were of the Smuckers ilk. But for me the absolute best was fig jam though rare and hard to find. For a treat, whenever available we would eat Italian bread instead of white.

On the weekends Mom would buy specialty pastries from Elmwood Bakery in Lakewood. They were French like turnovers with various fillings and some pastries were encrusted with pecans and covered with delicious white or maple sugar icing. In my earlier years I was a bit on the chunky side from over indulging in these amazing pastries or more likely from not exercising enough as I would later prove in my medical research.

On other occasions, my grandmother Caravella often provided nut rolls made with immense amounts of crushed walnut filling or poppy seed. Her "nut rolls" where chuck full of the tasty nutty sweet filling far better than any bakery would make.

When homemade baked goods were not available, some excellent pastry and bakery shops were scattered around most communities. Some of the best pastries came from Hough Bakeries that were city-wide though unfortunately eventually apparently went out of business when they could no longer compete with the newly built large grocery chain bakeries from a cost perspective that slowly began to show up on the scene. Hough Bakery had many masterpieces though with the most memorable one to me being a luscious chocolate cupcake with a white thick rich central cream filling topped by an amazing thick fudge like chocolate icing. This creation was very similar to chocolate Hostess Cupcakes but to a far more decadent degree with thicker richer chocolate topping and an even better white creamy filling. This elegant masterpiece was priced higher but was substantially superior in taste and quality to other cupcakes of similar appearance usually sold in local grocery stores. I could not get enough of them.

A terrific line of Italian grocery stores by the name of Fazios also had fabulous baked goods though because of their success were later purchased by a larger national food chain. Their excellent pastries in my opinion were later mutated to a lesser quality and beyond all recognition once big business took over. Some casual observers may have referred to this pastry travesty as the very first "FUBAR" (fucked up beyond all recognition).

In the final analysis, Cleveland's excellent bakeries have nearly disappeared from the landscape with only a few privately held family operations that I know of. In any case, as a child I overindulged in these pastries enjoying every blissful taste and bite to their final conclusion. Now that I can afford these wonderful miracles they are not to be had. Life can be a real "bite" - or maybe not!!!

Getting back to Dad's skill as a barber and an innovator in the art of cutting hair, he proved to be as good as they came. He was a master at cutting the "flat-top" hair style of the "50's." This was a variation of the "butch" in which the hair was closely cropped taking on the shape of one's head and was popular for boys active in sports and for those who wanted to keep cool. Shaving heads had not come into vogue. Short was more often worn in the summer. The "flat-top" differed from the butch in that the hair was cut on top perfectly flat, similar in appearance to the deck of an aircraft carrier. It was sexier and more stylish than a butch with the butch being more boy-like and less attractive. The flat top was more difficult for barbers to perfect and more time consuming to perfectly cut and thus never gained a lot of favor though it was one of Dad's masterpieces. The front of the flat-top would require a gel or moose like substance that would dry and keep the hair straight up over the forehead. The front of the cut was about one inch long and tapered to a shorter cut as it progressed to the back of the head. It was worn by boys, young men, and sometimes by middle aged men as well.

This cut was worn during the same era in which long locks of hair were worn up front in a wavy fashion with the rest of their hair combed all the way to the back on the side of the the head into a DA (duck's ass) style. As the hair reached the back of the male's head, it met the other side looking like a duck seen from the side or back. The hair would come together at the very back of the head like a duck's ass and then would be slightly swept downward at the midline in the back of his head. The hair was combed in a fashion as to not be combed upward like a real duck's backend. The style was quite attractive, catchy, and different. It would be fun if it resurfaced in today's day and age.

Some women in contrast wore a similar cut with their longer styled hair swept backwards and then upwards in the midline at the back of their head; more like a duck's ass. The women looked very sexy with their "DA's" whereas the men thought they looked cool. Many people however did not care for the male's version but the woman's version had a very hot and sexy look that could not go unnoticed. Now this style should definitely come back. It was clever and amazing. Let's go ladies! Wear a "DA."

For a very brief time I wore a similar man's style when I wasn't wearing a flat-top.

During the 50's, my dad invented the "razor cut." He discovered that hair could be sharply cut on the side of the head in a very clean and in an even way, using a straight razor rather than shears. It took a bit more time and a lot of caution but he soon mastered the cut. His reputation grew and several articles appeared both in *The Cleveland Press* and *The Plain Dealer* newspapers. Soon actors of stage and screen were occasionally coming in to his shop for a "razor cut." For a while it was a lot of fun. It is fun to note that Lucille Ball of 1950's television fame, heard of my dad's expertise and occasionally invited him to New York to style her hair. Her glamorous red hair was always as perfect as it could be during the 1950's era. She was the "Bell of the Ball" and Dad was thrilled to work with her.

The fun ended in the 60's when the Beatles arrived on the scene. Sporting long hair almost killed the barber industry when many took up the style for themselves. Barbers survived by cutting hair for businessmen and younger children. This period was a dark time for my father in that he worried from then on about his business continually going downhill. Being forced out by hairstyles worn by major singing groups, that also spread to men of the general population was very hard on Dad. His business never failed but from that point on he seemed to think that it would. This personal burden may have contributed to his early demise at a fairly young age.

My mother equally interested in financial success believed that her children should be earning money for their future. She didn't care how we did it but she expected results. Both of my folks had started working early in life and they felt that it was important for us to establish the importance of sound financial planning to secure a future. With their families suffering through the depression in by-gone years, it impressed upon both of them that life could be difficult but preparation would ease the way. My sister Phyllis started babysitting and I picked up other jobs from occasional lawn cutting, car washing, and later followed by more high paying and more reliable work. Reliable meant a real job.

One of my earliest jobs was delivering newspapers beginning first with *The Rocky River Herald*, a small local paper with limited news other than local stories. This was sort of a boring job but it was linked to one very interesting customer.

In a small apartment building on Wooster Road between Hilliard and Center Ridge lived a famous or infamous customer, depending on your viewpoint. He been recently released from prison. It was none other than Dr. Sam Shepard who had at first been convicted of his wife's murder and later released from prison on a technicality.

I met and talked with him during those days when he became a professional wrestler, learning a few tricks of the trade while incarcerated. He had been an important surgeon in the neighboring community of Bay Village before the murder conviction.

His entire trial had a circus like atmosphere about it with Dr. Shepard being convicted by press accounts which were believed by many to have adversely prejudiced the jury. His conviction was later reversed by the U. S. Supreme Court which for that era was quite a surprise. My brother knew Sam's son through a school connection. His son always believed in his father's innocence as do I to this day.

After a bit more experience in the newspaper business, I took over a *Cleveland News* route to earn more money. About a year or so later the paper went out of business. Fortunately, a *Cleveland Press* route became available. This being the second largest newspaper in the area was a shot in the arm for me. About a couple of years later, it went out of business. I then graduated to the big time, the Cleveland *Plain Dealer* having a Sunday edition. This worked well and later when I had grown older and moved into other work, the paper route was taken over by my younger brother.

My most famous customer of Cleveland fame was the baseball player and pitcher, Bob Lemon. I delivered one paper or another to him and would collect money periodically on weekends. He rarely came to the door, but on one occasion instead, his "hot" blond wife showed up. She handed to Bob a baseball I had with me and he also autographed my favorite baseball glove which I still have to this day. The Lemon's seemed to have plenty of money but certainly not compared to athletes of today's standards. I often had to go back several times because they never had cash or the right change as I was told. Due to his position on "the club," they were rarely seen outside and apparently didn't kibitz with their neighbors. Fame, even in those days was more of hassle than it was worth.

With these newspaper routes, I was able to save up a lot of money that my mother banked for me. Other monies from holiday gifts were commingled in this account so I never knew how much I had earned over the years. It was all to go towards a college education.

Traveling to Grandma Rose's home remained high on the list of things to do. These weekend events were rarely missed by my folks, but as we aged it became more of an ordeal since we were developing our own friendships and activities. The trips were more enjoyable after the birth of my brother, Louis Philip Caravella, Jr., who was a delight in most ways, with an affable personality and an endless playful way about him. We always got along well. He looked up to me with some degree of admiration and would later go on to follow in my footsteps in many ways. The three of us including Phyllis also enjoyed the major holidays of the year.

My folks were so happy to have us, that they went out of their way to have each and every holiday or birthday be special in many ways. They sacrificed their own needs and desires, to please us but they were just as pleased in doing so.

As children we rarely received gifts from our parents other than on all of the major holidays and birthdays. This achieved the result of increasing our thrills and expectations, as they would arrive without us becoming fixated on material things as a reason for existence.

Though in truthfulness, he did break the rules with my youngest sister, especially when the rest of us had already left home for school or jobs. In retrospect it was a good thing that he did so, since fate would ultimately deal a terribly unexpected blow a few years down the road.

The real fun began every year with the advent of Thanksgiving and a treasure trove of amazing food and friendly visits from both sides of the family. It was such a "riot" to help mom put together a big juicy bird that we would help her select at the butcher shop next to Dad's barber shop. We loved turkey, but then who doesn't.

Actually, I did have, as difficult as it was to believe, an uncle who never ate turkey and instead had a great big juicy steak on Thanksgiving. He just was not with the program. I guess that steak diet would work for a few people but it would never work for me.

Turkey was such a treat and unfortunately it was not usually available more often during the year, at least in the form of a big juicy well-browned chestnut stuffed delectable delight. Then mom would also include amazing mashed potatoes covered with a delicious mahogany colored thick gravy made from the simmered juices of the turkey's liver, gizzard, neck, and other usually uneaten parts that would provide the perfect base for the best hot mouth-watering gravy you could ever hope to whirl a tongue around. Yes, it was fabulous. Her dinner rolls were just as good of course, accompanied by heavenly Italian heavily thick crusted and thick sliced bread that was incomparable when it came from the bakeries of Little Italy on the southeast side of Cleveland.

Well, that was not the end of it by any means. When we were more stuffed than the turkey with salad, fruit, green beans, and all the turkey trimmings, there was still desert. Now dessert took on a life of its own. We are talking here about the finest cannoli's you could ever bite into. The brown flakey cylindrical shell holding a fabulously creamy chocolate laced pure white cream filled delicacy had been deep fried to perfection. Everyone loved the cannoli's as much as the main course since they were only available around the traditional fall and winter holidays. The cannoli were never to be alone on the dessert menu.

Mom's perfectly created pumpkin pie did not take a back seat to any other dessert, especially when accompanied by delicious creamy smooth vanilla ice cream as a side car nestled close to that wedged sliced piece of pie with a golden-brown flaky crust that would shatter into little bitty pieces as the fork broke through the amazing crust.

Yes, we were spoiled. Dad and mom did not skimp on the food. We almost never went to restaurants because if for no other reason mom was a cook "par excel lance."

By the time we were all through eating, the men would gravitate into the living room to fall asleep while watching the usual football games of all descriptions. I would join them for a bit but often-spent fun visits with my cousin Sam or my cousin Roy, if they had also been invited to the festivities.

To some degree, Thanksgiving rotated from home to home depending on variables I never had the privy to understand nor worry about since it was generally good. No sooner had we enjoyed the delectable delights of Thanksgiving would Christmas Eve and Christmas day be just around the corner to kick start the rest of the entire festive season once again.

Life was not always quite as perfect as I have implied. There was always the travel back and forth between homes, from Westside to Eastside or the commotion that goes along with fifteen to twenty people being together in close quarters for many hours. In another vein, smoking cigarettes, cigars, or pipes by the men folk was commonplace if not involving at least half of the World War II generation. During my childhood, smoking by the grownups did not seem to be very annoying because it was so commonplace. In today's age it would be annoying should you not be a smoker.

Also, there were the inevitable hugs and kisses from grandparents, uncles, aunts, friends, and nearly any and all adults that were within reach of children under the age of fifteen. As children grew older, they were often spared the barrage of affectionate gestures from all sides of the adult population.

In the final analysis, these were all fairly minor inconveniences when one looks at the larger picture. Fun is usually fun no matter where it surfaces. Family was fun, safe, rewarding, and had a comfort about it that most would love to experience. There were some families where holiday festivities were the exception and not the norm. Ours was not one of them.

Christmas day was one of the best examples of my parent's generosity. On the Eve of Christmas when I was about six years old, dad not being mechanically inclined, attempted to put together a fairly complex Lionel train set. After a few too many glasses of deep red vino, his abilities deteriorated from a high of terrible to a low of impossible. He got on the handle and called Uncle Bob to the rescue. Uncle Bob, the generous soul that he was, drove across town a cool distance of at least twenty miles on 1950's style streets and avenues composed of endless stoplights, rugged potholed streets, and variable weather conditions that were standard fare for Christmas Eve in Cleveland.

Bob was always ready to give his brother a hand as woundable ready to return the favor at any time. After uncle arrived, the two of them started the project with a few more glasses of deep crimson-red wine from the usual barrel residing in Dad's "very cool wine cellar". They were able to somehow figure out how to assemble the entire train system after an hour or two of somewhat tedious attempts not in any way improved by the effects of the wine. I suspect that more than a few colorful words laced their speech during the tedious process that today could have likely been managed by any twelve-year-old.

The young have an innate technical ability that gives them an edge early on, yet ultimately diminishes with time or the advancement of technology. However, with patience and determination the men completed the railway construction project way before midnight and just in time for Santa to squeeze down our red brick chimney. Being fairly wasted by the time the evening was over had its advantages by taking the edge off of the assembly ordeal. Dad knew it would all be worth it. Uncle Bob being a generous soul was happy; I mean really happy to help, assuming he could remember anything at all.

When the Christmas festivities would begin, they really began in earnest. Either Louis, Jr. or I would be the first to awaken on Christmas morning. The other would quickly awaken the other unless the other woke up first. Soon we rousted Phyllis and then the three of us would run into mom and dad's room on the first floor, jumping on the bed and getting them moving. We could not wait to see what Santa had brought. There was an unwritten rule that no one would enter the living room where the tree stood before we all entered together. The living room was separated from the rest of the house by a pocket door that slid into the wall with a gentle push. It was a clever and unique answer avoiding a swinging door in a location of limited space.

We children never broke the rule of sneaking in early on Christmas morning, at the risk of ruining the fun for everyone else. On Christmas morning, after awakening our parents, we all went into the kitchen adjacent to the living room but was separated from the kitchen with a sliding pocket door. Dad would first enter the living room closing the sliding door behind him. He then would light the Christmas tree to add to the festivities.

We all fed off of everyone else's fun and enjoyment and no one wanted to ruin it for the others. Once the pocket door was opened, we would all run like crazy towards the wonderful Christmas tree to grab a strategic spot on the floor to sit our derriere down on just the right location we chose. The good news was that there were many perfect spots to sit and every one of us thought their spot was the best. Of course, my spot was the best. I mean let's get real!

My parents spared no expense at loading us with presents. Mom saved every penny all year to spend on birthdays, Christmas, and Easter. She was the real deal. To save some money, Mom would wrap every gift, every holiday in plain white paper without bows. Our names would appear on small tags. We would then get into the larger gifts. Each Christmas, someone would receive a new bicycle, electric train, large doll or some exotic gift.

On this Christmas morning, it was a thrill for all of us to see in action the new electric train Dad and uncle had assembled the night before. The Lionel train rolling on its track, circled the ornament encrusted and multicolored Christmas tree. A whitish smoke arose from the locomotives chimney being released via a clever hot electrical element deep within the smokestack that heated a white tablet placed in the bottom of the stack. Lionel trains were the "Cadillac" of hobby trains of that era. The train engine itself was incredibly heavy for its size and quite powerful as well easily pulling any number of cares that were attached to its rear.

Mom or Dad began the gifting by sliding the proper Christmas filled stocking to each of us with our names sewn onto a very small "stockinette" attached to the top of the larger stocking. In the small stocking was a five-dollar bill for each one of us. Five bucks in those days was huge considering an ice cream cone could be had for a dime, bread was ten cents a loaf, and gas was about fifteen cents a gallon. A "fin," as it was called by many, was big money in those days; big money. Each stocking was overloaded with always two or three gifts protruding from the top barely able to fit inside.

Dad even had a stocking. Mom did not have one and none of us ever questioned that. I wonder why, now as I think back. It hurts me to think about it but mom was a generous sole and lived for her family. Mom always arranged for each of us to have a large stocking filled with amazing goodies and small gifts but never included herself in that enjoyable activity because, so to speak, she was really the Santa Claus of the stockings. It would take us at least one hour to open the gifts found in our stockings since we all shared in each other's delight. Wow! Those were the days.

Each one of use would open one small gift at a time from our stockings as the others looked on. It was a lot of fun but since there were at least ten to twelve small gifts and treats in each stocking, the effort would be prolonged but worth it. Each little treasure was wrapped in Christmas paper to add to the thrill of seeing what Santa brought for us. This little fun filled gifts were always the best part, since no one knew what secret treasures the stocking harbored. Mom went out of her way to find the best and coolest small toys and gifts we thought were all from Santa.

Dad partook of the same adventure with his stocking, not knowing either what Santa had in store for him. Mom was a wiz at coming up with little surprises that would tickle our fancy for every single holiday. Of course, during our childhood years, we all thought it was due to Santa's efforts. Who would have "think it"? After the stockings were ransacked, it came time to get serious with the other gifts which filled up the bottom surrounds of the Christmas tree. There were always at least six to ten gifts under the tree for each of us children.

Our parents had a few less to open. As we grew older, we would bring home gifts for our folks that we crafted at school. Eventually we would save up money from various sources and then shop for a gift for Mom and Dad. They were always so thrilled by anything they received. Either thrilled they were or great at acting. Christmas was just a super blast. My folks cold not have been better to all of us. Each Christmas was a jackpot of gifts and fun.

We always had many gifts for each holiday but as a result did not receive gifts during the year. My parent's generosity exceeded most limits and would never be forgotten. This keen sense of helping others to feel loved and respected would influence all of us Caravella children in our future lives going forward. Giving became a given and not an option.

As the day would progress, the tree was not the only thing that would be lit. Dad loved to have a good time and sometimes had one or two more drinks than he could handle though problems never occurred that I can remember. Mom sort of policed the entire operation during holidays ensuring few if any problems would surface.

Mom loved dad dearly and was able to manage his errant ways. They rarely fought, but once, while at grandpa Caravella's home, uncle Bob on one occasion had to intervene during a royal fight between dad and mom that was rare and out of character. The dust would settle and family life would go on. If anything, odd happened at home, mom was there to right the wrongs, fix the broken, smooch the sad, help the busy, structure the unstructured, and pardon the errant children that sometimes went amuck. Dad was also a child that fell occasionally into this category.

Men will be men, unless they are boys. Growing up is rarely an option for most men but generally a requisite of being a woman when they tend to more often take the reins of their children while also reining in their men.

Not to be too jaded, after opening our gifts, we cleaned up, got dressed, and drove about two miles to Saint Christopher's Church on Lakeview Avenue for Christmas Mass. The Church was always so beautifully decorated with reams of poinsettia's covering the alter, while a Christmas tree stood off to one side of the alter. Red bows were hung in various locations to add another colorful Christmas touch to the church. We all felt great respect for the Catholic faith and loved to attend mass and specially to receive Holy communion by our priest.

No sooner was Christmas over when New Years was just around the corner. Mom and Dad usually went to a night out "dressed to the nines" for a Knights of Columbus blast at a local hotel. Over the years, Dad had become very involved in the Fraternal Order of Police and "the Knights" where he achieved the level becoming a Fourth Degree Knight. He was very proud of his efforts. Our parents had a few great times several times a year involving these two organizations.

Easter was equally as festive with an Easter egg hunt and glorious cellophane wrapped baskets in beautiful pastel colors. Each basket was covered with a pastel-colored pink, yellow, or purple colored cellophane wrap, held together with a bow at the top. They always looked beautiful and even too good to open. After about thirty seconds we got over looking at them and got into their contents with great vigor.

Cleveland had a wonderful chain of chocolate shops known as Fanny Farmers that had the best collection of candied Easter eggs ranging in size from one-fourth pound, one-half pound, and one full pound apiece.

There were about four varieties. One had a dense chocolate filling sprinkled with nuts and covered with a thick milk chocolate outer shell. Another had a similar outer thick chocolate shell but the center had a maple sugar and nut like composition. The third huge chocolate Easter egg was milk chocolate wrapped with a fruit and nut creamy center. And the fourth amazing Easter egg had a thick dark chocolate wrapped around a white sugary filling with a yolk-colored sweet center. The last was my favorite with the chocolate and nut egg coming into second place.

These Easter chocolate treats were so good. The store carried many other varieties of pure chocolate bunnies, yellow and pink marshmallow peeps, and any number of other treats including multicolored jellybeans of every description. Somehow that chain disappeared into oblivion or was possibly absorbed by a competitor who could not really compete. The real and amazing chocolate Easter eggs were gone for good.

The holidays were all very special to us. We all knew that Mom and Dad were financially stable but lacked additional money for some things that many others in our neighborhood thought were essential and they took for granted.

For example, to save money the parents made do with one car. Mom would drop Dad off at the shop and take the car twice a week to do her banking and grocery shopping. We rarely if ever went out to eat at restaurants. Only on two or three occasions during the first ten or twelve years of our lives did we go out to a restaurant. On a special birthday we did go out for dinner, however not more than a couple of occasions each year.

I can remember going to nearby "Frisée's Big Boy" a couple of times with the mom. For myself, a fancy hamburger, French fries, and a milk shake was the order of the day. These dinners out were so rare that they were a phenomenon in their own right taking on almost a holiday atmosphere.

Vacations were also nearly nonexistent. The family took only two vacations during my entire childhood and adolescence. We went on a long weekend to Niagara Falls and a one week visit to Washington D. C., to visit my and Phyllis's birthplace. I still remember both of these trips vividly since they were so special.

I have not been back to Niagara Falls since those days, though the Canadians were very hospitable as I am sure, they remain. Passing through the American/Canadian border, by stopping for review by the border guards was to us children very odd indeed. Staying in a Canadian hotel was a highlight since that was my first experience in doing so. I was around ten years of age.

The Washington trip started off with a degree of difficulty. My Uncle John Koesel, Aunt Edith, and their children Roy, Dolores, and Joyce followed us in their car on the trip. In 1957 my dad had just purchased a brand-new Plymouth Belvedere two weeks earlier from his Chrysler Plymouth buddies in Lakewood. At the time I was about age twelve. Sitting in the front middle seat of the new car gave me a great view while mom rode shotgun. My other siblings were in the back where the view was likely nearly nonexistent but too bad - if they couldn't take a joke.

Shortly after beginning our drive down Center Ridge Readjust south and perpendicular to Gasser Blvd., after traveling only two miles from home, I noted a red light appeared on the dash. "Hey Dad, do you see that red light? "I asked. "Sure do, but that's nothing. "Don't worry about it," Dad retorted.

He was never mechanically inclined. Well shortly after leaving Ohio and arriving in Pennsylvania, the car died. My Uncle in the other car behind us, pulled over, assessed the situation, and with Dad's concerns, Uncle went for help. He arranged to have us towed with a wrecker from a nearby service garage. After a while, the tow-truck pulled up and the driver talked with Dad. He hitched the car to the tow hook and off it went. After arriving at the service station, the mechanics quickly determined that the generator had burned out though unfortunately they did not have one in stock for that model car.

Fortunately, it would only be an overnight stay until the part arrived in the morning and our trip again would resume. The next morning the defective generator was replaced and the trip resumed.

We arrived in Washington the next day and stayed at a Marriott Motor Inn that was relatively new. It was amazing to me, since we had never stayed at anything approaching this in quality. It had an outdoor pool that was huge and crowded. I will always remember this one fellow that was swimming and diving off the board. He was the hairiest human I had ever seen. Being just a bit south of being a gorilla he sported thick black hair overrunning most of his otherwise normally formed body. We couldn't stop looking at his out-of-control hair. We felt bad for this guy but he didn't seem to be shy so apparently all was well. I have never since seen anyone so fully endowed with thick black hair from head to toe. It was crazy. I mean it was crazy!

We eventually went on to Mount Vernon to visit George Washington's home. I was admonished by a security guard for whistling near the tomb and not paying due respect. He was certainly right in his warning to me. It was a lesson I never would forget.

Even more amazing than our two trips out of state, were the major holidays and birthdays we celebrated at home.

With each holiday Mom put together a fine breakfast. Church would always follow. Though it was a routine for us to attend Mass every Sunday. We sometimes went to the 8:30 AM Mass but the 9:45 was a possibility while not to the exclusion of the 11:00 AM mass either. The 7:00 AM was too early and the noon was too late. By then we would have been starving since we could not eat before communion.

The three of us children would attend confraternity class at Saint Christopher's School every Monday night. This was always a chore but was mandatory and it went on for years. Many of the kids in the class came from other schools so it was a bit of fun getting to know them. Being shy, I spent more time looking at them rather than meeting anyone.

There was a very cute lass with dark brown hair and well-developed breasts that went noticed by all of us guys. I am not sure how God would relate to our voyeuristic views or even our thoughts. But boys will be boys. God made us that way. Right!!? Well, we would make every effort to sit next to her. My sister was always around however and she would grab a seat somewhere. I always felt that I should sit with her; my sister of course.

My view of Miss Sexy was rarely as good as it could have been and it was a good thing because I probably would have learned little if anything during class. I remember this sexy little thing more than anything else about the class. Going to confession became a regular duty of each week.

Growing up involved an extravaganza of visits, social gatherings, and family frenzies of all varieties that as children we all looked forward to the fun. Many of my cousins were memorable and fun to be with but none was more colorful than Salvatore Louis Torrisi. He was the first male grandchild to show up in 17 years and was born at home at 14317 ¾ Kinsman Avenue in Cleveland. Can you believe that address?!?

His folks had three acres of land for "Sam" to explore. His family had suffered tragedy on more than one occasion with his first sister Lillian dying shortly after birth. The only pall bearer was his father carrying the small white coffin with tears in his eyes. This would not be the last death of a child. Uncle Jim and Aunt San would try again with little Stella (named after heavenly stars) Jean being born one- and one-half years later. They would have two other daughters including Rosemary and Nancy.

Sam was a character in many ways but felt that family good, bad, or charming was the basis for all things Italian. A holiday would not be one without Sam taking part from being a young child to later on as an adult. Sam has had more interesting stories and adventures than the rest of us in total.

As a child, Sam was a bit rough and tumble while growing up as a Torrisi. For various reasons they struggled at times to make ends meet. In a very memorable incident, Aunt Santina, purchased a pair of Red Goose sandals that due to Sam's nature and maybe some design flaws along with acres of explorable land, were trashed within three days.

Not being flush with cash and also dismayed over the short life expectancy of the shoes, aunt felt betrayed by fate or fun. Either way, it seemed like a costly adventure. She returned to the shoe store requesting a free replacement but the shop owner would have none of it. Aunt and Sam walked back with the broken shoe tied on with a rope.

By chance, Uncle Jim's cousin Jimmy Montano, was sitting in the kitchen sharing a few beers when in walked the dejected pair. He never seemed to have a job, but money was never a problem.

Cousin Jimmy drove a black sedan with white wall tires and was usually dressed to the nines with a Black Stetson fedora, black shirt, dark suit, and two Colt 45 automatics, strapped under his jacket across the sides of his chest. After walking in, he usually removed the Colts, wrapped them in his jacket, and placed them in the coat closet on a shelf, to avoid scarring unsuspecting guests.

Santina offered Jimmy some biscotti to go with his beverage and they began to talk. Aunt "San" told him about the shoe fiasco and he softly spoke casually like it was no big deal, "Don't worry about it. When Jim and I are through, I'm going to pay the proprietor of the shoe store a visit."

A little later, Jimmy started to get up and leave. "San, see yak later sexy" and he kissed her on the cheek, grabbed his coat, loaded holsters and all, and walked out the door. He liked to peel out of the driveway, fishtailing with flying cinders everywhere, often causing a bit of a commotion wherever he went. He was a spectacle in the way he dressed and more so with his Italian flare and bravado.

Jimmy drove the short distance to the shoe store, walked in, leaned onto the counter, and seeing the shop-keeper, Mr. Goldman spoke in a few soft brief sentences. He related San and Sam's problem with the shoes that had occurred earlier in the day. Pulling the shoes from his black overcoat pocket and throwing the broken pair on the counter, he began to voice his concerns for a bit. After a brief second or two; the shop-keeper said, "the little shit is rough on shoes, get out of here. I'm not going to give you nothing. " Jimmy unbuttoned his coat, pulled back the jacket enough to show at least one Colt and said, "You know, I can't help it if you're going to be out of business by tomorrow". He turned heading for the door. The proprietor began sweating and, in a panic, yelled, "You're right. You're right. They don't know how to make nothing now a days. Let me look at those shoes again. " He went to the back room and returned with three pairs of new shoes. Each was a different style but all matched the size of the broken pair. "I hope your nephew likes these. " "Cousin, not nephew," Jimmy retorted and he took the shoes and while walking out said, "You're all right. I'm glad we could do business."

Sammy was a likable kid, and grew up with many close friends some of which would show up when I was visiting. We would go out in the yard and play but on occasion we and his sisters would play together.

Nancy was the oldest, then Rosemary, and lastly Stella. They were all cute as buttons and friendly beyond reproach. As time went on, the girls would understandably become quite friendly with guys and even friends of Sam's. Nancy had a remarkable figure that was enviable and difficult to ignore. Her sisters were not too shabby either. Unfortunately, as time went on, Nancy's life would be terribly altered as would a nephew's life, and her brother Sam's, but not so profoundly.

At age eleven, Sam awakened one morning with a sore throat. Aunt San sent him to school anyway though he returned home for lunch, not feeling well. He began to eat a sandwich but could not swallow. His mother gave him some water to drink but it came up and out through his nose. He choked further on food and he was taken to Saint Luke's Hospital ER for evaluation. He was diagnosed with bulbar polio, the deadliest form of polio and was immediately transferred to city hospital for a long stay, surviving but not without difficulty. He never required an "iron lung" (an external machine surrounding the chest to assist breathing) but we were all worried never-the-less.

Stella, Sam's little sister, was also shortly thereafter diagnosed with polio but a milder case. In the 1950s, the injectable Salk vaccine and later the oral Sabin Vaccine were God-sends becoming available for most Americans. They proved to be one of the greatest medical triumphs in history by nearly eliminating polio completely.

The rest of us escaped the terrible polio epidemic by receiving lifesaving vaccine distributed at schools nationwide. We all happily waited in long lines on several weekends to receive the precious vaccines provided free of charge by good old Uncle Sam. These were shots that no one minded.

Polio of that era was feared by all until the vaccine was available. This disease in those days caused very similar fears as in modern times dealing with the notorious Corona virus.

Finally, the Covid vaccine and other treatments have come available towards the summer and fall of 2020, which has done a great deal to lessen, though not eliminate the disease completely. New strains continue to surface making our pandemic now endemic that will require ongoing annual or biannual vaccines forever. Our current batches of vaccines weaken in efficacy within a few months and must be repeated at regular intervals. Over one million people have died from Covid, most of which refused the vaccine. These people's fears were unwarranted, compared to the danger of the disease itself and has put us in the mess we are in today.

Hopefully newer varieties will last longer and may even someday provide a cure from Covid-19. We are on the right track. This will get done.

In my Rocky River neighborhood, playing baseball, football, and some basketballs were nearly daily events. Directly across the street from our home on Gasser Boulevard, lived as fate would have it, twin boys named John and Jim Kirk. They were ironically the same age as my sister and I. The four of us being the same age and living on the same street were therefore to be in the same grade and at the same school.

As I recall as twins, sometimes one or the other twin would be placed in a different class room to somehow abort any and all bizarre circumstances that could occur from confusing the teacher, to promoting mixed behaviors, boys being boys. However, this rule did not always apply. My sister and I were always in the same classroom during the early years. Guess why? It was easy to tell us apart.

The Kirk twins and I would become the best of friends as time went on. We were fairly inseparable. We played together most of the time and visited each other's home on a nearly daily basis until high school when our interests went in different directions. We were much alike in many ways, though the Kirks were Anglo-Saxon in their heritage and they often teased me about my Italian heritage. Over all, we got along well.

One of the Kirks grandfathers I believe invented the large stadium lights seen in professional football and baseball stadiums of years gone by. The Kirk family also managed and owned what was then The Astrum Awning Company; the largest maker of canvas awnings in America at that time. They handled canvas products for many other purposes as well.

Mrs. Kirk was very kind, attractive, and I was often invited to their home for lunch and other treats when I was around her children. They were always generous and fun to be around. Boys being boys; we occasionally got into squabbles and a rare fist fight or two where little if any damage ever occurred. Our feelings were only temporarily affected and we always remained friends.

On another note, between Gasser Boulevard and Wooster Road was an undeveloped piece of land about twenty-five acres in size inhabited by rabbits, raccoons, mice, ponds, frogs, and claiming a few abandoned nearly collapsed old building as its only "real" estate. Broken glass, concrete footers, and rotting wood laced the level ground. There was old broken down, falling down, dilapidated greenhouses covering a large expanse of land that would in later years become developed into new homes. Walking barefoot was foolish and we fools learned quickly not to embark on travel without proper protection. The Kirk twins and I would spend endless days and months and years in this amazing wilderness.

On the Southern half was a wooded area with apple, pear, and cherry trees along with an old collapsed unused well. Grasshoppers, potato bugs, spiders, praying mantises, and a few small non-venomous snakes went unchallenged most of the time. There was an old water-well on the property near the Center Ridge Road end of the land expanse. We kept our distance from that fearing the possibility of falling in. Nothing like that ever happened.

Two distinct groups of kids lay claim to the same area not infrequently challenging each other over petty issues. These two groups chose this area as their haven of activity and occasionally challenged each other in more childish ways than in any serious attempts to gain any control. The Gasser Gang controlling the Western side of the terrain, consisted of myself, my twin sister, along with the Kirks, Bob D. (now an attorney), David. D. (to parts unknown), and a couple of others. We would cross paths with the less than notorious Wooster Gang roaming the eastern side of this same terrain and was primarily led by two brothers one being named Jerry Rensberger.

They owned a German Shepard named Sergeant, which the two kept at bay and the group consisted of several others including a cute little ten-year-old female that I liked a bit more than was practical considering the circumstances and the rivalry. She was starting to develop and was noticed by the guys. Puberty was kicking in for her though not as apparently for us lads. However as in my case, some sort of juices was apparently flowing. With time, Jerry Rensberger became one of my best friends though I never thought again about asking him about the young lady in his "gang".

Being inquisitive of each other's territory of course led to forays into the other "gangs" area and sometimes a stone-dirt throwing melee would ensue. These stone throwing wars consisted of tossing small pieces of dried mud like chunks at them and they returned fire with equal vengeance. Rarely was anyone struck though the potential was always there. These wars went on for years with neither gang getting the upper hand. No one in memory was ever hurt, because close in combat never occurred, and only a bit of name calling and teasing ever transpired. Often the so-called gangs fought each other in a good-natured baseball game, as time went on; old rivalries dissipated and were forgotten. The gangs became a thing of the past. These childish antics would lose their steam over time and thus eventually dissipated into history.

In those years the bicycle was the chosen mode of transportation for most male children and adolescents. Teenage girls would not generally be seen riding bikes using instead two legs as their primary mode of transportation.

Schwinn's were the "Cadillac's" of bikes, though many similar brands were available. When growing up I was given a Murray bicycle for Christmas one year, painted red and white and was of similar design to a standard Schwinn of the era. The large 21" wheels sported white-wall tires with front mounted springs to absorb road shock. It had a long narrow bullet shaped battery-operated headlight and a horn mounted inside a center mounted compartment, similar in shape and location as a motor cycle gas tank, but of course much smaller in size. These bikes were heavy, heavy duty in construction, and heavily into carrying passengers or any variety of items from books held on with rope (bungee cords had not made their arrival) to boxes or any item that could be secured with a minimum of effort.

All of us acquired whatever skills were necessary to jerry-rig all sorts of packages to the rear end of bikes. Most of us were too lazy however when it came to being overly creative. These were bikes for most of us and not pack mules.

Bike theft was unusual, so bikes were found almost everywhere one looked, parked outside of homes, businesses, or shopping areas. A few would lock their bikes to any stable object with various combinations of locks and chains, though most let fate roll the dice.

Forget fate. I was a bike locker.

Many had baskets hanging from the front handlebars. Some had baskets of various designs, attached to a chrome plated steel grate attached to the bike frame, just behind the seat and above the rear fender. Many bikes had battery operated horns and a few had headlights. All had rear light reflectors.

American style bikes were much heavier in construction and differed from European foreign designs by incorporating a very effective, reliable, convenient, and fool proof brake, built into the rear wheel assembly and activated by reversing the bikes peddles. It wouldn't hurt to add this form of rear brake to compliment the front hand brakes on current bicycles to help prevent fishtailing when stopping due to front brake lock up.

"English racers," similar to modern twelve speed bikes were rarely chosen as a mode of transportation because they were relatively flimsy, more expensive, and useless when it came to carrying items or any passenger of any size. Their hand brakes were less reliable and constantly in need of adjustment.

Peddling the American style bicycle contributed to the trim figures most of us children had when growing up. We were rarely driven anywhere. Obesity was on the unique side among my generation of friends and acquaintances, so when it occurred, it was noticeable and sometimes rudely noted by those with poor manners.

There was a minimum of four ways to carry the driver and one to three passengers on an American style bike. A common method was to place the passenger straddling atop the handle bars in front of the driver and hanging their feet over and about each side of the front wheel. This method of riding was at best unsafe and at worst stupid, since cornering and turning was precarious but possible with a skillful rider and a cooperative but also stupid passenger. In additions to the obvious risks, the forward visibility was limited by the size of the passenger sitting in front of the driver. A larger passenger compounded the stupidity of this arrangement. Of course, none of these risks would deter most of us from attempting these juggling acts with friends or relatives.

Should your passenger by chance or intention be a young female, this changes everything. Under these unusual and rare circumstances, the preferred method for a variety of reasons that I will not expound on, was to carry her side saddle over the main bike frame rails so that she sat between the handle bar and your seat. This provided for many opportunities to become more closely acquainted with her. Not having a girlfriend during my bike riding years did not allow for experimentation on my behalf, though I keenly observed others perform various mating rituals that I will leave to your imagination and to my dreams.

Another method was to carry a passenger on the back rack behind the seat. These American built bikes were strong enough to handle a passenger probably weighing in at up to seventy-five pounds or more depending on the peddling power of the driver. This was the safest way and usually the most common method of carrying a trustworthy passenger. Trustworthy was the operative word when carrying a passenger behind you. Your passenger would sit on the back rack and place their arms around your waist. Again, should your passenger be a female rider sitting behind you (assuming you're male), any number of possible interactions could have occurred that I will leave again to your imagination. Some could have been good. Some could have been not so good. In most instances, the quality of the ride was usually dependent on the skillful selection by the driver of the appropriate passenger be they male or female.

Should your bike not have a rear rack over the back fender a passenger could stand on the extended axle projecting on either side of the rear wheel, while holding on to your shoulders. This arrangement was again stupid, precarious, and not recommended except for short distances or when selecting passengers that were expendable. Passengers would either hold on to bike parts or driver's parts for balance and security.

Bike riding outcomes were often related to a degree of natural selection when biking with one or more passengers. Common sense, being an oxymoron under most circumstances, often resulted in one or more of the three "F's" coming into play when it came to biking with passengers: fear, falls, and fractures.

Carrying passengers was an art form mastered by most boys and few of the other gender. Young ladies were more likely to walk places rather than ride bikes. As we grew into adolescents biking would fall into disfavor losing its coolness. Bikes, as age progressed were viewed as modes of transportation only for losers. I being a first-rate example of one. Only "dorks" would ride bikes. Skate boards and similar mobile devices for boys had not been invented and thus we're not an option.

My Murray bike and I became intimate friends for several years before I reached high school age when bike riding was considered taboo for older adolescent boys.

I put literally thousands of miles over many years on my two wheeled friend, since my parents were not prone to driving me anywhere within reasonable reach of a bicycle.

Today, adolescents and older kids have many styles of bikes that are cool that we never had. Times have changed for the better in the arena of biking for fun, sport, and exercise.

As my bike riding days evaporated, my dreams later in my teen years would be to acquire a driver's license so I would never have to peddle again or so I thought. I never owned a car to drive to school and as I implied, I never again rode a bike to school either.

On another note, when still young, the Kirk twins would occasionally steal a few smokes from their mother's mentholated "Kool's" lying around their home. We would each take one, grab some matches, and head for the fields behind our home. Though with time, none of us ever picked up the smoking habit.

In grade school I believe it was John who pulled one of the most dramatic though possibly cruel practical jokes on me that one could pull. He claimed to have snuck into a teacher's classroom desk and looking around, founding some sort of IQ test, noting that I had below average test grades approaching the rank of a babbling idiot. I never forgot about this and still at times wondered about myself.

The lack of sports acumen and the low IQ theory all probably eventually helped me to become somewhat successful later in life, depending on definition, as time would later bear out. Somehow, I had to pull myself up by the boot straps and get it together.

As we grew up and actually were commingled in school classes together At Wooster School the rivalry also dissipated and the groups (gangs) disappeared from the landscape. I never learned of the young lass's name from the former Wooster Gang and never remember seeing her again, as time went on. She likely morphed into an even prettier young thing over a summer and I guess I will never know the answer to that adolescent mystery.

As a youngster I also tried but could never mastered a game using a knife called "mumble peg." It is a game of skill requiring a straight knife with a two- to three-inch-long blade and a fixed handle. The knife needs to have some heft to it without being bulky. The trick is to balance the pointed sharp end of the blade on the boney end of a part of your anatomy such as the distal end of a finger or even the outer boney surface of your wrist or elbow. The trick is to flip the knife end over end from the tip of a finger or from a point about two to three feet off the ground. A successful flip would result in the knife tip sticking into the ground holding the knife upright in the grass or soil. The winner had the most successful flips in a row. If the knife struck the surface and fell over, then the turn would shift to the next contestant. A skillful player could start with each fingertip and progress to the wrist, elbow, shoulder, and even their chin. This was all well and good and would often amaze an occasional young lady in our presence. Of course, a few were unimpressed and had other concerns about our perverted intellect.

On one very impressive attempt, I tried to show off when a pretty little thing was in my presence. Early on, during the game, the knife flipped but failed to stick into the ground. Instead, all three to four ounces of the brown handled knife twirled end over end while dropping the usual three feet or so, stuck into my right foot. I guess that counted, but the sight of blood and the screech of pain failed to impress the young lady nearby. My mumble peg days had ended and I moved on to other ways of impressing the fairer sex. None of them worked either, as I was not a girl magnet in any sense of the word.

Getting back to baseball, one incident bothered me no end for years. We were playing baseball one day and along came an adult that lived nearby. He asked if he could use my Adirondack baseball bat, given to me by Dad, to take a few hits. He went on to break the bat after a few swings. The scoundrel never offered to replace it. What a jerk. It was my favorite and my hitting was good with that particular bat but not so with others. It seemed to have a magical quality about it. Not giving up, I took the bat home, drilled two holes in the bat and countersunk two screws. Then I heavily taped the handle using black plumber's tape. All to no avail. It was never the same. I was never the same as a batter. I believe that led to my downhill spiral as a hitter, from which I never recovered. This sad event occurred even before I had entered little league. It may seem trivial but every hitter goes through various procedures with special attention to whatever it takes to allow him to hit effectively. In those days all bats were made of wood with thicker handles and rarely broke if the bat was held properly with the manufacturer's label held skyward when the ball struck the bat. In this position the grain of the bat was linear and gave the bat its power and strength, when accompanied by a good swing and solid contact. This was a great theory but putting it into practice was another matter.

I for a variety of reasons never got into sports on the junior high or high school level. The Kirk boys on the other hand were into sports at a much higher level than I, but for reasons that few would ever know about. As a child I was found to have a heart murmur and my folks were told never to allow me to play in contact sports. They discouraged me from doing so. Neighborhood sports were fine but the more organized sports other than Little League baseball and Pony League baseball were off the table.

The first baseball team I played on at about age eight or nine was called the Indians as fate would have it. Rocky River built a fantastic little league field between Detroit Road and Lake Road a short distance from downtown River. It had two dugouts with built in water fountains. The dugouts were covered with a world and shingle roof. Chicken wire covered the front of the dugout to prevent wild balls from striking unwary players and coaches sitting inside. The dugouts were sunken in the ground about 20" or so.

There were two sets of stands, a clubhouse, and a loud speaker system with a score board in the distance manned by helpers. The baselines were chalked before each game just as in the big leagues. There was always an official umpire and an infield official calling each game. An announcer sat in the upper club house using a public address system to give the name of each batter and to announce the balls and strikes. We wore uniforms early on patterned after and named after big league teams. Later on, in years the names reflected the names of our team sponsors. We wore metal cleats in the early years.

Games were always played during sunny times so field-lights were not needed. It was fun to play but the coaching was sometimes substandard or more likely I was a real loser because my batting always stunk. I never seemed to get any coaching to help me to improve my hitting. Being left-handed, I occasionally played first base or played right field.

Baseball for me was very entertaining though I always felt bad about my terrible batting skills. My Dad had no sporting abilities, never having time to play as a child, and thus was not able to help. Being a baseball cripple, I broke the record nationally for the most strikeouts in a season though walking was not beyond my ability. As an outfielder I wasn't much better. I dropped more than my share of fly balls but I never quit trying to do better. Quitting in any venue never appealed to me.

I always rode my bike to the games and my parents rarely if ever saw me play. Mom was too busy and lacked her own car and Dad was probably too embarrassed but I'm not sure what really was going on. He worked long hours and seemed exhausted every night when he came home at seven to seven thirty PM. It didn't seem to bother me as I recall, but maybe it did. In fact, it was a relief for me not to have them following my lack of progress.

Come to think of it, my twin never saw me fumble or play either. Phyllis always looked up to me as did my little brother Lou and it wasn't due to my sports ability. My greatest enemy was myself and the almost total lack of self-confidence I felt throughout most of my school years.

My sister Phyllis struggled as well with her ego, though my younger brother Louis would more than make up for our lack of self-confidence. He often played alongside of me in pickup games and became skilled in most sports. He was big boned, tough, and loved competition. He had the confidence thing down cold and probably as time would show, he would become a very prominent Caravella.

The closest I came to being part of a winning team was on July 5, 1956, at age 12, when I played for Luke's defeating Kyle Insurance one to nothing in seven innings and winning some sort of a title. Those were my glory sports days.

When I was still an adolescent, my father would have one of many opportunities to prove his wisdom and patience. One day, two neighbor friends dropped over to pay me a visit. They brought with them some balloons and suggested that we fill them with water and have a bit of a water balloon war. It sounded like fun, so we filled up a few.

As fate would have it, a young lady was riding down Gasser in our direction and the others coaxed me into tossing a balloon in her direction. Not wanting to be a bad sport about it and being inexperienced about danger, it hadn't occurred to me about the possibility that anything could go seriously wrong with this prank. So, I went ahead and threw it. The little girl when seeing it and becoming fearful of being struck by some object flying through space, swerved to avoid it. Unfortunately, she swerved into an oncoming car, striking the bumper and was thrown into the windshield and over the roof. Fortunately, God was overlooking this fiasco and miraculously allowed her to avoid serious injury. Apparently, her bike absorbed most of the forces and was totaled in the process, though she remained intact though likely fearful for the rest of her life from the likes of me.

My father, learning of this stupid escapade and realizing that I had been severely shocked by the incident, and rarely in trouble, decided not to scold me. He knew that I knew. My father bought a new bike for the little lady. The parents of the other boys, one being an attorney, refused to pay any part of the damages though it seems to me that their children were equally at fault. It is interesting to note that one of the boys involved eventually became a practicing attorney just like his father. It is a bit odd that the attorney father could not see his responsibility in the entire incident: or is it?

At Rocky River High, John, Jim, and Jerry would become excellent wrestlers and all-around athletes. I became a bore.

The lack of sports acumen and the low IQ theory all probably eventually helped me to become somewhat successful later in life, depending on definition, as time would later bear out. Somehow, I had to pull myself up by the boot straps and get it together.

As time went on, the fields and limited woods behind Gasser were built into two streets connected by a horseshoe extension on the north end of the undeveloped area. The city of Rocky River, being always interested in civilized forms of play and entertainment contracted with some firm so one day heavy equipment showed up and a park was built on about twenty acres of land. A baseball backstop, benches, and a field were added. We had discovered baseball, playing games nearly every day with as few as four to six players.

Signs blossomed at each end of the park warning residents with dogs that droppings were not acceptable. With and without their masters, dogs came anyway patrolling the park from one end to the other. The park also had some slides, teeter-tooters, chinning bars (of all things), and a rotating wooden merry-go-round that we enjoyed for hours on end. The trick was to rotate the gizmo so fast that the parties holding on would be flung off. Yeh, we knew how to have fun. Another cool trick was to jerk and thump the butts of the kids on the other end of the teeter-tooters. This sounds a bit mean, but some of us had a warped sense of what was fun. What can I say? I must have learned a few lessons on how to behave while growing up, but I'm not sure what some of them were.

The park was always busy with activities during all seasons of the year including winter. The city had built a hill in the center of the park intended for sled riders to use after heavy snows. In the peak of winter, small children with friends or relatives made many trips up and down this specially tuned slope. The park was special in so many other ways and became a focal point for years during my childhood.

My sister and her many friends also frequented Morley Park having fun day in and day out. At times they would picnic back there and play on the park equipment during endless hours of spring and summer fun. They were also members of the secret Gasser Gang but held lower-level positions and tended to be less aggressive. Heck, they were girls. What do they know about having fun? Later on in our adolescents we started to appreciate girls and having fun but it took a while for most of us to even get a clue about having fun much less about getting anything else.

In the 1950's River played musical schools shifting us back and forth from the old Wooster School, to gold wood

School, and later back to the new Wooster School all within a period of four to six years. We got to meet many new kids with this circus going on but it was a bit confusing at the time and it was hard to get a good foot-hold on to what was going on. The school system was respected and effective so somehow, we still came out ok even though my IQ was a bit in question.

In sixth grade I had an interesting teacher named Mr. Hoffman who served duty in the lunch room during lunch of course. He had an interesting way of getting the attention of a student with a big mouth (me) but in a very subtle way. While eating with a bunch of kids along a long table he would come up from behind an unsuspecting student and clamp his large hand around the back of their neck if that individual was talking too loudly or making a fool of himself. His fingers would dig in with noticeable pain, getting the attention of the victim but not with any fanfare of sorts. He would gently say, "Phil, I think you're a little loud and I would like you to tone it down a bit for the benefit of the rest of us. " His grip was very persuasive and yelling rapidly became mumbling or near speechlessness. After two or three of these vice-like episodes, I learned a lesson and my behavior as a sixth grader was permanently attenuated. In retrospect, this was a clever technique and probably could be recommended but parents now-a-days are bit on edge about every little inconvenience to their loved ones, especially in a school setting. It may be time to introduce school uniforms and a bit of discipline as in days gone by.

Respect of teachers and older adults seems to have gone lacking but not during my childhood. Coaches even drew more respect and led athletic teams in local schools with skills approaching those of drill sergeants having a bad day.

While still young, many playful activities lingered in our past. However, few events occurred during the year that were more fun than sled riding down "Gasser hill". The top of the boulevard rose into a fairly steep hill that from top to bottom was about 500 feet in length. The Rocky River police placed a flame driven pumpkin sized oil fueled lantern in the top center of the street preventing vehicles from going straight down the hill. Cars would have to keep to the far right heading down the hill avoiding all the wild children having fun. This was done after every significant snow fall that covered the street creating ideal conditions for sled riding. In the early 1950's kids would then congregate at the top of Gasser hill after snow falls that were inevitable and frequent each winter in the Cleveland area. They brought their sleds and would body slam, coast, ride airplane style, or train style down the hill. Body slamming involved running a few feet down the hill and then dropping to the snowy surface on top of the sled and heading down the hill as fast as you could go.

We turned sled riding into an art form though you have to remember the old fashion sleds that were four to six feet in length with a wooden steering handle connected to the front runners. The runners were waxed with candles to improve speed. Some sleds were faster than others.

It was typical to cross one sled on the back of another airplane wing style with one of us becoming the pilot sitting upright on the winged-sled crossed at right angles to the bottom sled. The pilot would place his or her feet on the wooden steering bar to guide the "airplane" down the hill. Another would push against the drivers' shoulders to get the whole thing going and the then he or she would hop on the rear while holding on to the driver for balance. Sometimes two other smaller kids would balance on the wings and it became a foursome. The airplane eventually would be chased down by some "wise guy" chasing it downhill and then grabbing the "wing" of the craft and pulling the contraption apart until everyone fell off. It was hilarious.

Another thrilling fun thing to do was to ride a train down the hill. The train effect was achieved by several sleds connecting to each other with the person in the front sled placing their boot covered feet into the front spaces forward to the wooden steering bar of the sled. They would do this in successive order locking the train together sled after sled. Usually, three to four sleds would lock up in this manner. Then all of the riders would push downward and backward with their gloved hands on the snow-covered street to get the train going. That was a real "riot" to say the least. "Man" did we have great fun for hours at a time.

Traffic be damned. Nothing got in the way of us sled riders. We would bundle up to stay warm and we would coast down the hills for hours during the evening from about seven PM until nine PM when car traffic was lighter.

The night time was special with the backdrop of the street lights, the falling snow, the yelling, and laughing that always made for a winter night of lasting and happy memories. There were few if any injuries, though the potential was always there considering all the horse-play going on most of the evening. The girls and boys all played together during these happy winter evenings. Sooner or later a snowball fight would break out to add more fun to the entire event. There were always a few parents hovering around for the evening directing traffic and keeping the entire even under control.

Man, we had a blast. These amazingly fun filled evenings went on for at least ten years until eventually the practice of sledding on Gasser Hill was terminated and relegated to Morley Park adjacent to Gasser Boulevard about one block east of the street.

I'm certain the fear of law suits in one form or another ruined the freestyle sledding for us kids in the same fashion as removing diving boards from most public pools in the area. Scrooge lives on in many ways. A lot of fun has been legislated out of existence gratis the few, at the detriment of the majority, but what is new about that!

Cleveland's weather was perfect for snow ball fights, making angels in the snow while lying on our backs and waving our outstretched arms into the snow up and down or building huge snow men with carrots for noses or buttons for eyes. We all made the most of these opportunities. It was fantastic.

Other fun events for the Caravella's during our growing years involved owning an endless stream of pets of every description including a few dogs, the infamously pink or blue dyed chicken peeps that were popular around Easter in the 1950's, turtles, fish tanks, a guinea pig, a cat or two, a captured snake from the woods; you name it. The chickens would die for unknown reasons as time went on thought to be sure, they never looked like a healthy lot to begin with. Dye your skin purple and see how well you fair.

As time went on, other creatures of various descriptions would take their place, later to be given away or meeting a timely demise as the case would be. There was one critter that remained the most cherished for the longest time and it was a mixed dog breed named Holley by little Jennifer. The critter was purchased as a pup just before Christmas one year. When fully grown, she weighed about twenty pounds, had black hair with some patches of white and brown on her face and lower abdomen accompanied by long trim legs and a bushy tail. She rarely whined and had a good disposition.

Over time my mother grew tired of putting Holley out on a fifteen-foot chain in the back yard to do her business. She finally decided to have a chain linked fence installed in the back yard to keep Holley corralled there so she would not run away.

Americans the Beautiful

One day a crew arrived and began the task of fence installation; no inexpensive event for the family. Towards the end of installing half of the five-foot-tall fence mom decided to let Holley out into the back yard to relieve herself. Standing about eighteen inches tall from the ground to the top of her body, Holley was no giant. Holley approached the newly installed section of fence, sat by its base for a moment, and then casually and easily leaped straight up into the air without so much as a walking start much less a running start and like Super Dog easily cleared the top of the fence finding herself on the other side. Holley proceeded to romp around the rest of the unfenced yard. Kangaroos would be pressed to match this feat. On frequent occasions Holley would jump the fence whenever the whim struck her. The fence remained as did the chain. No fence in history has ever been more entertaining and less effective for its intended use.

Holley would live a very long life, just a year or three short of twenty while providing a source of great love and enjoyment for each family member. The fence would outlast Holley though it never seemed to have any practical use other than keeping away elephants.

A few years after moving into our new home on Gasser, the open lot across the street from our home was separated by a short two-hundred-foot-long dedicated street that was more of a driveway than anything else. Though to this day I have never learned the name of that very short yet functional street adjacent to our home and terminated just the other side of our driveway into a four-foot-tall grass covered hill that backed up to the home behind it.

The unfinished lot just south of our home on Gasser became a target of a new builder in the area. Mr. P. decided to build a new home on this very lot across the drive/street from our home. He was a portly fellow who ran around in a sweat stained t-shirt, often unshaven, and looking a bit drab to say the least. He was not college material but certainly made a good living in home construction! I think? He built a two-story brick home on the empty adjacent lot. After completion of the home, he had the odd habit of leaving his unsightly mud-laden dump truck parked on the driveway "street" where my mother had to look at it all day when looking out her kitchen window. The neighbors felt equally unhappy but did not know what to do about the atrocity. This vehicle would be out of character for most bedroom communities and certainly not typical of what would be expected in what was otherwise a city of beautiful well landscaped homes, elegant trees, boulevards, and sidewalks with curbs lacing all streets.

Dad on several occasions asked him to park the truck elsewhere. He was either hard of hearing or couldn't understand the perfect English of an Italian immigrant. There was one language he would understand however. One dark night someone wielding an ice pick inflicted a disturbing number of insults to the truck's tires of this disgusting and filthy atrocity. It was not known who wielded this environmentally altering instrument but it's possible that Louie was as adept with an ice pick as he was with a razor.

The truck was never parked there again. After that incident the relationship which barely existed to begin with, deteriorated to a point of near extinction between my dad and Mr. P. Little was lost by this entire event since we "neighbors" shared nothing in common with the Mr. P. family and the beauty of the street and neighborhood had improved immeasurably with the artistic flash of a sharp if not almost surgical procedure giving new meaning to the word "message".

Not being vengeful, I shall never however forget a terrible tragedy that occurred to Mr. P. and his family. He had built a swimming pool in his back yard and unfortunately a young girl wondered into the area, fell into the pool and drowned. It was a horrible tragedy never to be forgotten by the local residents. Shortly thereafter a fence was added and city regulations were changed accordingly to mandate fences to encircle private pools. May her sweet little soul rest-in-peace. What a shame!

Over the years Dad enjoyed watching his children develop into useful citizens. He was proud of all of us. When mom turned forty-two, she surprised Dad and the rest of us with a late comer to the party. Little Jennifer, named after Mom's mother Generosa, arrived with fanfare and devotion. She was about ten years younger than her youngest brother Louis. Jennifer was always happy, smiling and a real treasure.

As time would go on, Jennifer would unexpectedly fill a big hole in the family tree.

Dad and Mom enjoyed watching television, a new novelty of the 1950's for our family. They both enjoyed watching Bishop Fulton J. Sheen in his weekly program, *Life Is Worth Living*. There were many families shows and even Disney was getting a foothold with made for television movies such as the Davy Crocket series. Dad watched the fights on the weekends and heavy weight greats such as Floyd Patterson and Rocky Marciano. Everyone liked The Ed Sullivan Show and of course Bob Hope specials. Lucille Ball was an American actress, comedian, studio executive, and producer. She was the star and producer of the television program "I Love Lucy" as well as occasional comedy television specials.

As fate would have it, she eventually would contact my father about having him style her beautiful hair on occasion for her shows, when she was living in New York.

These were the good old days as I knew them.

Dad had a special love for the movie industry. My mom would never go to the movies with Dad thinking the cost was too great. It was sort of a pity when I think about it. On many occasions Dad asked me to accompany him though I rarely did so as a young boy because his taste and mine were so different. The one movie I remember seeing with him was a boxing movie entitled something like, *The Bigger They Are the Harder They Fall*. Typical of most teens, as I grew older, I wanted to be with my friends and would later regret not spending as much time with Dad as I could have. It bothers me to this day.

Dad hated doing any form of yard work and rarely did any. For the most part I handled these chores and did so with relish. I felt our home should look as good as the others and many of the others were beautifully maintained. I was no stranger to fertilizer and pruning. I also washed the cars and again this was not something Dad would give much attention to. He was always tired when he got home and had little free time that he would ever devote to home chores of any type. He and mom delegated many chores to both Phyllis and I. We carried out their wishes believing that it was important for us to contribute to the wellbeing of the family in any way that we could.

Dad became interested in some home improvements. Years after finishing the basement he tackled the huge empty attic space on the second floor that became a fourth bedroom. He failed to properly insulate it though he tried. His knowledge of home construction projects was grossly limited though he did the best he could. I guess the insulation battings he used in the walls and ceilings were not correct for the task. It felt like an igloo in the winter and bordering on the Mojave Desert in the summer. This room would become the bedroom for my brother Lou and I. It was very large in size and two single beds were lost inside of it.

The room in the summer was akin to Death Valley until Dad installed a Feder's room air conditioner into the southern facing window of the room. It did the job. The electric bills had to sky rocket but Dad never complained. He tried hard to make the room special and he did. The beds Mom purchased for us were "Kool" twin beds, very rustic and Western in design, made of what looked like heavy duty hand carved wooden posts at the corners that were indestructible. These beds will exist somewhere at the end of time.

Dad's most important achievement other than being a good father to all of us was his devotion to America. He excelled in being a good American. He loved our country so much he never talked of Italy except upon questioning. Dad was more of an American than the majority of those born here. He never spoke negatively of this country but only spoke of our freedoms, opportunities, and life style. Dad spoke nearly perfect English, mastering grammar, the written word, and abolishing his Italian accent. He was the master American in thought, word, and deed. He was a beautiful American.

Mom, in her own way was cool and a beautiful American as well. Being born in Cleveland gave her a special opportunity to meet my father. An all American she was as well, but did not having the same hurdles as Dad had to overcome. She was a bit less intriguing but never the less another example of what makes our country what it is. Mom never put on that she was anyone but herself. Her abilities were never more poignant than when looking at her skills in running a home. She was a genius in conserving money, banking, paying bills, and managing accounts. Mom was thrifty but not selfish, nor foolish, nor extreme. It was sort of a good thing because Dad tended to be overly generous when it came to giving away money to help out relatives and others. Mom was loving, smart, and innovative.

Mom though frugal in many ways had an eye for the arts and wanted us to be exposed to some of the finer things in life. On a few occasions as young children, my mother took Phyllis and I downtown to the Palace Theater in Clevelands "theater district". What a magnificent place it was with high arched gold encrusted ceilings, dramatic light fixtures, and magnificent red draperies. We saw Walt Disney's Peter Pan and The Lady and the Tramp playing on a huge movie screen of that era. Once again Mom would spend money for our benefit but rarely for her own pleasure.

She loved to cook or so it seemed. A pleaser she was in every way but neither she nor Dad ever went overboard. They knew how to do the right thing without spoiling us. Good food, nice clothes, good shoes, and a clean and pleasant home were the rule of the day. They never tried to compete with the neighbors but in many ways they did better in how they raised us. They were strict but only until we understood the rules of the household. Repeat performances for bad behavior were not necessary for us to learn what was expected of us. We all knew who the bosses were and they gave us leeway but were able to instill the important values we needed to succeed. Trouble makers we were not. All of us kids were well behaved and a credit to the family. We never got into significant trouble and never picked up any bad habits. Having said all of that we still enjoyed a good time when it was to be had.

The most memorable party I ever attended as a child was at Jennifer's and Judy's home, a few doors down on Gasser from where we lived. Jennifer was a very good friend of Phyllis. This party was for Jennifer's seventh or eighth birthday and most of the neighborhood kids were invited along as well as a few others from our grade school class. There were about fifteen to twenty kids there having a great time with food, drinks, and party games such as pin-the-tail-on-the-donkey. At one point and for only a few minutes, a classmate and gorgeously attractive Pamela A. (you got it, the same last name you're thinking about) came and sat on my lap out of the blue. I could tell that she sorts of liked me and I was able to sneak a kiss on her left cheek from that precious little thing. It was the one and only and it never occurred again. As we grew up, she found others "of interest. " Pam would remain immensely popular throughout her school years and I believe she may have been a home coming queen at The Ohio State University during the 1960's. After we graduated from high school, we never saw each other again. In fact, she disappeared and would never return to any of our school anniversaries for unknown reasons. No class members have ever been able to locate her. She just disappeared. She was my first love though I am certain she never realized it. To make the situation even worse there was a terrifyingly long gap until the next love would eventually surface when I was about twelve years old.

I never took a date to the Beach Cliff movie theater in downtown Rocky River with the single exception of Mary Kaye S. that I met at a Knights of Columbus family picnic through my father's membership. Dad was a Fourth Degree Knight and loved his involvement in a terrific Catholic organization intended to promote the faith in many productive ways. Mary Kaye was attractive, sweet, and fun to be with but without a car it was not practical to see her again since she lived in Bay Village, a bit too far away to make anything work between us. She attended a Catholic high school and was quite the lady. She was the cutest little thing with a figure should we say that was very advanced for her age. For that one date, I talked Mom into picking her up in Bay Village, of all places, and she drove the two of us to a movie show for an evening.

My clothing was neat, clean, and typical though in the 1950's many teenage boys wore their hair swept back or closely cropped as with a butch or flat top. My hair style was cut close. I wore kaki-colored pants with a brown belt and buckle pulled way over to my right side, lying just below my right arm pit area as was the custom of the day. I still remember well where Mary Kay lived.

She lived on Osborn Street, a tree lined nicely groomed street typical of this cute little bedroom community though notorious for the home of Dr. Sam Shepard and the small hospital this innocent surgeon practiced at. He had been imprisoned for the murder of his beautiful wife though after many years was released through a reversal of his sentence by the US Supreme Court. It was believed due to so much adverse news about the crime, that he never received a fair trial.

The innocent part is my opinion and worth only that. I did have the opportunity of meeting him and delivering newspapers to his small apartment on Wooster Road in Rocky River. After his release he somehow met and married a beautiful blond woman of German extraction. Debbie is also of German extraction, and I can vouch for their beautiful women.

Getting back to Mary Kaye. Both of us sat in the back seat of my parents Chrysler while my mom kindly chauffeured us around and dropped us off at the Beach Cliff Theater. I do not even remember the movie that we saw, since I could only think of Mary Kaye. Other than drooling about romantic possibilities nothing interesting happened on my very first date.

Mom would never be a chauffeur again. Once was enough, since traveling back and forth to Bay village was a lot to ask of any parent for a movie show date. Mary Kaye must not have been too impressed with me because she never again went out with me. However, I do not remember asking her out again the car problem being what it was.

Much later in life I would meet her again. My romantic touch or behavior apparently needed polishing. First dates are probably more often than not last dates as well. Experimentation is just that and only practice improves the species. All was not lost though. We would meet again in an unexpected place about two decades later under unusual circumstances.

Fun is fun, though Phyllis and I often participated in chores delved out by mom on a regular basis. We were involved in cleaning all rooms of our home at least weekly. Once a year we tackled the garage as well.

Lawns were cut, manicured, and trimmed. Walls, base boards, floors, and windows were cleaned annually. As "Little Lou" grew up, he helped a bit with some household duties, but would take on a more important roll later on.

Phyllis was involved in more regular superficial cleaning such as dusting and kitchen duties though we all washed and dried dishes on a daily basis.

Mom knew how to get all of us involved in house work but no one seemed to mind since chores became a regular responsibility and thus arguments or debates never materialized. Our participation was expected and not negotiable. It was simply taken for granted and that was that.

In my spare time I would wash and wax cars finding this duty to be more fun-like than work. Okay, I'm somewhat warped, but cars for me were always too cool. Detailing cars became an obsession at times knowing that when my time to drive would come, I wanted to drive the sharpest and the best.

The slightest imperfections were repaired and corrected upon discovery.

Mastering car tuning, radiator flushing, replacing worn belts, and contaminated fluids all became important and not usually difficult to perform on cars of the 1950-1970 eras. Dad liked performance cars but had no clue about how to work on them while relying usually on me for most car repairs and maintenance. Routine maintenance prevented road side breakdowns. I know how much dad appreciated my auto mechanic skills.

Soon I would be entering Rocky River Junior High School to further my education into the real world. And what is that all about? This two-year experience was relatively bland but it was another step into a life aimed at hopefully making a difference in some way for others. I became interested in science and mathematics and fared fairly well not really knowing what my future would hold for me. My social life in contrast to Darwin's theories of evolution, did not. My fantasies evolved but that was the extent of it.

The junior high was memorable only from the movie industry perspective. Rocky River school systems had very innovative ideas when it came to educating and entertaining their students. As students we each had a one-hour lunch break. Thirty minutes was spent eating in the cafeteria and thirty minutes was left to watching a single reel of a first run movie that we paid about five cents to see. In a weeks' time, we were able to see the entire movie. The movies were excellent and were shown in a two-hundred seat theatre via a standard movie theater projector and sound system. This was big time being in our own back yard and it proved to be very enjoyable.

No refreshments were permitted and everyone was well behaved. An interloper or teacher was always in attendance to make sure there was no funny business or romantic interludes to speak of. It was amazing. Going to the movies while still in school. What a trip!

My parents gave each of us a small allowance every Sunday to spend as we so desired. Most of it was spent in my early adolescent years going to see movies at the Beach Cliff. We would go with friends to the Saturday matinee. A couple of special treats were purchased before the movie but rarely popcorn due to its excessive cost usually exceeding my means. Popcorn was available in relatively small boxes or was provided in a larger cup when "butter" was to be added. Cheaper choices were my targets such as Juicy Fruit candy, JUJU Beads, Nocco Wafers, or Goetz Caramel Creams that I favored the most.

As time went on my prowess and financial means continued to be lacking.

The movies were still fun when I went with Joe, Lowell, or a couple of other lesser friends. Joe and I spent many a weekend going to the Beach Cliff to see the latest movies. The Saturday matinees were the best starting off with a news reel or two, a couple of cartoons, (my favorite being the Road Runners), the main feature, another cartoon and a second feature film. It was standard to get to the show just before one in the afternoon and stay until five. These were all day affairs, so to speak. All of this was to be had for about 25 cents.

Joe later on worked part time at the Beach Cliff. Those were the days. Joe would eventually become an usher at the theater and this occasionally paid dividends with free entry now and then.

My love for the movie industry began at this point and never waned. It was the start of new adventures sparking amazing family traditions and kick starting a future family movie interest that would take on a life of its own. Well soon that brief educational education would evaporate into another more important adventure.

It was time for high school.

In the old days Rocky River High was a football, basketball, wrestling powerhouse ruling the Southwestern conference for years and years. During my tenure at "River" we won or tied many if not most conference championships in the popular sports.

I never played in any of these sports much less the tamer varieties and thus I deserved no recognition of any type in the sports arena. In not playing on the playing field, I fared no better on the dating field. The jocks new the benefits of being jocks and the rest of us thought we knew the benefits but who's to say.

Exaggeration is the mother of fantasy. The truth is that I was a slave to reality but experienced fantasies that were wonderful in some sort of a perverse way.

The Bay Village Rockets were the Rocky River Pirates primary nemesis and usually the Rockets finished second place as I wish to recall. No attempt has been made to review the actual records so I will rest comfortably with any and all delusions or half-baked memories I feel serve my needs and purposes. "Never let the facts get in the way" as many have said before me. "Memory" is more often than not warped by the passage of time and diminished by overzealous egos.

High school progressed but with only a few solid friendships. My twin sister's history according to her met the same fate. Neither one of us were social giants and we essentially passed through school going unnoticed and unrecognized. We were successful academically and at the end of the day that is what school is all about. Social circles be damned. Let's move on into the future.

Lowell eventually moved to a nearby city Fairview Park where he became a class theatrical leader performing in several theatrical performances. This had its benefits, since he met several beautiful young ladies and managed to introduce me to a few that left me with lasting impressions.

As well as my friendship with Lowell, Joe and I spent a lot of time together. He became very close to our family and my folks enjoyed his presence. At times he seemed to be like one of the family.

He and I were both intellectuals or so we thought. After a Friday or Saturday night show, I would take him home in whatever car I had and we would sit and talk in his driveway for hours on end discussing the universe, space travel, mathematics, and science. We must have been a bit fruity since we rarely discussed women. Neither one of us ever seemed to date so it wasn't as though we had any experiences to discuss.

In fact, to show you how far off the mark I was, later in my teen years my dad once said to me. "I don't care what you do with your girlfriends (there were none), just don't knock them up. " I said "Ok Dad, sure. " The problem then was I didn't know what he meant by not knocking some girl up. I was shall we say too naive to have even a clue about what he was talking about. Thus, I had no idea about what sort of questions to ask about any advice he may have had for me. I just left it alone and went about my business as usual.

Louis Philip Junior or little Lou was a cool kid and a good brother. Being five years younger, he was catered to but received his share of good-natured teasing from both Phyllis and I. Lou was big boned as was his father, good natured with a cute smile and sported an attractive personality. Being intelligent he learned quickly and always found ways to entertain himself. His friendly disposition always won over other children and as time went on, he would become a leader by endearing many to his cute disposition and effective way of handling all sorts of situations be they recreational, educational, or organizational. Being strong willed but usually right about most situations gave him the ability to succeed where many others would have failed.

As a child he and I interacted with friendly play and while trying to equal my behavior, he would learn quickly and was soon competitive under most circumstances.

Lou like the rest of us was usually well groomed. Mom took care of keeping us clean and neat while providing an endless stream of freshly cleaned clothes.

Dad would cut our hair every two weeks in the basement on a tall chair near a bare light bulb hanging above our heads. He sometimes treated us to a little shoulder massage with the coolest mechanical and electrical massager. He would slip this strange gismo on the back of his hand, being held in place with two rows of flexible steel sprung cords that would fit around the palm and back of his right hand. He would then flip a switch on the device making it vibrate like crazy in one of two possible speeds; vibrate or serious vibrating. His vibrating hand would gently grasp the back of our necks and the base of our heads. The vibration of his hand and fingers was relaxing and amazing.

Dad always kept us looking sharp, cleanly cut, with the latest of hair styles. We must have been the envy of the neighborhood feeling clean, properly dressed, and groomed as best as possible.

One of my favorite childhood memories that Lou regularly reminds me, of occurred when I was about seven or eight years old. Tying white lightweight kitchen towels around our necks and draping them over our backs allowed Lou and I to run around playing Superman. Standing atop of a hassock in front of my dad's favorite chair, I leaped off jumping downward to the floor and then proceeded to crush unknowingly our pet turtle resting on the carpet below. This was followed by a moment of shock, a few tears, and later a brief burial service after which the remains were placed in a shallow hole beneath a bush in our back yard. That escapade has never been forgotten by the family, nor should I say Lou who brings it up at nearly every Christmas Eve dinner.

Lou did well in school. Being the youngest at that time, he learned from our misfires and thus became more secure with himself as shown by his rising popularity and charisma. Lou's smile could knock you over. In sixth grade he became the Captain of the American Automobile Association Safety Patrol at Wooster School. This was a prestigious position, akin to being class president.

The patrol members being of both sexes were trained to cross school children at intersections near the schools. "Patrolman" wore a white band across their waist and another band crisscrossing their chest from one side to the opposite shoulder and then down their back. The bisecting white band held a police style chrome badge and was authorized by the State of Ohio.

Lieutenants wore red/chrome engraved badges, while the captain of the patrol wore a blue/chrome engraved version. These authoritative insignia were bold enough not to be visually missed by motorists or pedestrians. All motorists were required to respect the direction of these student police and did so without question. Being a member of the patrol was considered important, prestigious, and a position on the patrol was awarded to those in good standing.

Lou's leadership skills grew rapidly and he became very popular with everyone including his teachers. He was good at baseball and as life went on, our parents having more time on their hands as we all grew older were able to see him play successfully in many games. As Lou grew older, he began to look more and more like our father.

In high school Lou would amaze his friends with athletic achievements in wrestling and football. Being very competitive he on one occasion pinned his opponent in a matter of seconds finding his name in an article on the front page of the *Plain Dealer*. The paper awarded him with a free meal for him and a friend to a downtown restaurant. He graciously asked one of his lovely lady friends for an evening out.

Americans the Beautiful

His sporting accomplishments were also tested on "Rivers" football team where he played an offensive guard and a defensive line backer. His strategy was simple. On the first three plays of every game, he would viciously and soundly attack his opponent with serious hits or tackles that would take that player psychologically out of the game. This technique worked quite well for Lou making the rest of the game more leisurely while developing his reputation as a maniac on the playing field.

During those years River would remain a dominant force not to be taken lightly by our arch rivals. Lessons were learned on both sides of the field that would influence Lou in years to come.

Becoming President of his senior class was another important achievement that showed his leadership abilities and would prepare him for a future role in life with a major Cleveland institution. Lou was not only smart but coldly calculating; letting little escape his attention. He knew how to make a big splash when he had to but also on occasion new when to keep his mouth shut - now that is a feat in its own right.

He was a master of the political aspects of most situations but not as fully secure about the families' emotional needs at times. Lou was a good kid and always still had the best interests of his family at heart.

A few years later little Jennifer, the youngest of all, would surprise my un-expecting parents with her conception and birth. She was not planned but decided to make her presence known anyway. Little Lou was happy to relinquish his position as the youngest to his new sister. The Caravella family would not be denied little Jennifer. Jenny was cute, blondish at birth, happy-go-lucky and a sweet and wonderful gift to the family.

Being the youngest of four, she was attended to by all and given the treatment of a princess. Dad catered to her every need as did Mom. At about age two or three Dad would come home from work and each evening offered her an opportunity to select a coin from among several in his outstretched hand. She would select whatever caught her eye and then she would place it in a small bank found in her room. This game was always amusing to watch since the coins intrinsic value had no meaning to her.

On Wednesdays when Dad was off from work, he often took Jennifer to a small kiddy park in a nearby town where they would ride children's amusement rides for a couple of hours at a time. Dad got more of a kick out of this then Jenny and spoke of it on many occasions. One Wednesday, Dad and Jennifer arrived at the park and found it to be boarded up. They were both so heartbroken they held each other in their arms and cried for the longest time. It was her first loss but it would not be her last. The memories of this park would last forever within Jennifer's heart.

Her good nature and loving character made her easy to be around, fun, and special in many ways. She had and still has an artistic bent with an outgoing personality allowing her to perform in theater before large audiences; a thing that terrified the rest of us especially Phyllis who was always so shy she could never have considered such a harrowing experience.

Lou being the consummate extrovert, leader, and intelligentsia was a hard act to follow. Jennifer did something the rest of us could never do including her brother Lou. At the Beck Center in Lakewood, Jenny became at age six a member of a troupe known as The Peter Pan Players. This troupe performed on stage with exquisitely designed sets and elegant costumes.

At age ten Jennifer auditioned for and played the role of the Pied Piper of Hamlin. She stole the show with her singing and acting. The play ran several days and was a source of pride especially for Dad who had played in operas during his earlier years in Cleveland. Dad could see a lot of himself in Jennifer. She had his jaw line, his love of people, a cute sense of humor, and the gift to allow self-expression in so many ways.

She always liked to dance and sing her way into others' lives by showering her charisma and caring ways onto them. Jennifer was good in the fine arts as well, often bringing home from school beautifully detailed works of art completed in a variety of media from water colors to oils and acrylics. Two of her most striking examples deserve museum recognition.

She would later hone her skills to create new works of art that would be sold to others for a pittance of their real value. Being a generous and caring person, her motivation was not money but rather the beauty of creation.

Jenny being about fourteen years younger than I, became somewhat lost to me in the shuffle. I was able to make up for some lost opportunities in getting to know her better as time would allow. Being gone at The University of Dayton during her later teen years reduced my memories and much if any direct influence I may have had on her. Maybe that was a good thing? Maybe that was not?

In life, Jennifer would accomplish one of the greatest achievements anyone could and one that so unfortunately passed out by mother. I believe in her heart, by putting her family first, mom was never able to overcome her desire to become a nurse. Jennifer graduated from Bowling Green University with a degree in nursing and has practiced the profession with care and dignity for over thirty years attending to women and their children in the well-known maternity center of Fairview Hospital; a Cleveland Clinic facility. She has made an indelible mark at Fairview Hospital acquiring so many friends and many more patient accolades than one could list.

Her caring ways continue to include frequent phone calls to family members when often promoting family gatherings throughout the year. She is not one to gloat over achievements but would rather listen to the rest of us rave about our own. Long phone conversations with Jenny are the rule rather than not because she wants to remain so much a part of our lives. In an ongoing way, she loves to know what is going on. She is so loving that she craves every moment she can glean from others' lives.

Now you're in for it. My family and friends have been the best anyone could hope for but for some unknown reason my passion and fanaticism for automobiles has been a trademark of mine since early childhood. The male side of the Caravella family must have a genetic penetrance when it came to the automobile. My father loved high performance coupes and sedans as did his brother. They passed this passion on to us Caravella Boys with little if any effort. It was indelible. Once it hit, it would go unquenched for life.

From the moment I got my driver's license I would always have access to something with at least a bit of a punch to it. Dad bought home a new 1959 Chrysler Windsor, red over white, with a red interior, swivel seats, push button torque flight tranny, Golden Lion 383 cubic inch V-8 with 305 horsepower. This car had huge tail fins and roared when floored.

I kept this car absolutely flawlessly cleaned, polished, swept out and wiped down at all times. My friends would comment on this near obsession with perfection on so many occasions. My high school buddy Lowell Gaspar especially noted this many more times than once and he still does to this very day.

Most of my classmates were into cars as well, though some of their parents were a bit more financially solvent and a few of them drove some pretty nice wheels. Many of them were very talented mechanics in their spare time and also new something about body works other than what their girlfriends had to exhibit.

Two classmates come to mind that towered over the others in skill, knowledge and ability when it came to auto mechanics 101. My distant friend, Eric Mauer was a car genius and this is even diminishing his ability by a long way. He totally rebuilt a 57 Chevy Bellaire convertible to perfection painting it candy apple red, and refitting the interior with white bucket seats, a white interior, white canvas top, and then threw in a 327 cubic inch Corvette engine with a four-speed floor shift, dual exhausts, postreaction, and finished it off with fuel injection for good measure. This puppy put out really good, easily laying twin strips of black rubber in two or three gears almost at will.

His close friend, Bill Westley was no slouch either rebuilding a gorgeous "59" Pontiac convertible with beautiful maroon paint, a four speed as well, postreaction (both rear wheels would be power wheels rather than just one of the real wheels as in most cars of that era), dual exhausts, and a 389 cubic inch killer mill with three two-barrel carbs. Posi traction is a set up in which both rear wheels would be power wheels rather than only one of the real wheels as in most cars of that era. Thus, both wheels would provide amazing traction for the car to gain speed rapidly without just burning rubber.

These magnificent machines were sometimes seen drag racing in River while filling the air with sweet music roaring out of their twin exhausts, and billows of black smoke churning forth from their cars hot molten rear tires.

Not all car times were good times. Two weeks after reaching my sixteenth birthday and obtaining my driver's license, I had my first and only accident. But it really wasn't my accident so to speak. One day when driving the big "59 Chrysler" with one of the Kirk twins' ridings shot gun, I got into a bit of trouble. I was driving down Center Ridge Road heading away from Westgate Mall on a rainy afternoon when a Volkswagen Karman Gia in front of me was slowing down too quickly for me to notice any brake lights and I rear-ended this piss-ant thing they called a sports car, totaling it with ease. It was no match for the huge Chrysler. There wasn't a scratch on the Chrysler's bumper. The Police were called and arrived on the scene though a ticket was not issued to me but to the driver of the other car. The Karman Gia's brake lights weren't working, which was not unusual for a Volkswagen and so I was not apparently to blame. The driver of that vehicle was issued a citation though fortunately no one was seriously hurt in either vehicle.

Man, that was too close for comfort. I was dumbstruck about how suddenly something could go terribly wrong even when you least expect it. However, no brake lights, no worries; a least for me.

As fate would have it, one of my fellow classmates with the initials J. B. was driving by and seeing what had happened, he waved to me and incredulously laughed as well. His laughter didn't last too long. Not paying attention as he passed the accident scene while turning left into the next street Lakeview Road, he proceeded to ram an oncoming car approaching the intersection. J. B. would eventually receive a citation for failing to yield the right of way. He wasn't laughing the next time I saw him. As they say in the vernacular, "He who laughs last, laughs hardest."

More police soon arrived to deal with the entire mess.

After arriving home, a short time later, I confronted Dad with what had happened. Fearing the worst, I was quite upset but Dad took me aside and said, "These things happen. I don't want you to have a fear of driving from this accident. Let's go for a ride." Dad was the best. He never embarrassed me. After this accident I would never be involve in another one.

Street drag racing was big at the time. Chevy owners always thought they were hot shit. I often gave them a few things to think about.

Once on Lorain Road just past Fairview Park Hospital, I was sitting at a light at 150th and Lorain Road and what pulls up next to me but two "greasers" (known for having hair covered with some greasy like hair cream of the day) in a white

Chevy II with six-cylinder emblems on the front fenders. This guy revs up his "mill" (engine) while we were sitting at the light and by then I knew this was no six-cylinder slug. I thought alright dude. You're going to learn a lesson here. He looked at me. His buddy looks at me with a shit eating grin on his face. I looked at him. The driver flipped me the bird. The light changed. I mashed the accelerator to the floor and we both pulled out of the hole with tires screaming and black smoke spewing everywhere. In first gear he was ahead by a half a car. My 361 cubic inch Plymouth V-8 Fury started to really get serious hauling like a freight train from hell. So long suckers. The push-button torque flight tranny, fed up with first gear, jammed into second, melting the rear tires with dual exhausts howling like two wild hyenas while screeching white-wall tires were laying down a thick ribbon of black tread down Lorain Avenue. When this "mother" took over, it took over. He watched my tail lights the rest of the way down Lorain until the next red light flickered. At the light, he yelled, "What in the hell are you running." I told him the bad news. He was running a 327 small block Chevy with a big Rochester carb and four on the floor. Too bad for him. I thought. This guy needs a real car; not that piss-ant 327. He couldn't believe my car was stock. Worse, he couldn't believe losing to a Chrysler product. Little did he know it was a rare Fury with a special engine that he would not likely face again.

On another occasion late one evening, I was coming home from visiting Nadine, the sweet young lady I met from a friend, who new another friend, that finally I befriended.

I came to a stop at a light once again near Fairview Park Hospital just before the Lorain Avenue Bridge and overlooking the Cleveland Metro Parks. What in hell pulls up next to me but this honking red Plymouth Satellite with a big block ram-charged 413 cubic inch killer mill, running street headers with dual exhausts. He revved the Mopar a bit, blipping the clutch now and then with the car sort of lurching forward and extending its suspension like it would leap into the air. This was no one to mess with. My Fury was dog meat next to this. The light changed and he dropped the clutch at God knows what engine rpm bringing the rear of the Satellite to life. His tires which were really slicks (bald tires made for drag racing) lit up and after biting in to the pavement, the Plymouth launched forward like a rocket sled blurring the surroundings with smoke and vanishing within seconds across the other side of the bridge while I was sitting there in disbelief. This guy's toy was boss and I knew it.

Another memorable event occurred when my dad was driving his "59" Chrysler on downtown Carnegie Avenue when a minority American was sauntering slowly across the street supposedly paying no attention to traffic and taking his good old time about it. My brother and I were sitting in the front seat next to Dad. Lou was sitting on the central seat cushion and I on the other red swivel seat. Dad was a bit miffed knowing he would have to slow way down for this character to cross. The sand bagger knew exactly what he was doing as well which added fuel to the fire and a boiling anger within Dad. Dad said "watch this." He floored the big Chrysler. The front end of the Windsor lifted up, the engine roaring full speed ahead, and smoke began to billow out of the rear end. You never saw anyone move so frigging fast across a street in your life. This guy turned into a cyclone and within a split second broke the Olympic record for the 100-yard dash narrowly making it to the curb as we roared by. It's a good thing or he would have been mashed potatoes and gravy for the morgue. Admittedly sometimes Dad was a bit over the top.

All of this car stuff is one thing though more importantly was the history and academic record of schools with an emphasis especially on the high school. River public schools functioned in my day more like college prep schools, in that its graduation rate and college attendance rate was nearly unmatched by other school systems in the Cleveland area.

In the 1950's to 1960's it was unusual for a public school system to aspire to such its lofty goals for its students and graduates. Most of the citizens and leaders of Rocky River were college grads and they expected the same for their children. Going to college or a university upon graduation was the rule and not the exception. More significant was the fact that upon graduation students were so well prepared for college, at least academically, that their freshman college year for many would be redundant.

An unusual way of celebrating academics was to de-emphasize other commonly practiced social events occurring at most public high schools. We never celebrated homecoming at Rocky River High nor did we ever select a king or queen for that matter. The president of the class always being academically at the top of the food chain and in popularity was the path the "River" schools wanted to follow. Homecoming with a queen or king was considered irrelevant and out of place. It was not in keeping with River's mission which was to graduate the finest students possible to enter the work force or to move on to higher education.

Teachers were excellent and well prepared. As good as River was in sports, it was even better academically. David Bichsel, an economics teacher and Charles Shelton, an English teacher were two of the finest I ever was fortunate enough to be taught by. The department of mathematics excelled in every way as did the science department. There were no academic classes that were losers. "River "was at the forefront of high school academia in its time. This is not being sentimental. This was a reality.

My class did have its share of practical jokers and a few that were academically challenged probably more related to attention deficit disorder than to anything else. Unfortunately for them I do not believe this disorder was recognized in that era or it would have been aggressively attended to one way or another.

Behavior problems of any consequence rarely occurred. In my day drugs were unheard of though a few classmates over indulged in alcohol at occasional weekend parties which I was not privy to. Lacking spendable income, a few social graces, and "status" among the elite, placed me in the unenviable position of a near social outcast akin to being a leper, though at the time it didn't seem to matter. Or did it? In retrospect I believed the lack of being less socially accepted by peers influenced my future in a favorable way as time went on.

Phyllis and I progressed through high school relatively unnoticed and moved on. Our education at "River" richly prepared us to succeed in the work force though at the time we were unmoved by our new found education.

In summary, equally as important as it was for my forefathers to come to America was the discovery by my parents of the community of Rocky River with the opportunities it had to offer. Phyllis would move on to Dyke College known for graduating elite business students and I would follow my cousin Roy Koesel already finishing his freshman year at The University of Dayton, a respected Catholic university in Southwestern Ohio operated by the Marianist order of priests.

The Society of Mary is the sponsor of the University of Dayton. It was founded by Blessed (meaning a person who reached Sainthood) William Joseph Chaminade (1761-1850), a priest in the diocese of Bordeaux, Francien 1817. The Society of Mary is the male religious branch of the Marianist Family. This university has been therefore respected over the years for the achievements reached by its students.

Besides academics, college, and breathing, there are other very important aspects of life that are more than worth mentioning as I have alluded to before. During my late teen years and early college years my two true loves were both ladies from Catholic high schools. The young lady I dated the most was Nadine. She was introduced to me by my good friend Lowell Gaspar through his girlfriend Rosemary. They both attended the same Catholic high school, Saint Augustine Academy. Nadine was tall with striking blond hair, a cute figure, and a brilliant mind graduating valedictorian from her high school class at St. Augustine Academy of Cleveland fame.

She was over zealous to a fault about her physical appearance. I mean she was nuts. Every hair and every part of her clothing and makeup had to be flawless. I mean perfect. Did I mention impeccable.

One magnificent summer day my cousin Sylvia Anne loaned her 1959 maroon Corvette convertible to me for a day so I could take Nadine for a ride. I mean who loans a Corvette to anyone, ever? I mean who does that??? Thank you, Sylvia. You were the best.

It was a last-minute thing and I wasn't able to contact Nadine by phone. Being impatient and anxious to take her for a ride I drove over to her home and coxed her outside. What could be better; a beautiful woman, a beautiful car, and a car nut with an unexpected chance to show off in the best car of the era?

What I forgot to take under consideration is that good old Nadine used hair spray about as often as you and I would drink water. Every aspect of her attractive looks had to be perfect. As I said before; perfect! When I arrived at her home with this magnificent car she flatly refused to go for a ride. It was out of the question. Her looks would not tolerate a single hair being ruffled. No amount of convincing would alter her mind. I was dumbfounded and hurt. The situation was unthinkable. The opportunity would never occur again.

We continued to date for about two to three years but our relationship took a turn for the worst one evening. We had a major falling out related to what I believed to be related to overzealous teachings of the sisters of St. Augustine who taught Nadine that boy's intentions are not always totally pure and chivalrous and may run amuck at times.

We had been in her living room on a comfortable couch and after necking for a couple of hours I decided with over two years of dating under our belts or should I say above the belts, that maybe it was time to investigate a woman's most intimate parts. Having never done so and being more than curious and being in my early twenties I felt the mysteries of sex were at hand and needed to be explored. I had managed to get up the courage and proceeded to unfasten a lower button on her dress over her lower abdomen. Fortunately, she was wearing a half slip and I managed to touch some of her soft, smooth warm flesh around her lower abdomen just below her navel. She was quite persistent in relocating my dominant hand. As time went on, she grew weary of stopping my advances and allowed me to grow incrementally close to her pubic area without touching it. I grew bolder still and gently slipped my hand under her lacy panties just a bit, barely touching the upper border of her pubic hair. That was it. She went berserk, standing up, and screaming for me to leave and to never return. Granted we had somewhat gone amuck here and it was obviously too much for her to deal with.

My apologies had no effect and she threw me out and that was that. Nadine felt our relationship was becoming a bit over-heated for her comfort and it went the way of the Edsel. I guess the sisters of Saint Augustine were right. They probably had a role in ruining more than one relationship.

This breakup was not exactly of my own doing (Yaa, right) but it marred my fragile ego for a couple of decades or more if not forever. I was totally heartbroken and scared from then on with my dealings with women. Interventions and conversations with my family priest, Father Emler of Saint Christopher's Church of Rocky River, and with Nadine were in effective. She had made up her mind that our relationship was over and she was not to see me again. Well at least that is how it seemed for a very long time.

After this experience, I was totally gun-shy for months but eventually dated one of her friends on and off, Johnna Mancini, named after her father John. She was equally as attractive if not more so, soft spoken, and an intellectual heavy weight just like Nadine. She was of Italian extraction and voluptuous in every way, filling out the upper part of any dress in a more than an ample way.

On one occasion she invited me to Ohio University for a weekend visit. She was such a sweetheart but the timing was not right. Our relationship though romantic, was never intimate in any way and it lasted on and off for years though it never progressed primarily due to career interests that were evolving for me and for her in different directions.

I was just not ready for a serious relationship and not capable of becoming intimate with any woman. I grew to love her and her family but not enough to further her cause. She was a gorgeous lady with character and beauty unmatched by most women. Her complexion and facial beauty were more than perfect.

Because of her Italian heritage, my family encouraged me to a degree to be with her but I was not ready to become seriously involved. As fate would prevail, her future tragic life would have a significant effect on me and would never be forgotten.

On another occasion, my good friend Lowell and I decided to double date for New Year's Eve. He invited Rosemary, his very special lady from St. Augustine Academy. She was beautiful as well as very classy and a sweetheart that he cherished no end. His father loaned him his brand-new Dodge for the evening. Uncharacteristically he arrived early to pick me up first at my home, before we would corral the ladies. It was a snowy and cold evening. He tooled into our long driveway cutting his wheels a bit too soon and landed a drift on a huge snow bank. The rear wheels were off the ground. You can be sure that there would not be traction here anytime soon.

While dressed in suits it took us the better part of an hour to dig this rig out. Our dates, Nadine and Rosemary, were not amused by the fiasco and nothing else was memorable about the evening.

As you can see there are so many great friends and stories about the Caravella family that it brings up the concept of what all of us, are all about, that live in America. We are a special and unique breed of people that will always make a difference in this world.

We are a country full of amazing people. America has the best of what there is to offer not just in land mass, opportunity, and freedom but primarily in its people. The best people of the world discovered us and laid the framework of what we have, what we mean, and who we are. I actually feel sorry for the rest of the world's people, not in a smug way, not in an arrogant way, not in an ugly way, but only in that it is a crying shame that others in many ways suffer at the hands of despots, or selfish and incompetent leaders. Many do not have and will not likely have the freedom, peace, security, and lifestyle that we have as Americans.

Americans the Beautiful

Sure, our history is not perfect. But compare us to any other country. We have the best intentions and generally try to provide for others in the world in the best way that we can. Sure, we want to export freedom. It is our greatest export. It is what we do. It is what we have been called to do. If not us then who would do so? Others do not step up as they should.

No others have routinely helped other countries unless there was something in it for them. Sure, we are not totally philanthropic but we have asked for less from Europeans, Africans, Asians, and from other countries that we have historically given. Does anyone remember that "the sun never sets on the British Empire." The French nearly conquered as much land mass in centuries gone by. The Spanish were the same. Remember the Conquistadors? The Romans likely controlled the largest part of the world for hundreds of years and beyond what other civilizations have ever accomplished.

America is different. When finished, Americans usually get up and leave unless the area is so militarily critical to our survival, we will take a long-time vested interest in a specific country or territory. We are not booted out.

We are usually often asked to return with open arms and greenbacks. The Vietnamese want us back. The Arab nations, sooner or later will ask for our help, presence, and guidance. It is what we have been called to do.

And so, it is today. Americans are good at heart and conscientious but should never be underestimated. We have never been interested in failure. Let others do that. Good families, good heritage, good leadership, and common sense under most circumstances have allowed us to succeed. We are the super race that Hitler could not achieve. Through immigration, genetic interaction, education, and hard work we are what others could not have ever hoped to achieve.

The only real blow to America's technological self-esteem was when the Russians narrowly beat us into space by launching Sputnik I. What a bite! President Dwight D. Eisenhower believed too strongly in the Navy's complex missile system, the Vanguard that misfired one too many times. Shortly after the Russian victory, Eisenhower gave the nod to Warner von Braun's Army Red Stone Missile program and he launched our first satellite with his first attempt.

During this period, I became very interested in missile and aircraft technology hoping someday to be a fighter pilot. Unfortunately, my poor vision would put an end to those dreams though all was not lost. An education would provide the ground-work required to achieve dreams and success never imagined by an immigrant or his family.

School had become a priority for the children of our family. Success and hopes for the future were all about a first-rate education. We were expected to do our best, complete homework assignments on time, never miss class, and perform up to our abilities. My parents encouraged us, guided us, but were never tyrannical or obsessed with grades.

They convinced us that the future lies in the present. Without a strong presence in school, there would be little hope of long-term quality living as we moved on in life. We were taught that you make life what it is. Life experiences do not happen by chance but by choice. The Rocky River High School coaches had similar views. One coach placed a sign on the doorway leading from the men's locker room into the gymnasium. The sign read, "I am not interested in excuses. I am only interested in results."

Results were what we delivered; but not on the playing field. Both Phyllis and I brought home fairly decent grades linked to a work ethic and showing up. Phyllis did well in social and business-like courses while the basic sciences and mathematics were my forte. English classes on writing essays interested me as well. Reading was not a priority, though I had to read before I could write. Critical thinking about literature became more interesting as time went on. The best theme I ever wrote was about the book, "The Heart of Darkness. " My English teacher, Mr. Shelton, gave an A+ plus to me for the effort. To this day the paper lingers after all of these years somewhere in my personal space waiting to be rediscovered again.

My sister and I were never part of the class aristocracy but only lingered in the commoner's domain. We went largely unnoticed but in some ways that was commendable. Being neither fish nor fowl resulted in neither fame nor misfortune. We simply existed in the "Twilight Zone" of those times. Our turn would come though we never guessed while still in school, an aurora borealis of sorts would show-case our abilities. A few gifted teachers were able to extract the best efforts out of us indicating there is sometimes more to a student than simply a conventional wrapping.

Socially, during my high school days, I was inept in wearing a flat-top haircut, dark framed glasses, average clothes, and twenty extra pounds of weight that did nothing for my ego or status among friends.

As time went on, I became interested in weight lifting, reworking the same lifts over a couple of years. My special secret lift was perfected by lying down on the floor, flat on my back, with my arms fully extended beyond my head. Grasping the seventy-five-pound bar-bell with arms extended, I could lift the weight off the floor to a point straight up over my head and above my shoulders and later returning the weights to the floor in the reverse manner. This seemed to have no practical application until one day after gym class one of the upperclassmen was bragging about his lifts. Gathering some nerve, I challenged him to the lift I was used to doing. Being an egocentric muscle-bound arrogant athlete, not that I didn't have a few similar characteristics, he took me up the challenge.

While lying down on my back on a floor mat and with my arms fully extended beyond my head and shoulders, I cooly lifted the loaded bar bell off the floor with seventy-five pounds on it. The loaded bar bell came off the floor and hovered straight upright over my head with little difficulty until I lowered it back down to the floor. This other wise guy laid down on the mat, extended his arms fully to grasp the loaded barbell, and could not budge it off the floor. The day was mine.

The unexpected result of this circus act was that my reputation for strength was established and I was left alone by the usual bullies who mistakenly thought I could be a bit of a bore should one of them consider taking me on. It worked for me and life went on. Outside of this cluster of jocks and agitators the social impact of this feat remained zero.

Phyllis and I continued to struggled socially. She lacked self confidence in her younger years and thus never flourished as others around her, though she was cute, trim, and sported a very attractive figure. She was clean to a fault and her language unlike mine, was never laced with colloquial expressions. In fact, to this day, I cannot remember a single deviation in her speech from anything other than acceptable language. Maybe that was another reason why as a child I called her Honey.

I had a few faults in the linguistics area but never cursed nor swore during classes or on school grounds. Occasionally thinking I was cute; a few less then complimentary expressions would pollute the atmosphere around my mouth when I was hanging out with friends with similar behavior though as a whole my use of the English language was respectful and acceptable.

My sister Jennifer also spoke with loving respect on all but the rarest of occasions, though my younger brother Lou picked up a few salty words either from me or from Dad who at times spoke with less than a reverent tongue.

My mother like Phyllis never swore nor cursed and was raised well in this regard. Her mother, Generosa was a living saint like individual raised in an orphanage by the "Nuns."

While at River, it was a foregone conclusion that Phyllis and I would be eventually applying to college. College would require a sizable amount of money that in fact I had been saving for over the years, just as my sister had done through her baby-sitting jobs.

Mom being aware of how important money was and having free time on her hands as all four of us children had grown up, decided to take a job at the Higbees Store at Westgate Mall. She worked in the housewares department for over twenty years bringing in much needed funds for a variety of household causes.

In my last two high school years, I worked as a woman's shoe salesman also at Higbee's Westgate Mall. This was not my forte. I couldn't bring to bear the necessary forces required of a persuasive salesman. My sales numbers were never sparkling though I did enjoy the ladies' legs.

While working in the women's shoes department, I met a fascinating young man who was one year my senior in age. He had the same first name as I, which was fascinating since I had never met another Philip. Philip Marquardt from Fairview High School was a cool stud; handsome, self-confident, with a gorgeous girlfriend and a brand-new Chevy 409 convertible, with a 4-speed transmission, 409 horse power, a white top, light green or pastel yellow exterior, dual exhausts, and a white interior.

I couldn't decide which was neater; his girl or his car. In any case this guy was not hurting. To my unexpected surprise, his future though would play into my hands many years later. At the time I'm sure I thought that I would rather have his girl then his future. On the other hand, his Chevy 409 wouldn't have been bad either.

Not doing so well in woman's shoes, I was later transferred to children's shoes where less salesmanship was required though a bit more skill was necessary when it came to fitting the correct sizes. I made a meager amount of money at the time; fifty cents per hour, which was even on the low end for that era. As for my father, he like I was always worried about money and for good reason. Life is always difficult for most people that are not independently wealthy.

As time went a few family issues became apparent. Dad **had a few medical** problems that began to surface. He had increasing wrist and hand pain related to his occupation and was apparently due to carpal tunnel syndrome less recognized in that era when nerve conduction studies were in their infancy. He, on many occasions would mention to mom about his symptoms. His long years of barbering had taken its toll.

His bilateral wrist and hand pain today would have been diagnosed differently than an arthritic condition that he was told that he had.

Dad never exhibited any joint changes so he was clearly misdiagnosed by Dr. N., his internist. He complained of this often and usually relieved the discomfort in the evening with a tumbler or two of rich red Italian wine to help him sleep through the night. Mom often complained about his drinking on the weekends though he never drank excessively during the work week and he never drank to intoxication. Dad was never abusive in any way and I really believe the drinking was intended to reduce his horrible wrist and hand symptoms that today is an easy diagnosis and correctible with surgery.

In the same vein, once as children on Christmas Eve, we were driving home through a major snow fall after visiting the relatives. We were heading south just after turning off Cleveland's Shoreway running parallel to Lake Erie. We began heading west onto Clifton Boulevard when Dad being a bit pickled, lost control on snow- and ice-covered roads while our car turned two or three complete donuts in the east bound lanes. It landed against the opposite curb while other cars flew miraculously by without so much as a whisker of contact. Mom took over from there and of course scolded without mercy you know who. His drinking and driving days were over.

Another area of concern to Dad were the Beetles with their long hair resulting in cultural changes that shocked Dad and the hair cutting industry to its roots. Men began to lengthen their locks to a point that haircuts were relegated to the frequency of oil changes. This of course led to more worry and less income or at least that was the perception by many in the business.

As time went on, Dad began a new career in woman's hair styling though never abandoning his main profession. He went on to study in New York and later at Higbee's Department Store saloon in downtown Cleveland. He was quite the artist and developed a creative way with hair techniques that would be the envy of contemporary hair stylists today. This gave him security and he along with a friend began a hair styling school in Lakewood.

Dad's two businesses always did well and we never went wanting. His business**es** never interfered with his new found love of golf. He and Uncle Jim, cousin Sam's father, played the game about twice a week not only locally but often traveling to Florida in the colder months. He loved the game and kept up with trends in putters and clubs to improve his score. Lessons and driving range visits were not strangers to him. He always leaned in the direction of perfection when it came to most tasks and golf would be no exception. I never saw him play which is heart breaking, since it meant so much to him, but I often noted the glimmer in his eye when he headed off to some local course. It became a way of life but never at the sacrifice of his family or at least I never felt that it did. Mom may have believed otherwise.

Golf is in many ways a reflection of life. They are both beautiful yet ridiculous in so many ways. They are filled with pain and aggravation yet the small successes keep golfers coming back for more. Life and golf are both tantalizing though impossible to perfect regardless of the effort put forth. They both require an ongoing learning process fraught with ups and downs and bewildering choices. Being unpredictable neither golf nor life can be boring. A perfect game of golf though never achievable by the average golfer - or even the pros for that matter - is far easier to play than is living a life of perfection. Golf was never my foray. Life has been more of joy.

During that time of my life Phyllis and I were entering our mid to late teen years and knew that the time was coming for us to begin to make a couple of important life choices. Time has a way of inevitably moving forward with or without us. This change of events would likely not only separate me from the Caravella's but would also for the first time separate us in away as twins.

As youths, we were always a stone's throw away from each other passing back and forth thoughts and ideas as they arose but now this would all change and maybe for the better. We both had to function independently from each other and this is always I suspect an interesting change of events that only twins can truly understand. Twins like no other beings other than triplets have an unusual bond that goes beyond the usual brother-sister or brother-brother or sister-sister thing.

It's different and much stronger and never really changes with time. It is indelible in a way and remains a gift between twins or triplets that is nearly genetic in its expression. Only we can know. The bottom line is that we were both in for a change and change it is. My change came with the influence of my first cousin Roy Koesel who had already transitioned from home to college.

My cousin Roy was matriculating through freshman year at The University of Dayton in computer science. He approached me one day about joining him there and living together with another friend or two in off- campus housing. I took the SAT and ACT, passed with adequate grades and become accepted as a freshman student with a major in chemistry. Why chemistry you may ask.? Well as I have portrayed before, Phyllis and I were introverts in that our social skills took forever to develop in that we had difficulty in associating and becoming good friends with others of our own age group. Some of that may have been the twin thing since we did pretty well on our own and did not need others to expand our horizons or provide the social stimulation that other non-twin children or adolescents required.

In any case Roy was very convincing plus he was a known commodity that I trusted and felt comfortable with. He knew the ropes and his experience and advice would be sound.

So, you guessed it! Dayton was the only school I had applied to. Maybe that was a bit presumptuous at that time though I didn't know better and hadn't received any other advice on the matter. In the 1960's, it was not the norm to apply to a string of colleges or universities as far as I remember. Applications cost money and there was precious little of that to go around.

After my acceptance to UD, my cousin Roy took me on a tour of the campus after arriving in Dayton. He drove me around the grounds or campus as he put it and it was a bit depressing. All I could see was huge buildings that appeared dark and somewhat abandoned in a way. There was little if any sign of life. "Well, what do think Phil," Roy questioned. "Well, it seems a bit different than I had imagined. I thought there would be more grass. It seems odd." I was a bit dumbfounded because I had expected something else. "Okay Phil, the jokes over. This is the NCR (National Cash Register) complex and not the university. We always pull this stunt driving new students around the factory grounds rather than the university to throw them into a bit of an uproar."

He then drove me to the real campus nearby and it was quite a relief to see what seemed more appropriate with grassy knolls and architecturally and artistically designed buildings for the different schools of engineering, science, mathematics, social sciences and the rest. They were impressive and exciting to see. NCR they were not. Quite a joke as I think back. It wouldn't be long before the action started.

Freshman year would begin with an orientation, a stack of books, and a blue beanie with red UD letters across the front. We would be asked to learn and sing the UD fight song by upper class-men whenever the whim occurred to them. This would last until homecoming. Fortunately, no one ever asked me to perform and I was happy to ditch the beanie when the time, came though it was a tradition that should have survived because it gave us a feeling of belonging. After homecoming I was one of them.

Living in off campus housing on Brown Street in Dayton, Ohio was interesting, affordable, and convenient. I shared a bedroom with my buddy Joe Quinn; a mathematics major. Joe was brilliant, not exactly charismatic, though a gem in many ways.

My other roommates included my cousin Roy Koesel and his best friend, Richard Knecht, who shared the other room of the apartment. We all got along well taking advantage of on campus meal tickets, and strolling to campus for dinner on a daily basis. I will never forget the Thursday special; "mystery meat." It was some sort of hammered beef steak, cooked well and smothered in gravy. I liked it and it liked me. Eating at the cafeteria added a few pounds. But I will tell you I like everything when it comes to food. Fussy I have never been, and everything with rare exceptions appeals to my taste buds. Beer was not one of them. Dayton is a beer drinking school but so are most college campuses. I never became very acquainted with the brews that many other classmates enjoyed.

The year I started as a freshman, the first girl's women's dorm Mary crest, opened on campus allowing for the fairer sex to have a reasonable presence at UD. I never saw so many beautiful girls in one place in my life. Maybe my social life would take on new meaning?

A new field house opened that fall on UD's campus. The Flyers Club, named after the Dayton Flyers sports teams was a great place to meet coeds. The Club became known for serving legally available watered down 3. 2percent alcohol laced beer. Being lower in alcohol content than standard beer, it was cheap, well-tolerated, and less likely to overwhelm the average college student.

Along with the beer, playing wonderful music of the era, and offering opportunities to mingle with coeds was the draw attracting everyone there and to each other. It was the mingling that was the problem for me. Not being much of a dancer and lacking self-confidence made it difficult for me to blend in and mix it up. That was because I was more mixed up than was the actual situation. Not really learning how to dance or even how to fake it put me on the sidelines during the playing of "fast dances" of the time.

By the time the slow dances came around, most of the babes were picked over and they didn't want to dance slow dances anyway. Rejection by women, like paying taxes, was just as painful and became the norm once again.

My social life remained a shambles. My grades were not suffering since I had plenty of time on my hands to study.

ROTC (Reserve Officer Training Corps) was mandatory for freshman male students and I took to it with relish. Women still were not permitted to participate in ROTC. You have to remember this was the 1960's. Scoring well with my ROTC grades and doing well on the drill field allowed me to excel becoming one of the top two cadets to finish sophomore year. Thus, I had the option to go into Advanced ROTC but mistakenly passed on that because it would have led to a direct commission as a second lieutenant into the US Army upon graduation.

Now that was not a bad thing but once again, I had little understanding of the significance of that adventure and thus I did not pursue it. Also, as I recall, the Vietnam War was in full swing and that may have also been a deterrent to me since I had other ideas about my future that did not include fighting a war.

Freshman year went well and my chemistry professor and pre-med director, Dr. Carl Michaelis convinced me to switch to pre-med. I made the switch and my courses were going well except for American history in my junior year taught by a Marianist Brother. His class was a bit different in that all tests were essays. They explored the scope of time rather than specific data. Being used to memorizing dates, names, and trivia as opposed to theoretical historical hypothesis led me down a road of confusion when it came to test time. As a result, I did very poorly on the first two of four tests for the course. I knew that if I got a D or even a C for the course I would not be going to medical school. I met with Brother and he gave me some insight on how to do better on his tests. Pulling two as on the final tests gave me a B for the course and that was that.

Going to medical school would require not only good grades but also money; lots of it. I knew I had to find a more lucrative line of work other than selling shoes during summers off.

My summers became more interesting as well as lucrative when one day I found in the Cleveland *Plain Dealer* a summer job opportunity to work for Nabisco (The National Biscuit Company) filling in for salesmen that were on vacations for the summer. The plan involved working as a salesman for Nabisco for two-week stints going sooner or later into every grocery store, small or large, from West 25th street in Cleveland, west to Vermillion, south to Grafton and eventually all parts in between.

My duties included ordering cookies, crackers, and biscuits for the stores, stocking the shelves, and clearing the back rooms out of overstock, as much as possible. I learned quickly and became very efficient, often starting at my first store at 7:00 AM and finishing a day's work by 3:00 PM. I was sometimes ahead of the Nabisco delivery truck, which would then put me a bit behind in my hopes of finishing as early as possible.

At large stores I shelved hundreds of boxes of Oreos, Fig Newton's, Premium Crackers, and every product Nabisco made. My boss who was a fairly good guy wanted me to spend more time rubbing shoulders with the store managers which I rarely did. I tended to shun the thought, thinking it was not my responsibility but the responsibility of the full-time salesman who really owned the route.

Besides, who am I to press the store manager to buy more products? Due to my lingering insecurities stemming back from childhood I remained uncomfortable when it came to small talk since store managers were always hands on folks and had little time to kibitz. If it meant getting an extra display or an end cap on a store aisle, I would go for it. I did the best I could in "snoozing" the big boys if I thought it would better my cause and the cause of Nabisco.

Being good at the job, the boss tolerated my lack of palm greasing and gave me a bye. I was rehired each summer. Eventually my brother Lou would take over for me when the time came for moving on.

During the early 1960's, my mother's father, Luciano Franzolino would pass away from liver cancer. He was a kindly gentleman that would be missed by my parents but a man that I would never truly know other than what I was told by others since I lacked a grasp of Italian. He was quiet with a good sense of humor and new the meaning of a good day's work. He liked to smoke cigars which must have played a role in his demise, since he likely died of metastatic liver cancer rather than suffering from a primary tumor originating in his liver.

Grandpa was a ton of fun. In his living room he often sat in his own chair reading the Plain Dealer while in a fun way guarding the passage to the front door. It was not possible to reach the front of the home without passing good old granddad. Luciano got a kick out of kicking us in our little behinds as we walked by; chuckling each time he gently struck his target in a good-natured way. He turned this ritual into a science or better yet, a sport rarely missing his target and always laughing heartily each time he struck pay dirt. Our field ball kickers should be so good since he had to kick a moving target and rarely missed. One day his kick would no longer be felt as he grew sicklier though he would leave a memorable legacy that mom would later reveal to me.

In the "old days" women became secretaries, teachers, nurses, or airline "stewardesses. " Phyllis was very hard working, and doing very well in her studies.

She took herself very seriously, though occasionally took time to have some fun. At Dyke she was a premier student mastering the skills of shorthand and typing. Shorthand was a language of its own, a lost art but remarkable for what it could do before the days of voice recorders, dictation equipment and now computers.

Phyllis could set her typewriter keys on fire and along with her other skills, upon graduation, she found work as an executive secretary for a large company in the Cleveland area. My twin sister was doing well in her new line of work as a private secretary finishing at Dyke College before I had graduated from Dayton. As fate and timing would have it, Phyllis would be the first Caravella to graduate from college.

After changing majors at UD and coming a bit late to the party, I was behind in two premed courses and took summer school after freshman year to catch up. One summer was spent at Case Western Reserve University studying the subject of quantitative analysis. This course required precise measurements of "unknowns" and was difficult at best. During the course, I had to work on three or four determinations that required many hours of lab work. A determination was referred to as an unknown substance that was assigned to each student. During the course of one or two weeks, we would struggle to identify through extensive laboratory testing, the makeup of our specific substance or "unknown" as it was referred to. The course study was difficult and the lab was worse with many hours dragging on into the day in hot non-air-conditioned labs.

That class nearly did me in. I made a nearly tragic error in one determination but figured it out before I was doomed. During a one-week lab determination I was supposed to use an "ash-less" filter paper that would totally disintegrate when baked under high temperatures in an intensely hot oven, leaving only the final chemical. The final residual substance had to weigh within two to three decimal points of the intended final mass to receive a passing grade.

Unfortunately, by I choosing the wrong filter paper, the residual ashes would not disintegrate, increasing the weight of the final product. Recognizing this error late in the process, did not allow enough time to repeat the entire weeks work since the course was only about six weeks long to begin with. I decided to bake a piece of regular filter paper of the exact same form in a laboratory oven until it was only ashes. I then weighed the residual material and subtracted its weight from my final product. I received a C for the determination and a C for the course. That would be my only C grade as an undergrad. One more C and I would remain a chemistry student and not be going to med school.

The following summer, I took comparative anatomy at John Carroll University and received an A grade which bailed me out of trouble. Dissecting a small shark, a cat, and lastly a small pig during the course was fascinating though not exactly my idea of fun. Not having a car, I rode several buses from River each day to get to John Carroll on the East side of town. The cat was carried back and forth in a see-through plastic bag. It carried a strong formaldehyde odor and drew more than its share of attention. People riding next to me on the bus, being often crowded together, must have thought I was a serial cat killer at best or a lunatic at worst. They seemed to keep their distance.

When it came to the shark it was another matter. I still remember dissecting the inner ear ossicles of the shark. The trick was to remove the semi-circular canals of the shark intact which I was able to accomplish. It was a learning experience that most closely approximated sort of what I may be doing in the future.

My grades after three years at UD were not remarkable but reasonably competitive and hopefully good enough for me to be accepted into medical school, a dream that was never contemplated upon my admission to Dayton.

During Phyllis's adventures in college, I was patiently waiting to see how my future would unfold. Mom and Dad were very supportive and were proud of my efforts and hoped that I would succeed, though the competition to get into medical school was keen then as it is now and available positions were relatively meager.

During my first two years at the university, I was also interested in the military and joined a special group of ROTC cadets known as the Counter Insurgents, a take-off on the Army's Special Forces. ROTC was mandatory for freshman and sophomore men. Being a member of the Counter Insurgents, I was able to train with the U. S. Army Rangers, Special Forces, and Green Berets. US Marines of the era, jokingly referred to us with our beanies, as the "The beanie boys".

Our team took part in a number of two-three day training sessions, learning repelling, combat skills, and other survival skills. My first introduction into the military would leave me with lasting impressions. The Marines or the "Donald Duck Boys" were a well-trained bunch and remain so but no tougher than the Green Berets.

The most memorable training event was a cold snowy weekend toting rifles, back packs, sleeping bags, portable two-way radios, and all the gear necessary to defeat an "enemy force" tracking our every move. The nights were long, cold, and cautious. No smoking at night was permitted to avoid giving up our positions.

At about 1:00AM on the first night someone lit up and we took all kinds of small arms fire and machine gun fire from a nearby ridge. It sounded quite impressive but they were only blanks. The CO wasn't impressed and laid into us for being so stupid. It was so cold the second day that my feet were nearly frozen. During daylight a couple of us made a small fire and toasted our toes and boots to warm up. This didn't go well, when being too close to the fire, the end of my right boot caught fire. I put it out before things got too hot. The commanding officer did not go for that brilliant maneuver either.

During Phyllis's adventures in college, I was patiently waiting to see how my future would unfold. Mom and Dad were very supportive and were proud of my efforts and hoped that I would succeed, though the competition to get into medical school was keen then as it is now and available positions were relatively meager.

My cousin Dolores having pity for me and also a fellow student at UD introduced me to one of her roommates. Though she was sweet, pleasant, and reasonably attractive she did not do much for me and the chemical reactions simply were not there. That relationship was brief and not noteworthy in any way.

My experiences in kissing women were so limited. Ok I'm lying. Romantic dealings with members of the opposite sex for me were rare enough that any and all of them was always a worthwhile experience; well, most of them.

After Dolores's friend, I parted ways and somehow met Sue early my senior year and we dated for most of it. She was a first-grade school teacher who very fairly attractive and sported a fantastic figure. She possessed as I would soon discover an unending need to be kissed incessantly. During these escapades, not a shred of any other type of touching was tolerable to her apparently again related to the teachings of the good Nuns she had become educated by. Her large D cup breasts fitted nicely into numerous low-cut dresses she wore on too many occasions, considering she wasn't willing to share her attributes and God given gifts with me. She had a perfect figure with a magnificent waist line and amazing long legs to go with the entire package. She was intelligent and what few conversations occurred between kissing extravaganzas were laced with clever thoughts and ideas. She was a sharp lady.

Sue was also a staunch Catholic and no touching of even the most benign type was acceptable regardless of the passion created with the most extreme forms of kissing she enjoyed showering upon me. Kissing she liked. Nothing else worked for her. Anytime one of my hands drifted into questionable territory, she wasted no time in moving it to less provocative areas. This form of no fondling torture was more than what most mortal men could endure under the circumstances and began to lead me towards braking off the relationship. Marriage seemed to be what was on her mind but not mine, especially considering the emotional and physical torture I would have to endure long before intimacy would be allowed.

Sue invited me to her parent's home for a weekend. It was large and impressive with fine furnishings. Her father was quite wealthy making his money raising pullets for resale. These are small chickens that would be sold later as I recall for egg laying purposes. He liked my politeness and ability to converse with him.

Feeling good about a future long-term relationship with his daughter he made me an offer I could refuse. Before the weekend had ended, he and I had a nice little chat about my future and hers when he sorts of implied that should his daughter and I develop a permanent bond he would be in a position to pay for my medical schooling. Not feeling like beholding to anyone, this for many would be an offer to good to refuse but for me it was like the kiss of death. After that conversation I never felt like dating her again, coupled with the reality that my time for serious bonding had yet to arrive. It was sort of a shame because she was overall very fine in every way. I never saw her again nor did I ever look back.

The good news if there was any, was that I was becoming more comfortable with dating but even more comfortable with looking forward to going to medical school if the stars and moons aligned appropriately.

My grades held up well during the first two years and I was offered an opportunity to join Alpha Epsilon Delta, the pre-med honor society. It was quite an honor and I wore the black sport coat with the society's emblem with pride to many functions. My mentor, Dr. Carl Michaelis, guided me through the process of course preparation and preparing for post-graduate work. My grades continued to hold up well enough that I took the MCAT (medical college admission test) exam and passed.

Throughout my university years I had worked hard and was eventually able to forward applications to medical schools. I knew of no physicians to ask for help and likewise my parents were unskilled in any of these un-chartered waters.

A friend and Marianist Brother at UD suggested that I look into Saint Louis University School of Medicine. A few other inquiries as well, led me in the direction of Saint Louis University, The Ohio State University, and the University of Cincinnati. They all had reputable schools of medicine. Not feeling overly confident I decided that I would accept the first offer if any at all would come my way.

Before any offers were forthcoming however, the interview process had begun. I hopped on my first ever airplane flight leaving out of Dayton, Ohio and headed to St. Louis, Missouri. I dressed in a sport coat with tie and a white shirt as was customary of the day. This flight was bizarre to begin with in that it was on a commercial airliner without any passengers. Upon my arrival at the airport and checking in at the gate I learned that I would be the sole passenger; the only one. Can you believe it; the only one. The aircraft was large even by 1960's standards so apparently other cargo was being carried to offset the deficiency of passengers or possibly cancellation policies were too strict to overcome in that era.

The captain of the aircraft approached me and said, "You will have to sit in the back of the plane with the stewardesses, to maintain proper aircraft weight distribution." He winked at me casually as he pointed to the three attendants on board for the flight. I thought this is going to be really tough. How will I get through it? In the early era of commercial flying only the most glamorous women were selected as flight attendants then referred to as stewardesses. They were always beautiful with sensual figures, and cool personalities.

We all sat together in the very rear of the plane and we shared lifetime adventures. I told them of my upcoming interview and they told me of their interesting sagas as well.

The flight went smoothly though being caught up in my own nerve-wracking interview the next day, being shy, and lacking confidence, I failed to acquire any phone numbers still having major difficulties in being comfortable with the opposite sex. Most men knowing of this error in judgment would have had me ostracized from the male persuasion and they would have been correct in doing so. I mean enough is enough with this shyness rubbish. "Get a life" Dingbat!!!

Arriving in a timely fashion at the Saint Louis airport I gathered my grip and took a cab to the hotel for the evening while awaiting my morning interviews. After arriving bright and early at the medical school on South Grand Boulevard I found the Dean's office and introduced myself. I was given a tour of the Medical School by an assistant and was informed that it was the very first medical school established west of the Mississippi. It was a grand old lady with old style tall windows, old-fashioned wood trimmed hallways, and a unique flavor of education as it existed in the present as well as in the 1850's and was over one hundred years old at the time. Saint Louis University is a Jesuit institution of the Catholic Faith.

After the tour and returning to the Dean's office I was briefly introduced to the Dean of the School of Medicine and then I was directed across the street to the University's psychiatric hospital of all places to be interviewed by a psychiatrist. He was a gem of a man and made me feel comfortable and at home almost immediately. We chatted for quite a while about my thoughts, my aspirations, and my background. After a while I learned that it would be my only interview. This seemed a bit odd but time was precious and I guess they felt that was all that was needed to finish me off. Not feeling uncomfortable with the process though I was feeling a bit unnerved by the brevity of it, I returned to Dayton to finish my last year and to await my fate.

I would also be interviewed by Ohio State but never by Cincinnati as I recall. The more I thought about the situation as time went on, the more concerned and the less comfortable I felt about my future. The waiting game becomes nerve wracking. Finishing the year and graduating with a Bachelor of Science Degree in Pre-medical education, I returned home to begin working for the summer and awaiting my fate. If this didn't work then what the heck would be next. What good is a degree with a major in pre-medical studies and nowhere to go?

One warm day, I was working out in the back yard and unknown to me was that a postman had just arrived at our home. My mother came to the door and was looking through the mail and saw a letter addressed to me from Saint Louis University. It took her breath away knowing this was what we had been waiting for so long. She ran outside to the back yard screaming for me and I was frightened that something terrible had happened. She yelled, "It's here, it's here, it's finally here. Philip comes over here. " Running over and looking up she handed me the letter addressed:

Mr. Philip J. Caravella

2785 Gasser Boulevard

Rocky River, Ohio, 44116

I saw the name and crest of the university on the upper left corner of the white envelope. I did but did not want to open it fearing the worst. It was exciting but horrible at the same time. I opened the letter and it read:

December 30, 1965

"Dear Mr. Caravella:

It is a pleasure for me to inform you, on behalf of the Admissions Committee of Saint Louis University School of Medicine, you have been accepted as a member of the class which will enter our Medical School in September 1966...."

I blurted out, "Mom, I can't believe it."

The rest of the letter was a blur and not memorable. I'm sure it offered a few important details, like whether or not I would need a tutor but the meat of it was in the first sentence.

Our wildest dreams had been answered. We immediately called my father at the barber shop, "Louie this is Ad. I have a surprise for you. Philip has been accepted into medical school at Saint Louis University. Can you believe it. " There was a pause and we heard Dad yell out. "My son is going to medical school. I can't believe it. My son is going to medical school. " You never saw a prouder American.

Coming from Sicily, working hard as a barber, his wife toiling at his side and if all went well, they would have a physician in the family. This was beyond anything they could have ever hoped for. It was more than they could believe. An Italian immigrant would have his first-born child going to medical school in America. It doesn't get better. It was more delightful than anything they had ever known as parents other than the birth of their other treasures. At least that was the feeling I had gathered.

This is what it was all about. This is what every parent hopes for; to have a child reach a dream that before was not thinkable, barely reachable if not even realistically tenable for most, much less an immigrant's son. In the past college seemed to me to be a leap of faith. Medical school would have never dawned on me during my high school career or even after. College in the 1960's for most was a pipe dream, that is unless you were from "River."

That very day I sent a letter to Saint Louis University School of Medicine excepting the position. There was no second thought. There was no hesitation. There was no reason to wait for any other response from Ohio State or Cincinnati. Saint Louis University was in my mind the best, because I knew of another physician that had graduated from there and besides, it was a Jesuit school. What could be better?

Rocky River Schools had done their job as my parents had hoped. Their plan had worked, as far reaching as it seemed, back in 1949 when they discover Rocky River and its fabulous school system. To this day, the Rocky River Public School System is ranked number three in the state of Ohio, higher than most private schools.

All of the stars had come together. Now it was my responsibility to make their dreams a success and take it to the next level. I knew medical school would be difficult but I felt I was up to the task. Mom was super excited but also knew this would present a challenge; a financial one. She knew we would find a way no matter what it took. There is always away when it came to something like this. She had always been frugal by counting every penny and saving every nickel. She always made a list of every purchase before going to a store and never deviated from it. For her impulse buying was an unknown. For Dad it was a bit different but not by much. Mom saw to that.

Mom also new in the back of her mind, that there was a special surprise awaiting me soon. A surprise she never mentions to anyone; a surprise of unusual significance but one never to be suspected by me or any other family member.

During these challenging years my twin was engrossed in a changing job market and varying opportunities of her own. She first worked for a brokerage firm in Cleveland that was bought out by a competitor and her job was consolidated. Being so good at her work, she had no problem finding a similar job with Cleveland's Union Carbide. As fate would have it, after two years her boss was transferred and Phyllis was back on the street again. During this same period, my first cousin Delores Keisel, also a student at UD graduated after finishing her studies as a secretary/office assistant.

During a job fair at Dayton, the CIA was recruiting for secretaries to serve in positions in Washington D. C. Dolores being quite persuasive talked reluctant Phyllis into leaving Cleveland and heading off to Washington.

After arriving in Washington, they were tested by "The Agency". Phyllis scored a perfect on typing and shorthand resulting in an immediate offer. Dolores doing well, as well, was also offered a position. Passing exhaustive security clearances, physical exams, polygraph tests, psychiatric evaluations, and extensive background checks by the F. B. I., they were given positions with "the government" working at CIA headquarters in Langley, Virginia. Being cleared at the highest levels they would become knowledgeable about some of our countries most important secrets.

Their new jobs proved to be interesting and again a topic of conversation for years to come. Phyllis began her government career by working for one of the heavyweights, the Assistant Director of the agency and thus required a top security clearance. She carried a special phone number to be used in time of any emergency if she felt her safety was threatened. Using this number would bring on the full force of special agents in her vicinity to help her in time of need though the phone number was never required.

She loved the agency but could never, for security reasons, reveal to others whom she worked for. When asked what she did her response was always, "I work for the government. " Most people in her circles knew this meant she was with the CIA. They would not nor would others pursue the issue knowing that no further information would be garnered.

Dolores and Phyllis would never speak of the secrets they held. Becoming trusted in the service of our country, they were later offered high level positions in the foreign-service. Phyllis, quite concerned about leaving the U. S. decided not to accept. In consultation with Dad, he advised that she leave "the government" and return to Cleveland. She would later regret this move but on the other hand she met an agent that she would later marry.

While at the agency she met her soon to be husband Paul Petrus, a Special Agent with the CIA. We all knew what a Special Agent was. Paul was a big man soaring well into the 6'2" + range. He packed a side arm as most agents do but never spoke of his work. Prior to his time with the CIA, he had been with the FBI for a number of years. Before that, he was with the U. S. Army's special intelligence arm serving in Alaska early in the cold war.

Even more interesting was the fact that before Paul worked for the government, he had spent time in the seminary planning to become a priest. He was quite pious and often went to church sometimes daily and of course weekly and more often during church holidays. He had a great sense of humor and could take a joke better than I and better than most others. There was no end to the teasing Paul and I got into over the years. He was a character and strong in many ways. As time went on of course, his mind was provoked by other needs. Paul was well educated, opinionated, but honest in his dealings with others.

Ironically, like Debbie's father, he was the product of a Pennsylvania coal miner, a fine mother, and several siblings. For unexplained reasons, his family ties with his siblings always remained distant.

None of his siblings were close and visits by them were nearly nonexistent. They all apparently struggled as children trying to make ends meet by helping their parents. Life during his childhood years was certainly more difficult than he had related to me over the decades that I knew him. Paul would marry but became a widower early in life. He had no children with his first marriage. Later in life Paul would struggle with poor health, but being very pious and kind he always wore a smile on his handsome face until the very end.

When my twin and Paul first met, he was very polite, and swept Phyllis off her feet. She was not used to such special attention by most men and soon they were engaged.

Paul was "offered" an opportunity to go to Europe as a special agent more than likely in a subversive way. It was about his turn to take a tumble in the barrel. This period was during the height of the "cold war" and his duties would have involved intrigue, special missions, and the like. With his impending marriage, he decided to bow out and leave the CIA and its intrigue to others.

After moving to Cleveland, Paul Sr., suffered a misfire or two in the job arena before becoming an insurance agent with Sears Allstate. Hey once an agent, always an agent. They married, went on a nice honeymoon, bought a house in Bay Village, of all places, and settled down waiting for nature to take its course.

Phyllis during this period, returned to the work force but in a much different career. She began a six-year work program with the Glidden Paint Company of Cleveland. During her tenure at Glidden, she and our family home became an important part of a research project conducted by the paint products division. Our bungalow on Gasser Boulevard had a large wood covered second floor peak overhanging the front left side of our home. It was due for a paint job. Glidden asked Phyllis and mom if they could test a new paint they had just developed. The officers of the company offered to provide this new paint, and they would apply it personally to our home as a test application to study its characteristics and wear-ability, at no cost to my parents.

This proved to be a good idea. After countless years, the Glidden paint failed to fade or wear appreciably. If anything, it turned out to be too good and was never marketed. I also believe the paint may have been a bit more difficult to apply than most paints, likely making it very durable but less marketable. This paint could have been applied to the nose cone of the space shuttle and it would have outlasted the tiles on re-entry. It became a joke amongst us family members over time, in that the house never had to be repainted. After several decades, the paint may have started showing some powder like aging, though no flaking or pealing.

My cousin Sam, being in the aluminum siding business offered to cover the white peak at his cost, and that was pretty much the end of the paint saga, though I suspect if the siding were removed, nearly perfect Glidden Paint would still be there.

The paint was never brought to market and may have, being of such high quality, compromised the company's ability to survive in a market that depends on occasional repainting most surfaces.

Our home and house were surviving nicely and the next order of business was in my way of thinking, how would my future move forward. The day finally arrived for graduation and I received a Bachelor of Science degree in Pre-medical Studies at the University of Dayton. My family members were in attendance and it was a great day just as it had been for Phyllis upon her graduation from Dyke College in Cleveland.

We traveled back to Cleveland and shortly after arrival my parents presented a very special gift that was amazing. It had been provided for by the inheritance left to mother from her father. Luciano would have been proud of my mother's generosity. Sitting in our driveway was a brand new 1966 fire-engine red Plymouth Barracuda. It had a black interior, a 283 cubic inch V-8, and four-on-the-floor tranny. To say that I was blown away would have been an understatement. Mom said to me, "You will need this in Saint Louis. " It was my first car. What a way to start my new career. Wow!!! She was fantastic and so thrilled to gift the car to me.

My brother Lou had yet to enter high school at this time being five years younger than I. He felt good about what I had accomplished and was taking notes. My sister Jennifer was just a few years old at the time but knew how important these moments were as well. Moving on to medical school would even distance me further from the family but not in my heart. We were close and would remain so forever.

At the end of the day, all four of us siblings wound up in the field of health care and have made a difference in helping others. Being the oldest (by a few minutes) I became a family physician and have practiced in the field in many different ways.

Atte height of my career, I became the first Section Chief of Family Medicine at the Cleveland Clinic's Westlake facility. In fact, the new department of Family Medicine at "the Clinic" was initially placed under the auspices of the Department of Internal Medicine. Later on in years it would become its own entity.

As time went on, Lou would graduate from Saint Louis University and then he became an ophthalmology resident in training for many years until he graduated and opened up his own medical office in the field of ophthalmology of course, you guessed it, near Rocky River. Louis would become extremely well versed in the field and was known to all local physicians as one of the best in his field. Later on, Lou would become very well known to the Cleveland Clinic and would become a leader as well, within the organization.

After many other jobs, Phyllis ultimately became trained and educated as an ophthalmology technologist and worked with my brother Lou for a very long career. She and Paul would go on to have two wonderful children, Paul David and Elizabeth. Paul David became a New York, Manhattan, defense attorney (and do those folks in New York need that) while his well-educated sister became an educator in her own right, making her mark in the school systems of Seattle.

Louis went on to become quite accomplished as an eye surgeon and an innovator in his field of choice. His brilliant surgical procedures remain a goal of many current specialists in the field. He has four amazing children and an entire raft of grandchildren.

Jennifer my youngest sister, became an RN working at Fairview Hospital Medical Center, Cleveland, Ohio, for her entire career. She has two amazing children that are very successful in their fields of work. Fairview Hospital also eventually became a Cleveland Clinic facility. Thus, it was interesting that over time all four of us worked for the Cleveland Clinic at one time or another.

Dealing with the care of patients is an honor and a privilege whether you serve as a professional or as a caregiver. It is one of the highest callings anyone could hope for. As you all know, the corona virus pandemic has required deep sacrifices by members of the health care field and when it's all over, if it is ever all over, the corona virus may recur again in some other deadly form. Health care providers are a special breed, going into their profession with their eyes wide open and yet not deterred by risks that many others would shy away from.

My wonderful children include Philip Louis as an accomplished systems analyst with an entire career of over forty years with Disney in California. He is married to a wonderful and beautiful wife, Kayo, of Japanese descent. They gifted to the family our first and amazing grandchild Emma. She is such a sweetheart just like her mother. Phil and family live in the Burbank area of California. Emma is my first grandchild and she is very special to me in so many ways. I am looking forward to seeing her soon.

My eldest daughter Kimberly Anne is married to her husband Scott of restaurant management fame and they have two fantastic children a little daughter Parker and her brother Dylan. Kimberly is a wonderful mother and house wife enjoying every minute of her work. They live in the Loa Angeles area.

Suzanne Karen a graphic designer and my youngest is married to Kevin an industrious gentleman with a love of children. They have presented to our family an amazing sweetheart of a granddaughter who is as cute as can be, Lennon. And as another fantastic surprise, we now have Chase, another wonderful grandson.

Our family is rounded out by Debbie's son Alec, a blond-haired wonder who is creating new and interesting strains of marijuana that will be coming to market in Colorado likely by the time this book is print. He has a gift when it comes to knowing how to develop, raise, and create new strains of the plant. Being in Colorado has been a great help to him as he progresses in the field.

The history and the circumstances we live reflect the brunt of our existence and thus we are the products of fate and family even more than we are the benefits of education and effort. It has been proven that hard work and timing are more associated with fortune than any other factors. If you're waiting for good luck to help you out, you may have a long wait.

We are not alone. I as am you, are our families and acquaintances recycled into a new format. Many of the great have little to cheer about for their successes, often evolved from the gifts of their parents. Many of us are not lucky enough to inherit a nickel from our parents. What we inherit and learn about hopefully is a great work ethic.

Try to be as loving and as perfect as a good dog. Though few if any of us can reach the dog level of perfection. We are often selfish. A dog is selfless (except when eating - keep your distance! Hey nothing is perfect).

In the final analysis, this story is about how people from a distant country were able to come to America to discover, live, enjoy, and exemplify what makes America great. America is great due to the love, ingenuity, skill, and hard work of its citizens. America represents the beauty and strength of generations of people that never took the easy way out. America represents the ideals and the best of the best people ever assembled in one area of the earth.

America has no peers when one looks at the big picture, or even at the little one. Some say there are other countries - a few northern European countries where their homogenous population is statistically more content and happier. Of course, that's likely but now we're comparing apples to oranges, a typical trick of many statisticians. It brings up the point again about statistics. "There are lies, damn lies, and there are statistics. " You see, few if any countries have the full spectrum of all races and nationalities that America engenders in its citizens. That is what makes America so glorious, strong, diverse, respected, and the place that most people wish to live.

I don't know of anyone from my past or present that has ever left America, has ever considered leaving, and did not return. Sure, because of American's diversity there will always be differences and different levels of what can be achieved by some or even by many.

Though most successful achievements are governed not by a person's race or nationality, but by their own abilities, drive, and desires. Many will make excuses for why they are not successful. Many complain about everything from soup to nuts.

Of course, education and many other variables play a role but at least in America most will have a chance, as small as it may be, to become successful regardless of how one's beginnings began. Sure, many have struggled that others will never understand nor care to. However, many who have had struggles are able to rise above the furor and find a place for themselves and their families to move above and beyond the masses.

"The harder you work, the luckier you get.," as my father Louis Caravella said to me on many occasions.

America is not a free ride. The harder you ride American, the greater your ride will be. America represents hope and a future for all of those who try their best to overcome adversity. Most successful people know what I am talking about. There are some men and women born into a wealthy and privileged family. So be it. The rest of us who become successful, have a greater love and story to relate to othermother we made it.

Americans the Beautiful

We are beautiful Americans. Americans the beautiful are the core of what makes America great. It is not about the mountains, rivers, lakes, slopes, beaches, desserts, or any other God made terrain, though they certainly count. America is great because it is composed of many of God's greatest creations in the form of men and women who have risen to the occasion and are proud of their lives and what they stand for.

Are you a beautiful American? I bet you are! Americans the beautiful are everywhere. Look around your neighborhood, workplace, school, and family: There they are! Say hello!

Finding a great American soulmate to fulfill our wonderful lives is not without challenges, as most of you already know.

As time went on, I eventually found my true love; a woman that loves me more than anyone has ever loved me.

Debbie is from Pittsburg; a strong minded, tough, unyielding group of determined Americans who live a life devoted to a cause, a challenge, a belief, and a worship that is God like when it comes to their city. People from Pittsburg stand together and will not be pushed aside. If you put them in a corner, and you had better not, they will "Go Pittsburg on you". The backbone of "the Steelers" is as tough as they get. The Steelers, likely the best football team ever fielded over time, has a winning ethic not unlike America. Pittsburg is full of grit, full of history, full of those who know how to win.

Pittsburg is a microcosm of what makes America great. Now Debbie being born and raised in the "Steel City" fits the mold of a determined, tough minded, person who does not like to be crossed. However, she will love you like none other, and she will always have your back.

Debbie is a Caravella. She is a gift for which I am thankful for now and forever. Debbie and I met on the internet dating site, "Plenty of Fish". Her picture was gorgeous (see the front cover of this book) but not as much, as she is in real life. A picture is one thing but the real thing is way beyond in beauty, character, life, form, and thought.

If Debbie is your friend and you do not cross her, she can be counted on for life. Debbie is bullheaded but negotiable. Debbie is a beautiful American.

My brother Lou is equally as bullheaded yet negotiable as well. Debbie and Lou are not cut from the same cloth nor the same mold. But then none of us are. We are as individual as oil and water yet in a way, we Caravella's are all the same.

We believe in America, in values, in love; in each other. America wins because we are a unified force that will achieve its place in society and in all corners of the earth. In so doing other peoples throughout the world will hope to obtain similar freedoms and a comfortable life. We are tough, we are free, and we cannot be overcome by any outside force. That is because we Americans are the best God has to offer. We Believe. We fight for what is right. We are a snapshot for

Americans the Beautiful

others on this great planet to emulate and see what is achievable. I say to the outside world. Do not bite us!

Caravella's are Americans true to our heritage and that is what also makes America great; our heritage. America is beauty, power, and forward thinking. We always look beyond and deeply into what America can become.

Where are your wonderful people heading? I hope it is in the same direction with America and with all great Americans.

In this country the streets are made of gold. The gold is represented by the opportunities afforded to the finest people that have ever existed anywhere. The gold of America is malleable into many forms of people who love, cherish progress, adventure, and have no limits. Our gold is vested in our history, our natural resources, but primarily in a determined people that cannot and will not be passed by, by history.

We are Americans. We are the beautiful.

Younas well, my friend, are a beautiful American.

You are precious and valuable in your own way.

AND; when you eventually pass on and into heaven God will then say to you:

"You're an American. You have a higher responsibility here than others that have not been afforded your opportunities. I expect you to pull your own weight and then some. Welcome home".

The following poem was written by yours truly for my wife Debra and tells the story of how we met at the bottom of a tall staircase rising up from the beach, to the front door of a well-known watering hole, Drunken Jack's, in Myrtle Beach, South Carolina, on one fine Friday evening at 7:00 PM nearly precisely on the dot (It was the only time Debbie was on time for anything. LOL).

At the exact moment we met, she approached me for the very first time and without saying a single word, she passionately placed her arms around my shoulders, and kissed my lips while holding me as close to her as she possibly could. At that exact moment in time, we bonded forever.

Debbie and I have talked about this many times over the years and she said it was not planned and was completely spontaneous on her part. She cannot explain it, other than to say, "It just happened". I think it took her by surprise as well. She does not know what came over her! We have bonded for life.

I believe *God is what came over us.*

A poem written for both Debbie and I.

THE DEBBIE THAT I KNOW

On the cell she spoke to he.

Then crossed the beach to welcome me.

Her long blond hair stroked by the wind.

Blue eyes were there to welcome him.

She kissed his lips without a word.

We bonded there before the Lord.

Her *beauty* formed from *God's own hand*.

A gift from her to her loving man.

A living gift to be desired.

Between us two our love is sired.

And after life they'll always be.

A loving bond: Eternity!

Eternity.

Written by her loving husband, Philip.

Philip Caravella, MD, FAAFP, Lt. Col., US Army (Ret.)

Americans the Beautiful

The following notes are from members of the Caravella family that are pertinent to this book in demonstrating the success of the Caravella family and likely the future success of our children and grandchildren.

Submission by my *Twin Sister Phyllis Caravella Petrus.*

My wonderful Husband Paul David Petrus died November 3, 2002. He was a gentleman and an amazing father as proven by his intelligent and gifted children; Elizabeth and Paul David, Jr.

He was awarded a Bachelor of Commercial Science (BCS) Degree from Southeastern University, Washington, D. C. and he was an accounting major,1959; He also attended St. John's Seminary, Boston, Mass., and received a B. A. Education, Philosophy major, 1965.

Military. S. Army, Special Agent, CIC, (now MI); primary assignment the Pentagon, 902nd MI Group, ACSI. , 1959-61. Investigative and security assignments at direction of Assistant Chief of Staff for Intelligence. Attended Military Intelligence School., Fort Holabird, Md.

Paul Sr. is survived by his wife Phyllis and his Children.

Children of the Petrus family:

Paul David Petrus Jr., Esq., Attorney at Law; Manhattan, NY, NY.

Graduate of Cleveland-Marshall College of Law 2003.

Elizabeth Petrus Cano is a graduate of John Carroll University, Cleveland, Ohio, 1999. She is a principal of a local high school in the Seattle area of Washington.

Orlando Cano, the husband of Elizabeth is a graduate of the University of Washington, 1999.

He currently is Orlando Cano Consulting, LLC after years of working in the House of Representatives in the Washington State Legislature.

Grandchildren of Phyllis Caravella Petrus/ Paul David Petrus; Alessandra Adela Cano born on 2-8-2011.

Andre`s Victor Cano 8-14-20.

Submission by my brother Louis Philip Caravella, MD

I attended the University of Dayton, a Catholic college attended by my cousin Roy Koesel and my brother, the first of our generation to attend college. I majored in pre-med and subsequently attended St. Louis University, also where my brother had attended. I had applied to several medical schools and was uncertain as to my favorite. A St. Louis University representative came to the University of Dayton and interviewed students who had applied there for medical school, relieving us of the expense of having to travel to St. Louis. This was my first medical school interview, quite early in the process, and as the interview was concluding, the represented noted that I had not applied for early admission (it had never occurred to me to do so) but that if I agreed to attend St. Louis University medical school and cancel my other applications, that he was prepared to give me a position in the class of '74, then and there. How could you beat that? My worries were over and I accepted the position on the spot.

There were several areas of medicine that interested me but, in the end, I chose the specialty of ophthalmology. I am a gadgeteer at heart and I loved all of the instruments that are employed in the examination of the eye; surgery on the eye, recently being performed utilizing an operating microscope was slick; and the eye itself, as well as its interior, are beautiful. Plus, as I frequently joked, everything in the eye is "color-coded". Furthermore, the specialty appeared to me to be quite antiseptic and perhaps even the "gentlemen's practice of medicine. So as my fourth year of medical school began, I applied for a residency in ophthalmology in that ophthalmology residencies were not part of the match and because they were so popular, one applied for a position before even applying for internship. I was accepted at Ohio State University for my ophthalmology residency before I even had to begin applying for an internship, also required. I assumed that a surgery internship would be in store for me, however, Dr. Havener, the chairman of the department of ophthalmology and a nationally known ophthalmologists for his book on ocular pharmacology, advised me to take a medical internship with electives in neurology. Why neurology? Because the cubic inch of the eye and its eyelids have more neurons innervating it than any other square inch of the body and as an ophthalmologist, one needed to know neurology. With Doctor Havener's advice, I sought a medical residency and was accepted by Northwestern University in their Evanston Hospital medicine residency program.

I completed my internship and subsequently my residency in ophthalmology but wasn't quite ready to end my formal education. One of my rotations in ophthalmology included oculoplastic surgery which encompassed the plastic surgical repair of eyelid trauma, congenital and acquired eyelid and lacrimal (tearing) disorders as well as tumor removal of the lids and reconstruction. I very much enjoyed this rotation and elected to undertake a year of subspecialty study in the field. Dr. John Burns, an oculoplastic surgeon that I worked with while a resident befriended me and offered to have me as a fellow under him at Ohio State. He suggested that for an optimum experience it would be beneficial to study under more than one oculoplastic surgeon and even to spend time observing plastic surgeons operating on the face, as well as with maxilla-facial surgeons. In suggesting this, he helped me reserve time on the schedules of both such surgeons that he knew in the Columbus area and also a surgeon at New York Eye and Ear Infirmary as well as one in Manhattan Eye and Ear. As such, I became a peripatetic oculoplastic fellow. To top this off, Dr. Burns suggested that I obtain an in-depth knowledge of orbital tumors, which are somewhat rare but under the perusal of oculoplastic surgeons (as well as other medical specialists). The surgeon with the most experience in the world in this small subspecialty was a surgeon in London at Moorefield's Eye Hospital. Dr. Burns helped me arrange the first three months of my fellowship in London England where I attended the clinics and operating theater with Dr. John Wright, the aforementioned oculoplastic surgeon. On other days I worked with Dr. Richard Collins who specialized in pediatric eyelid surgery at The Hospital for Sick Children in London; with Dr. Richard Welham, a lacrimal (tearing disorders) surgeon in Reading, just outside of London and also with Dr. Glyn A. S. Lloyd, an orbital radiologist and ultrasonographer that worked closely with Dr. Wright at Moorefield's.

After having completed my training, I considered going to a number of alluring cities to begin practice but in the end, I was drawn to Cleveland, my Italian-family roots. In my research of practice locations, it became apparent that another ophthalmologist or two were needed in the area around the community where I was raised and so I began to look there. I spoke with two of the most respected and busiest ophthalmologists in the area and they indicated that partnerships in ophthalmology had not been very lasting on the westside of Cleveland and as such they would not be interested in a partner. But both Dr. Ken Kester and Dr. Ron Caravan also stated that they would be more than happy to send me emergencies that they could not fit into their schedules and also patients who needed appointments earlier than their schedules could accommodate. With this, I went into solo practice in 1979 and with the referrals of these two kind and excellent ophthalmologists, I became busy from the onset.

Interestingly, as time went by and these two wonderful doctors became less interested in running their own practices, they joined me in my practice – so we became partners after all.

I spent 34 years in private practice and retired just after reaching 65 years of age. Twenty years of that time included a monthly teaching appointment at Case-Western Reserve University where I was an Assistant Professor of Ophthalmology.

I met my wife, Patty, during the beginning of my second year in practice. I was attempting to extend my referral base a bit and began operating at Lakewood Hospital for the first time. I would operate there once a month and one day when going to the recovery room to write post-op orders on a patient that I had just completed operating upon, the new head nurse came up to me to introduce herself, as would have been customary. Similar to my father's experience upon meeting my mother, I was immediately overwhelmed by the beauty and pleasant personality of this young women. On leaving the OR after completing my surgeries that morning, I called down to the recovery room from the doctor's lounge and asked for the head nurse. I suggested that she let me take her out to dinner sometime but she assured me that she did not date doctors. I pleaded and was able to obtain her phone number and ultimately convinced her that she should allow me to take her to that dinner that I had mentioned. As they say, I was smitten and put on a full court press in the ensuing weeks. I even went so far as to propose to her on our third date – she laughed. Nevertheless, before the year was out, we were married.

My wife Patty had graduated with honors from The College of Mount St. Joseph, in Cincinnati and was class president. She was from a family of 8 children. When I met my future wife, she was in the process of obtaining her masters in nursing via a part time program, enabling her to work at the same time. This was interrupted by the fact that shortly after marrying we decided to begin our family. Subsequently we had four children. When the oldest, our son Louis, was in his first year of college, we decided to adopt a Russian orphan. Patty and I had felt that our lives had been most blessed and wishing to give something back, adoption seemed to be the way. Katya (Ekaterina) was adopted at age 9 years from an orphanage in St. Petersburg, Russia.

Like my father, I was all in favor of education and I told my children that whatever they wished to pursue in college or graduate school, I would be most happy to fund. For the most part, they all took advantage of this largess. My oldest son, Louis, attended Georgetown University majoring in American Studies. He graduated with honors and subsequently obtained a master's degree in in the same major at Columbia University. Louis later had a change of career and then obtained a master's in web design at Harvard University.

Our next oldest son, Robert, also attended Georgetown, graduating with honors. He did an internship with Key Bank and then worked for them for two years and subsequently went to the University of Chicago, School of Business where he majored in finance. He obtained his master's degree graduating with honors also.

Christina attended Elon University majoring in musical theater. She graduated with high honors and subsequently went on the road performing throughout the United States and Canada. She moved to Brooklyn to try to enter Broadway. There she met her future husband and was married shortly thereafter. Now, having three children her acting career is on hold.

Joseph attended Holy Cross College with a major in religion and a minor in Spanish. He spent his junior year of college in Spain, living with a Spanish family while taking a full course load – all in Spanish. During his fourth year of studies at Holy Cross, Joe decided to take courses that could prepare him for applying to medical school. Needless to say, he could not complete all of the pre-requisites for acceptance to medical school before graduating. So, after graduation, he enrolled at Case-Western Reserve University to obtain a master's in biology. With that he was accepted to medical school at Liberty University. Upon graduation, he began a residency at Laredo Medical Center in Laredo, Texas where his facility in speaking Spanish has been a wonderful asset.

Katya attended John Carol University, majoring in psychology and graduating with high honors. She subsequently attended Akron University and obtained a master's degree in industrial psychology. She is married and lives in Denver with her spouse where she works human resources for a national company.

Meanwhile, Patty and I have been retired for six years and are awaiting the marriage of our boys and more grandkids.

Submission by my youngest sister: Jennifer Caravella Helland.

The Caravella/Helland Family: The family of Jennifer Caravella.

1980, B. S. Degree in Nursing from Bowling Green State University.

Postpartum Nurse for 37 years; Fairview General Hospital/ Cleveland Clinic.

Daughter; Adele Brittany Helland: The Goddaughter of Philip Caravella.

Graduated college in 2012 from Bowling Green State University. Bachelor of Science in Education. Received a Master's of Art in Education from Baldwin Wallace in 2017. She works at Mentor High School in Mentor, Ohio; as a K-12 mild/moderate Intervention Specialist.

Son: Erik John Helland

Graduated in 2013 from Bowling Green State University in Business Administration and specializing in Supply Chain Management. Works in Columbus, Ohio for

Cardinal Health. His job title is Software Engineer IBP Global Demand and Supply Planning.

Husband of Jennifer Caravella Helland: John Michael Helland.

1981 awarded B. S. Degree from The Ohio State University.

1988 awarded MBA from Baldwin Wallace College, Berea, OH.

Worked over 30 years at Avery Dennison, Painsville, OH.

Submission by my oldest daughter Kimberly Caravella Kleckner

Kimberly Caravella Kleckner; Born September 5, 1979; Graduated from Kent State University in 2002 with Bachelor of Science in Electronic Media Production and Minor in Psychology; Stay at home Mom; Married to Scott Eric Kleckner December 12, 2015.

Scott Eric Kleckner; Born April 23, 1976; Graduated from University of Wisconsin Stout in 1999 with Bachelor of Science in Hospitality and Tourism Management; Retail and Restaurant Director at Belcampo Group, Inc.

Children of the Kleckners:

Dylan Bay Kleckner; Born February 14, 2015.

Parker Belle Kleckner; Born October 22, 2017.

Submission by my daughter Suzanne Caravella Bastian.

The Caravella/Bastian family: The family of Suzanne Caravella.

Lennon Bastian, born in Winfield, IL on 12/7/2018. She's an energetic, full of life, incredibly smiley 17 month old who spends her days running everywhere!

My husband, Kevin Bastian was born in Chicago, Illinois on October 29th, 1975. He graduated from Northwestern with a Masters degree in journalism and is currently working as a Marketing Manager for a B2B company called Thomson.

And then there's me, Suzie Bastian, born in Toledo, Ohio on October 15th, 1981. I graduated from Bowling Green State University with a degree in Fine Arts, and after 10 years working as a Graphic Designer in advertising, I made the career switch to recruitment and am currently working as a Design Recruiter with Amazon Web Services.

We also have an adorable Wheaten Terrier dog named Brewster, born here in Chicago on July 13th, 2015. He has more energy than our daughter, but no longer gets all the attention.

My final thoughts pertain to my wonderful grandchildren that have been gifted to the Caravella heritage and family. They are the most beautiful of all Americans in that with their youth comes grace, love, magnificence, charm, humor, and a mastery of what makes children the greatest Americans of all. For in them rests our future, our glory, our promise, our success, our values, and above all our destiny. "Go to it kids. We depend on you," Your Grandfather; GrandPa-Daddy — as my granddaughter Lennon named me.

GrandPa-Daddy;Philip Caravella, **GPD** April 8, 2022.

My RESUME or CV as we call it in the field of medicine.

December 22, 2022

Philip Caravella, MD, FAAFP, Lt. Col. US Army Medical Corps (RET.)

HOME ADDRESS:

12702 Granite Ridge Drive

Peyton, CO 80831

Email: phil.626670@gmail.com

The most significant contribution a family physician can make for any patient is to thoroughly understand all aspects of their lives, health, psychological profile, work status, and family life. It is just as important to be aware of a patient's level of fitness in order to fully develop an ongoing plan of preventive medicine, exercise, fitness, and health practices that will lead to a long and healthy life well beyond the standards currently used by most practitioners. This is what I am all about.

PRESIDENTIAL CITATION:

Awarded to me in April 2017 by President Barack Obama for my work with (VIM) Volunteers In Medicine, Jacksonville, Florida, from February 2016 through March 2017.

Letter of Excellence from Lt. General Robert W. Cone, Commanding, Headquarters, III Corps, September 25, 2009.

Army Commendation Medal awarded Dec 1, 2010.

—

EDUCATION:

• University of Dayton: Bachelor of Science Degree in Pre-medical Education. Matriculating from September of 1962 graduating in June of 1966.

• Saint Louis University School of Medicine: Matriculating from September of 1966 until July of 1970.

Medical Doctorate Degree. • Cleveland Clinic Matriculating from July of 1970 until July of 1971.

Serving In the US Army at the rank of Captain in the Medical Corps from July of 1971 until July of 1973. Rotating Medicine Internship.

- University of Illinois

- Peoria School of Medicine: Matriculating from July of 1973 until June of 1975. Family Medicine Residency.

• Fellowship Robert Wood Johnson Faculty Development Fellowship in Family Medicine: from July of 1976 until June of 1980.

TEACHING POSITIONS:

- Assistant Clinical Professor, Case Western Reserve University, 1979.

- Assistant Clinical Professor, The Medical College of Ohio at Toledo, 1980.

- Teaching Medical Staff; Fairview General Hospital, Cleveland, Ohio.

- Instructor in Advanced Cardiac Life Support, American Heart Association.

- Assistant Clinical Professor, Medical College of Medicine at Toledo, OH, 1981.

- Faculty Member: The Cleveland Clinic Lerner College of Medicine, 2004.

- Faculty CRDAMC, Family Medicine Residency Program, US Army Fort Hood, TX, 2008.

PATIENT CARE: During all teaching positions my primary responsibility was patient care (to pay the

bills) with teaching being 15% of my responsibility.

Private Solo Medical Practice: On Staff at Saint Johns Hospital and Fair view General Hospital for nineteen years, seeing about 20-22 patients per day of all ages. I initially practiced obstetrics for the first few years in practice. **Those dates are from 09/05/1977 until 04/15/1996.**

I became the first family doctor to practice family medicine at the Cleveland Clinic after leaving the private practice of medicine and started the Department of Family Medicine at the Cleveland Clinic Westlake, Ohio.

My dates of tenure were 05/01/1996 until 07/01/2012 (as verified on May 26, 2012 – by the Cleveland Clinic Human Resources Department).

One of the highlights of my career has been a cigarette cessation program I established when at the Cleveland Clinic and had well over 1000 patients quit smoking through the program I instituted. It was very well received and the success rate was well over 90%. The methods and medications I used prevented nearly any and all withdrawal symptoms which is why it was so effective.

I have rarely had hospital admissions during my entire career because of my ongoing and relentless use of all aspects of preventive medicine and wellness to improve most aspects of a patient's health and wellbeing. Because of my broad experiences I refer very few patients to other physicians.

CLEVELAND CLINIC: I was the first Section Chief of Family Medicine starting the department in the mid 1990's at the Westlake Family Health Center, Westlake, Ohio, under Medical Director Dr. Mary Walborn. Practicing at The Clinic for sixteen years with 95% of my responsibility involving patient care and 5% of my time involved hiring medical personal and managing the department of Family Medicine.

Overall, I have been in direct patient care for about forty years never having only an administrative position including my time with the U. S. Army. During my career I have worked in emergency rooms during my internship and residency program. I have see during my practice and during my military career countless patients with asthma, chest pain, angina, acute MI's, pyelonephritis, pneumonia, some with Covid, acute abdomens, TIA's, COPD, seizures, loss of consciousness, trauma, post car accident trauma, limb fractures, hyperthyroidism, and more. I am comfortable with treating all patients who present to where I am working as a physician. I know when and how to refer, when to transport, when to admit, and when and how to refer to surgeons, neurologists, and all other appropriate specialists.

Began Locum Tenens: defined as working for about three to four months at a time.

Staff Care as a locum tenens physician seeing patients full-time from early April 2017 into the state of Ohio beginning in 2020.

I HAVE WORKED FOR STAFF CARE AND CURATIVE in LOCUM POSITIONS on and off **FROM 2017 THROUGH 2021** in various capacities:

JACKSON MISSISSIPPI with the G. V. Montgomery Medical Center VA under Dr. Andree Burnett. LOCUM FOR from September 2017 until December 31, 2017.

1333 Meridian Ave, SAN JOSE, CALIFORNIA. Indian Health Center from February 5, 2018 until June 15, 2018.

OCEAN PARK, WASHINGTON general family medicine LOCUM for 3 months (dates are not available) but available from either Staff Care or Curative Locum providers.

TOLEDO, OHIO (The Toledo Correctional Institution on 2001 E Central Ave, 43608) for about two months as a LOCUM.

From parts of 2018 my wife Debra and I were working on opening a new business in Henderson, NV, called the Cannoli Castle. It officially opened in mid-August of 2019 and was forced to close by the state of Nevada due to Covid-19, in mid-March of 2020.

After the closing of our restaurant in March 2020 I went back into working for locum companies.

FEB. 2021-THROUGH APRIL 2021, I COMPLETED A working assignment as a Family Physician with the Sandhills Medical Foundation in Jefferson, South Carolina.

Locum Tenens:Dec. 21-22, 2021 In training with Dr. Rich Simovitz at Proactive Men's Medical ED, 4350 Glendale Milford Road, Cincinnati, OH. And worked an additional 4 days from 12/27-12/30/2021.

–

CERTIFICATION OF THE AMERICAN BOARD OF FAMILY MEDICINE: 6/1975 THROUGH 6/2015

LEADERSHIP ROLES:

- First Lieutenant, US Army Reserves, 1966.
- Chief of Clinics, Kenner Army Hospital, Fort Lee, VA. 1973.
- Captain, US Army, 1971-1973.
- Second in Command, Kenner Army Hospital, 1971-1973.
- Chief of Clinics, Fort AP Hill, VA.
- Chief, Medical Nuclear Attack and Decontamination Team, Eastern United States,

  Headquarters at Fort Lee, VA.
- Lt. Colonel, US Army, Medical Corps.
- Promotable; Colonel US Army, December 2009.
- Chief Resident; Department of Family Medicine, The Methodist Hospital of Central

  Illinois, Peoria School of Medicine; 1974-1975.
- Vice Chairman, Department of Family Medicine, Fairview Hospital, Cleveland,

  1978-1980.
- Assistant Director of Family Medicine Residency Program, Fairview Hospital,

Cleveland, Ohio; 1977-1980.

- Board of Directors, Ohio Academy of Family Practice, 1979.

- Delegate to the Ohio Academy of Family Practice, 1979.

- Youngest Elected at age 36, President of the Cleveland Academy of Family

  Medicine, 1980.

- DIRECTOR of Family Medicine Residency Program, Riverside Hospital, Toledo, OH. ,

  1980-1983.

- CHIEF; DEPARTMENT OF FAMILY MEDICINE, Riverside Hospital, Toledo, OH.

  1980-1983.

FIRST SECTION CHIEF, Department of Family Medicine, Cleveland Clinic. 1996-2002.

—

MILITARY SERVICE:

- United States Army, Medical Corps. Fort Lee, VA, Fort AP Hill, General Defense

  Supply Center, Fort Campbell, KY. 1971-1973.

- Lt. Colonel, US Army, Ford Hood, TX, Fort Campbell, KY. 2009-2011.

- Army Commendation Medal awarded Dec 1, 2010.

- Letter of Excellence from Lt. General Robert W. Cone, Commanding,

  Headquarters, III Corps, September 25, 2009.

- Medical School Award at Graduation:

- At graduation I was awarded the MAX GONSLOUSER AWARD FOR

  EXCELLENCE IN PSYCHIATRY from Saint Louis University School of Medicine, 1970.

–

PARTIAL WORK EXPERIENCE:

Worked in private practice as a family physician from July of 1975 through February of 1996 in Fairview, OH. Worked as Section Chief of Family Medicine for the Westlake, OH, Cleveland Clinic from May 1, 1996 through June 30, 2012.

Served as a Lt. Col. US Army Medical Corps from August 2009 through November 2011. Worked as a Locum Tenens Physician on and off from January of 2015 until 2021 under Staff Care and Curative Medical Corporation. During the above years while working part time as a volunteer in Florida and as a Locum physician I was also retired now and then between various assignments.

I have always maintained my CME studies for my entire career.

WORK IN THE FIELD OF WRITING:

- Editorial Advisory Board: *The American Breast Cancer Guide*, 2004-2005.
- Reviewer: The Cleveland Clinic Journal of Medicine.

PUBLICATIONS:

- TexasMD, medical journal, Shock and Awe, March/April 2016

- Weight No Longer, 266 pages; The Prescription for Amazing Fitness and Living,

  June, LuLu Publications, 2015.

- The Art of Being a Patient; Taming Medicine – An Insider's Guide, Author House

  Publications, 1999.

- Critical Issues in Family Practice, Cases and Commentaries, Let Them Rant and Rave,

  The Noncompliant Demanding Patient, Springer Publishing Company, 1982.

- The American Breast Cancer Guide: The Latest in Breast Cancer Prevention and Detection, 2004.

- Potty Train Your Child In Just One Day, forward by Philip Caravella, MD, author Teri Crane, publisher Simon and Schuster, 2006.

- Several Articles in Cleveland/Akron Family, magazine, Help Us Help You, Defeating Asthma Once and For All, Food Fight, Confronting the obesity epidemic, by Northeast Ohio's own "Dr. Phil.

- Americans The Beautiful, An Italian American Memoir, 76,000 words, 212 pages, 2020, Amazon KDP Select.

–

Developed a clear and workable method for people to maintain a healthy level of fitness, good health, and weight management. New Book; *Weight No Longer: The Prescription for Amazing Health and Living.*

New and effective system to assist patients in **quitting smoking** using bupropion hydrochloride, benzodiazepines, exercise, and doctor visits which have resulted in over 1500 success stories.

Preventive medicine techniques employed with every patient and at every patient visit with special attention to the prevention of vascular and heat disease, cancer, asthma, and diabetes.

Universal screening for cancers, heart disease, hypertension, elevated cholesterol, diabetes. Special intense **preventive management** of patients with asthma, nasal allergies, acid reflux, and respiratory infections.

Effective communication with patients, listening to their needs, and patient education through patient review of each important detail of treatment and prevention.

Teaching medical students, interns, residents the finest details of patient care and communication. Without communication there is little benefit. Albert Einstein said, "If you can't explain it simply, you don't understand it well enough".

Believed to be the oldest Soldier in history to re-enlist in the US military and as a member of the United States Army.

NPI: 133625931

Completion of Covid-19 vaccination series: Mid April of 2021. CURRENT BASIC LIFE SUPPORT QUALIFIED. Curent state medical licenses:

Ohio : medical license:35. 040427.

California: license number 151607.

Philip Caravella, MD, FAAFP, Lt. COL. US Army (RET.)

I am **AVAILABLE FOR SPEAKING ENGAGEMENTS AND INTERVIEWS FOR NEWSPRINT, RADIO, AND TELEVISION ON HEALTH, FITNESS, OBESITY, DIET AND GENERAL HEALTH RELATED TOPICS.**

www.ingramcontent.com/pod-product-compliance
Lightning Source LLC
LaVergne TN
LVHW021758060526
838201LV00058B/3148